Additions and Corrections to the W.P.A. Inventory of Brown County, Ohio: Georgetown

Jana Sloan Broglin

HERITAGE BOOKS
2026

HERITAGE BOOKS
AN IMPRINT OF HERITAGE BOOKS, INC.

Books, CDs, and more—Worldwide

For our listing of thousands of titles see our website
at
www.HeritageBooks.com

Published 2026 by
HERITAGE BOOKS, INC.
Publishing Division
5810 Ruatan Street
Berwyn Heights, MD 20740

(Originally Titled)
INVENTORY OF THE COUNTY ARCHIVES OF OHIO

Prepared by

The Historical Records Survey
Division of Women's and Professional Projects
Works Progress Administration

No. 8. BROWN COUNTY (GEORGETOWN)

Columbus, Ohio
The Historical Records Survey
June 1938

International Standard Book Number
Paperbound: 978-0-7884-4970-3

The Historical Records Survey

Luther E. Evans, National Director
John O. Marsh, State Director

Division of Women's and Professional Projects

Ellen S. Woodward, Assistant Administrator
Mildred M. Thrasher, State Director

WORKS PROGRESS ADMINISTRATION

Harry L. Hopkins, Administrator
Carl Watson, State Administrator

TABLE OF CONTENTS

The *Inventory of County Archives of Ohio* is one of a number of bibliographies of historical materials prepared throughout the United States by workers on the Historical Records Survey of the Works Progress Administration. The publication herewith presented, and inventory of the archives of Brown County, is number 8 of the Ohio series.

The Historical Records Survey was undertaken in the winter of 1935-1936 for the purpose of providing useful employment to needy unemployed historians, lawyers, teachers, and research and clerical workers. In carrying out this objective, the project was organized to compile inventories of historical materials, particularly the unpublished government documents and records which are basic in the administration of local government, and which provide invaluable data for students of political, economic, and social history. The archival guide herewith presented is intended to meet the requirements of day-to-day administration by the officials of the county, and also the needs of lawyers, businessmen, and other citizens who require facts from the public records for the proper conduct of their affairs. The volume is so designed that it can be used by the historian in his research in unprinted sources in the same way he uses the library card catalog for printed sources.

The inventories produced by the Historical Records Survey attempt to do more than give merely a list of records - they attempt further to sketch in the historical background of the county or other unit of government, and to describe precisely and in detail the organization and functions of the government agencies whose records they list. The county, town, and other local inventories for the entire country will, when completed, constitute an encyclopedia of local government as well as a bibliography of local archives.

The successful conclusion of the work of the Historical Records Survey, even in a single county, would not be possible without the support of public officials, historical and legal specialists, and many other groups in the community. Their cooperation is gratefully acknowledged.

The Survey was organized and has been directed by Luther H. Evans, and operates as a nation-wide project in the Division of Women's and Professional Projects, of which Mrs. Ellen S. Woodward, Assistant Administrator, is in charge.

HARRY L. HOPKINS
Administrator

PREFACE
2nd Edition

In 1929 after the stock market crash along with the Great Depression, crop failures and drought, which followed, President Herbert Hoover and his successor Franklin D. Roosevelt formulated relief projects, the most successful was the establishment of the Works Progress Administration (WPA).

Established as the Works Projects Administration in 1935, the WPA was the largest of the many programs developed during Roosevelt's "New Deal." In 1939, the agency's name was changed to Works Progress Administration, and continued as such until its demise in 1943.

The Federal Writers' Project, a division of the WPA (known as Federal Project Number One), created jobs for many unemployed librarians, clerks, researchers, editors, and historians. The workers went to courthouses, town halls, offices in large cities, vital statistics offices and inventoried records. Besides indexing works, many records were transcribed. One of these many projects was the *Inventory of the County Archives* which has benefitted genealogists and historians. The inventories listed the records, either by volumes or file boxes and years per record type, within the office. Although the WPA oversaw this project, the information for each volume of records may differ significantly by the information submitted.

For information regarding three of the "New Deal" projects designed to get people working, see: CCC (Civilian Conservation Corps), WPA (Works Progress Administration), and NYA (National Youth Administration) see: CCC: **https://en.wikipedia.org/wiki/Civilian_Conservation_Corps;** NYA **https://en.wikipedia.org/wiki/National_Youth_Administration;**and WPA: **https://en.wikipedia.org/wiki/Works_Progress_Administration.**

The information herein is verbatim except for obvious spelling errors. Records listed may have met the requirement for retention and have been destroyed as per the records retention act, while other records are considered permanent records. (*See:* **https://codes.ohio.gov/ohio-revised-code** Ohio Revised Code, sections 149.31 and 149.34). Records once considered "open" to the public, such as lunacy, idiotic, and juvenile cases, may be "closed" due to a revision of state laws. However, the records may be opened to family members with adequate proof of lineage.

PREFACE
2nd Edition

The addresses and website section of this edition list an up-to-date location guide to each office mentioned, if located.

This project was to encompass all of Ohio's 88 counties although approximately 30 of these inventories have been located while others may be missing or never done.

Mention is made of the Ohio State Archaeological Society now known as the Ohio History Connection, 800 East 17th Avenue, Columbus, Ohio, **www.ohiohistory.org.**

Jana Sloan Broglin
Fellow, Ohio Genealogical Society
Swanton, Ohio
2026

PREFACE
1st Edition

The Historical Records Survey began operations in Ohio in February 1936, and has been under the technical supervision of the State Archivist and Curator of History, Ohio State Archaeological and Historical Society. General regulations and procedures applicable to all project units in the forty-eight states have been followed in Ohio. In the sixteen districts of the Works Progress Administration in Ohio, the project was organized and operated by the district supervisors of the Writers' Project. In November 1936, the Survey became an independent part of Federal Project. No. 1.

The objective of the Survey in Ohio has been the preparation of complete inventories of the records of the state and of each county, city, and other local governmental unit. Although a condensed form of entry is used, information is given as to the limiting dates of all extant records, the contents of individual series, and location of records in statehouse, county courthouse, or other depository.

The *Inventory of County Archives of Ohio* will, when completed, consist of a set of eighty-eight volumes with a separate number for each county in the state. The units of the series are numbered according to the respective position of the county in an alphabetical list of the counties. Thus, the inventory herewith presented for Brown County is number 8. The inventory of the State archives and of municipal and other local records will constitute separate publications.

The principle followed in the inventory of county records has been to place a record in the office of origin rather than in the office of deposit. The records are arranged with those of the executive branch of the county government first, followed by judicial, law enforcing, fiscal, and miscellaneous agencies. Minor agencies are placed in the general arrangement according to function rather than according to constitutional or statutory responsibility to a major subdivision. The legal development of each office or agency has been treated in a prefatory section preceding the inventory of the records of the office.

The Historical Records Survey, under the direction of William S. Davis, District Supervisor of the project, was started in June 1936 and completed in April 1937. Field-workers under the immediate supervision of William Reed, Assistant Supervisor, carefully inventoried all county records. The final careful recheck of the inventory was made by George Reichert. The wholehearted cooperation of the county officials with the project workers has meant much in the thoroughness and completeness of the result. For the accuracy of the inventory, the project personnel in Brown County is entirely responsible. Members of the state editorial staff of the

Historical Records Survey, under the supervision of Russell S. Drum, Assistant State Director in charge of the administrative details of the project, and miss Winifred Smith, State Editor, compiled, arranged, indexed, edited, and reproduced the volume for distribution among public and semi-public institutions and organizations.

The various units of the *Inventory of County Archives of Ohio* will be issued in mimeographed or printed form for free distribution to state and local public officials and public libraries in Ohio, and to a limited number of libraries and government agencies outside the state. Request for information concerning particular units of the *Inventory* should be addressed to the Historical Records Survey, Old Post Office Building, State and Third Streets, Columbus, Ohio.

John O. Marsh
State Director
The Historical Records Survey

Columbus, Ohio
June 20, 1938

ADC . . . . Aid to Dependent Children
ad valorem tax . . . . according to value
adm. . . . . administration
am.. . . . . amended
Arch. . . . . Archaeological
Art. . . . . Article
c. . . . . copyright
capias . . . . a warrant or order for arrest of a person typically issued by the judge or magistrate in a case
CCC. . . . . Civilian Conservation Corps
certiorari. . . . . to be more fully informed
chap(s). . . . . chapter(s)
comp. . . . . compiler
Const. . . . . Constitution
ed(s). . . . . editor(s)
et al. . . . . (et alii), and others
et seq . . . . and the following
(et) passim . . . . and here and there
ex officio . . . . as a result of one's status or position
et seq. . . . . and following
fee simple . . . . full and irrevocable ownership
G. C. . . . . General Code
habeas corpus . . . . protection against illegal imprisonment
ibid. . . . . the same reference
loc. cit. . . . . (*loco citato)* in the place cited
N. P. . . . . The Ohio NISI PRIUS REPORTS
n. p. . . . . no place of publication shown
NRS. . . . . Nonresident Service
n. s. . . . . new series
nolle prosequi . . . . notice of abandonment by a plaintiff or prosecutor of all or part of a suit or action
NYA . . . . National Youth Administration

O. L. . . . . *Laws of Ohio*
op. cit. . . . . (*opere citato*) In the work cited
posse comitatus . . . . a group of citizens called upon to assist the sheriff
praecipes . . . . a written request for action
prima facie . . . . on the first impression
pro rata . . . . in proportion
procedendo . . . . sends case from appellate court to a lower court
pt. . . . . part
PWA . . . . Public Works Administration
quo warranto . . . . by what authority or warrant
replevins . . . . return of personal property wrongfully taken or held by a defendant
R. S. . . . . Revised Statutes
SS . . . . State Service
sec(s) . . . . section(s)
sic . . . . thus, following copy
supersedeas . . . . a stay of enforcement of a judgment pending appeal
TS . . . . transient service
v. . . . . versus
venires . . . . a group of people summoned for jury duty
vol(s). . . . . volume(s)
WPA . . . . Works Progress/Projects Administration
writ . . . . a formal, legal document, a decree
x . . . . by
— . . . . current, to date
4-H . . . . (Four - H)

ABBREVIATIONS, SYMBOLS, AND EXPLANATORY NOTES

Each chapter or section of "County Offices and Their Records" consists of an essay describing the legal status and functions of one department of county government and an inventory of the records of that department.

Each record constitutes a separate entry. Entries are arranged under topical headings and subheadings.

Each entry sets forth, insofar as applicable, the following:

1. Entry number. Entries are numbered consecutively throughout the inventory.
2. The exact title as it appears on the record, or if the record has no title a supplied title in brackets. If the title of the record is non-descriptive, misleading, or incorrect an additional title (in capitals and lowercase letters), also enclosed in brackets, has been supplied.
3. Dates show inclusive years or parts of years covered by the record. Breaks in dates indicate that the record is missing or was not kept between dates shown. A dash in place of the final date indicates an open record. If no current entries have been made the date of the last entry is noted. Where no statement is made that the record was discontinued at the last date shown, it could not be definitely established that such was the case. Where no comment is made on the absence of prior and subsequent records, no definite information could be obtained.
4. Quantity, given in chronological order wherever possible.
5. Labeling. Numbers and letters within parentheses indicate labeling on volumes, file boxes, or other containers.
6. Variations in title. The current or most recent title is used but significant variations are shown with dates for which each was used.
7. Change of agency. Occasionally a record is discontinued as a county record and kept by some other agency.
8. Description. A statement of the nature and purpose of the record and of what the record shows. As the contents of a record may vary, over time the description may differ somewhat from the record at any one period. Wherever feasible, changes in content are shown with dates. In map and plat entries the names of author and publisher and the scale are omitted only when not available.

9. Arrangement. Records said to be alphabetically arranged are frequently alphabetized only as to initial letter of the surname. This is true especially where there is a secondary arrangement.
10. Indexing. Self-contained indexes are described in the entry. Separate indexes constitute separate entries with cross references to and from the record entry.
11. Nature of recording. Changes are indicated with dates.
12. Condition. No statement is made if good or excellent.
13. Number of pages. Averaged for the series.
14. Dimensions show size of volumes, maps, file boxes, or other containers and are expressed in inches in every instance. The dimensions of volumes are given in order of height, width, and thickness; of file boxes in order of height, width, and depth.
15. Location. Rooms referred to are in the county courthouse unless some other building is specified.

Title line cross references are used to complete series where a record is kept separately for a period of time or in other records for different periods of time. They are also used in all artificial entries which are made to show, under their proper office, records kept in the same volume or file with records of another office. In both instances, the description of the master entry shows the title and entry number of the record from which the cross reference is made. Dates shown in the description of the master entry are for the part or parts of the record contained therein, and are shown only when they vary from those of the master entry. Artificial entries show only title, dates, and description.

Separate third paragraph cross references from entry to entry, are used to show prior, subsequent, or related records which are not a part of the same series. If, however, both entries are under the same subject headings, no third paragraph references are made. "See also" references from subject headings refer to entries in the same department which contain records logically belonging under that heading but which have been classified under an equally appropriate heading.

Few regions in Ohio have more picturesque and diversified topographical features than the land included in the present Brown County. Along the Ohio River near Aberdeen, cliffs rise almost directly from the water to a height of 300 feet. The three principal streams of the county, White Oak, Eagle, and Straight Creeks, run from north to south, have cut deep valleys, and descend them with comparatively rapid fall. There are hills so high and steep that they may be called mountains, but there are also large tracts of land which are level and well drained as well as certain area of swamps or "slashes." In recent years, however, most of the swamps have been drained. The highest elevation is in the northwest corner of the county and is 1,091 feet, while the lowest is 500 feet along the Ohio River.

Glacial deposits cover about eighty-seven percent of the area. The most characteristic feature of the drift deposits is the compact white clay which covers the flat lands in the northern sections. It is six to ten feet in thickness. These clays are rich in nearly all the elements necessary for vegetable growth, but require extremely scientific handling if crops are to be profitably produced. However, as the valley of the Ohio River is approached, the soils formed from the decomposition of the shales and limestones are quite largely represented and constitute some of the richest and most desirable land in Ohio. The geologic structure belongs to the Ordovician system with the Eden series represented along the Ohio. These formations are among the oldest in the state. The underlying rocks are thirty percent shale and seventy percent limestone, and their only economic products are road and building materials (*Report of the Geological Survey of Ohio*, Columbus, 1878, III, 942-944; Simeon D. Fess, ed., *Ohio Reference Library*, New York, 1937, III, 277-278; Roderick Peattie, *Geography of Ohio, Geological Survey of Ohio*, Bulletin, XXVII, Columbus, 1923. 1-21.)

Brown County presents an interesting archaeological study. A feature is the great number of burials of the stone grave type. So far as is known no stone graves as complicated and diverse in structure as these exist in any other localities. The stone grave method is not considered indicative of a different or distinct culture, but merely as a local custom, due, no doubt, to the fact that the conveniently flat stones were readily available. There are forty-one mounds, fourteen enclosures, five village sites, eleven burials, two cemeteries, and six stone graves in the county as evidence of the habitat of prehistoric peoples. (Gerard Fowke, "Stone Graves in Brown County, Ohio," *Ohio Archeological and Historical Quarterly*, IX, 1901, 193-204; William C. Mills, *Archeological Atlas of Ohio*, Columbus, 1914, 8.)

No historic tribe of Indians ever had a permanent settlement in this region, but it was a favorite hunting ground of the Shawnees and the Miamis. For a time the county was the boundary line between the lands of these two tribes. After white settlements had been undertaken in Kentucky the Shawnees penetrated into the counties north of the Ohio and held complete dominion over the whole region now included in Brown and adjoining counties. They frequently hunted and encamped within the region but made no settlement and the nearest Indian towns were in Ross and Greene Counties. Indian titles in southwestern Ohio were extinguished by the treaties of Fort McIntosh in 1785, Fort Harmar in 1789, and Greenville in 1795. (W. H. Beers & Company, comp. *The History of Brown County, Ohio,* Chicago, 1883, 220-224.)

The identity of the first white explorer to set foot in this county must remain a moot question. Undoubtedly several of the early voyagers of the Ohio River must have passed these shores but they left no tangible traces of their presence. However, several of the frontiers' most noted hunters and scouts passed over the hills and swamps of the county long before there was a white settler within its limits. Among these were Daniel Boone, Simon Kenton, and Neil Washburn. Kenton was captured by the Indians in this county on one occasion. In 1786 the army of Colonel Benjamin Logan passed through this region in a campaign against the tribes on the headwaters of the Great Miami. (Beers, *Brown County*, 226, 230.) In 1792 a noted Indian engagement took place at East Fork, close to the boundaries of Brown and Clermont Counties. The Indians were led by the able young Tecumseh, and the frontiersmen by Kenton, M'Intyre, and Downing. (Henry Howe, *Historical Collections of Ohio*, Norwalk, 1896, I, 328-330.)

Meanwhile, steps were being taken to provide for the survey and settlement of this territory. Four states, New York, Virginia, Massachusetts, and Connecticut had claims in the Northwest. Eventually these were settled by cession of the lands to the United States with certain reservations. Virginia's claim rested upon the vague expression in her charter of 1609 giving her the land "from sea to sea, west and northwest," but it had been strengthened by vigorous military action in the territory. In surrendering her claims north of the Ohio in 1784, she reserved the region between the Scioto and the Little Miami to satisfy the bounties promised to her Revolutionary War veterans; provided that insufficient lands remain in Kentucky for the purpose. (Eugene H. Roseboom, and Francis P. Weisenburger, *A History of Ohio*, New York, 1934, 71-72.) These land warrants were awarded by Virginia with consideration being taken of the rank and services of the veterans.

Thus, a major general received 15,000 acres, but a soldier or sailor serving less than three years received only 100 acres. (William E. Peters, *Ohio Lands and their Subdivision*, 2nd edn., Athens, Ohio, 1918, 109.)

The fact that Brown County was included in the Virginia Reserve had momentous consequences on its history. The lands were entered and surveyed under the laws of Virginia. General R. C. Anderson was appointed principal surveyor and he opened an office at Louisville, Kentucky, August 1, 1784. Before the close of 1786 it became evident that the lands in Ohio would be needed in order to satisfy all the warrants. In the winter and spring of 1787, John O'Bannon and Arthur Fox, two surveyors from Kentucky, explored the Ohio Country, and the former was the first to make a survey within the present limits of Brown County. This was made November 15, 1787, on a 1,000 acre tract entered by Phillip Slaughter. Seven different surveys were made by O'Bannon within the limits of the county before the close of 1787. (Beers, *Brown County*, 241.)

In 1788 Congress declared invalid all the locations and surveys between the Little Miami and the Scioto as it was believed that these lands would not be necessary in order to satisfy the Virginia warrants. However, after an investigation of the situation, Congress repealed the resolution on August 10, 1790. After this time, surveys proceeded rapidly, Congress making only one other effort to interfere in the matter. By an act of May 1800 it required all surveys for land issued prior to that time to be completed before December 1, 1803, but this date was repeatedly extended. (Peters, *op. cit.,* 110.)

Nathaniel Massie established a settlement at Manchester in Adams County in 1790, and surveys were made soon thereafter in Brown County; one of the surveyors being Duncan McArthur, later destined to become a governor of Ohio. The surveyors were given generous terms, keeping for themselves one fourth to one half of the lands entered. If cash were paid the usual fee was 10 pounds in Virginia currency for each 1000 acres entered. However, these fees were not excessive in view of the fact that the Indians were menacing until 1795, and surveys were often made in winter as the tribes were then in winter quarters. (Beers, *Brown County*, 241-242. For a description of these surveys see Rev. James B. Finley, *Autobiography*, ed. by W. P. Strickland, Cincinnati, 1859, 128-131.)

The evils in this haphazard system where numerous. The owner of a Virginia military warrant was permitted to locate it in such shape and in whatever place in the district as pleased him, providing that it had not been previously located. The only limitation was a Virginia statute which required the breadth of each survey to be at least one third of its length in every part. In consequence of this want of system there were interferences and encroachments of one entry upon another, and until recent years there was great difficulty in tracing land titles. Records reveal that some settlers were forced to pay twice for their lands, and that others lost them entirely. Furthermore, the surveys were usually for large tracts, a fact which discouraged the poor settler. Speculators dealt in these lands, holding the best of them for higher prices, and selling those whose titles were shadowy for as low as 25 cents per acre. (Beers, *Brown County*, 244-246.)

General William Lytle was a typical example of the land dealers of the early period, and tradition declares that as a surveyor he did most of his work from saddle with little regard for exactness (*ibid.*). John O'Bannons' records reveal the survey of 5,000 acres in one day, a feat that was physically impossible. He probably had hired others to work for him, but the net results of this haste were inaccurate surveys and faulty titles. (Nelson W. Evans, "Colonel John O'Bannon," *Ohio Archeological and Historical Quarterly*, XIV, 1905, 321-323.)

Indian hostility delayed the settlement of Brown County, and more than seven years elapsed from the time the first entry was made until it was safe to settle. The first settlers in the region were probably squatters, but Belteshazzar Dragoo was the first to settle under a land warrant. He located on Eagle Creek, about three miles from the site of Ripley in 1794. By 1799 there was considerable settlement on Eagle, Red Oak, and White Oak Creeks, and by 1803 it is estimated that there were about 2,200 settlers in the county. however, there was no great wave of settlers coming into the region, and as late as 1809 one traveler wrote that he knew of but one stone or brick building in the county and that was unfinished. (Beers, *Brown County*, 252-253.)

Nevertheless, by 1817 the population of this region had increased sufficiently to warrant its organization as an independent county. On December 27, 1817, the assembly created Brown County from territory of Adams and Clermont Counties (16 O. L. 29-31), its name being given in honor of General Jacob Brown of the War of 1812 fame (Beers, *Brown County*, 280). The county is bounded on the North by Clinton County, on the east by Highland and Adams, on the west by Clermont, and on the south by the Ohio River. Only one change was made in its boundaries. In 1874 the Highland-Brown line was re-surveyed and resulted in the loss to Brown of a small tract of land. This action was necessitated by the fact that early surveys did not make sufficient allowance for the variation of the magnetic needle. (Randolph C. Downes, "Evolution of Ohio County Boundaries," *Ohio*

Archeological and Historical Quarterly, XXXVI, 1927, 447.) The county has an area of 481 square miles.

The first town was laid out by Basil Duke and John Colburn, August 1, 1801, and named St. Clairsville in honor of Governor St. Clair. The name was later changed to Decatur. About nine miles down the river from Aberdeen is Ripley which was laid out during the period of the War of 1812 by Colonel James Poage of Virginia. At first this village was called Staunton, but later changed to Ripley in honor of a distinguished officer in the War of 1812. In 1804 Higginsport was laid out at the mouth of White Oak Creek, and in 1819 Georgetown and Russellville were organized. In the northern sections of the county many of the early settlers were Irish, and in 1811 some of them established the village of Fayetteville. In 1815 Samuel Gist, an Englishman, provided in his will for the establishment of a settlement for freedmen. In 1818 such a colony was attempted in Brown County but it ended in failure. (Fess, *op. cit.*, III, 278, 282.)

Ripley and Georgetown became the most populous villages of the county and both have experienced some unusual incidents. The assembly made Ripley the county seat, but in 1818 authorized a commission to locate the permanent seat of justice. The commission recommended a place since known as Bridgewater, but after many protests the decision was reversed and Ripley was made the county seat in April 1820. (Beers, *Brown County*, 284.) Meanwhile the assembly had accepted Bridgewater as the location of the county court (17 O. L. 151). On January 19, 1821, the assembly appointed another commission (19 O. L. 39) which eventually selected Georgetown as the seat of justice (Beers, *Brown County*, 286). Ripley had already built a courthouse and was forced to sell it at public auction (*ibid.*, 290).

Ripley became the storm center of a more serious controversy a few years later. While the majority of Brown's citizens were opposed to abolitionist doctrines, due, probably, to their economic ties with the South, there was a vigorous abolitionist minority. One of the most noted stations of the underground railroad was located at Ripley with Reverend John Rankin, the Presbyterian minister, and his nine sons as "conductors." The zeal of Reverend Mr. Rankin on several occasions placed him in serious difficulties but he maintained his position. His station is one to which Eliza Harris of *Uncle Tom's Cabin* fame is supposed to have fled. So great was his experience that William Lloyd Garrison presented him a book with the inscription "Rev. John Rankin, with the profound regards and loving veneration of his anti-slavery *desciple* [sic] and humble co-worker in the cause of emancipation." (Paul R. Grim, "The Rev. John Rankin, Early Abolitionist," *Ohio*

Archeological and Historical Quarterly, XLVI, 1937, 215-256; Wilbur H. Siebert, "The Underground Railroad in Ohio," *ibid*, IV, 1895, 55-56.)

The county witnessed other exciting days. It was visited by Morgan's Raiders in 1863, and $32,784 damages were claimed as a result, although no lives were lost. (Beers, *Brown County*, 340; Roseboom and Weisenberger, *op. cit.*, 284-285.) In 1888 a secret night-riding organization called the "White Caps" terrorized the county, but after the Governor discovered their identities they agreed to disband (Emilius O. Randall and Daniel J. Ryan, *History of Ohio: The Rise and Progress of an American State*, New York, 1912, IV, 387-388).

The population of Brown County slowly increased during the past century. In 1820 it was 13,350; in 1840, 22,715; in 1860, 29, 958; and in 1880 it was 32, 911 (Bureau of the Census, *Compendium of the Eleventh Census of the United States*, 1890, I, 34). Since that time the population has gradually decreased and in 1930 was 20,148 (*ibid., Fifteenth Census of the United States*, 1930, *Population*, III, pt. ii, 466). The birth rate exceeds the death rate so this loss is best explained by migration from the county (Ohio Study of Local School Units, *A Study of the Public Schools of Brown County*, mimeographed, Columbus, 1937, 17). In 1930 there were nine incorporated villages in the county: Ripley with 1,556 inhabitants, Georgetown with 1,531, and Sardinia, Mt. Orab, Aberdeen, Russellville, Higginsport, Fayetteville, and Hamersville having from 267 to 564 inhabitants (Bureau of the Census, *Fifteenth Census of the United States*, 1930, *Population*, III, pt. ii, 533-534). Less than one percent of the inhabitants are foreign-born. (*ibid.*, 479).

Since Brown is decidedly a rural county it is but natural that agriculture has been, and continues to be its chief industry. In the early days the chief difficulty was transportation. Beeswax, skins, and feathers were the principle articles that could be transported with profit to distant markets. Hogs and cattle were driven afoot over the mountains, and after a journey of a month or six weeks found an uncertain market in Baltimore. Corn rarely commanded more than 10 or 12 cents per bushel, wheat sold for 30 or 40 cents and other commodities were correspondingly low. (Beers, *Brown County*, 303-306.)

In the early years cattle wandered at large, sought their own food, and were without shelter in the winter. However, the Poland-China and Berkshire hogs were introduced in this county during the period 1816 to 1839, and the quality and quantity of pork produced were greatly increased. (Beers, *Brown County*, 305.) In 1846 Ripley was second only to Cincinnati in the amount of pork prepared for shipment to the plantations of the South. The meat was sent by flatboats, each carrying 1,000 to 1,200 barrels, and as many as ten or fifteen boats would leave Ripley each season. (*Ibid.*, 441.) Prior to 1849 the hills back of Levanna were famous for the wines made from the Catawba grapes grown there but this industry was abandoned (*ibid.*, 419). Tobacco was an important crop in early Brown County, and for some time prior to 1850 this crop was second only to corn in importance. The famous Burley tobacco was developed in the county (*ibid.*, 306), and in 1929 only two Ohio counties exceeded Brown in tobacco growing (Bureau of the Census *Fifteenth Census of the United States*, 1930, *Agriculture*, II, pt. i, 430-437).

In 1929 there were 3,302 farms in the county which utilized 92.3 percent of the entire area. Of this, 40.1 percent was in crop land, 8.5 percent in woodlands, and 48.4 percent in pastures. (*Ibid.*, I. 477.) These farms were valued at $13,959,350 (*ibid.*,) and produced crops in 1929 worth $3,892,881 (Bureau of the Census, *Fifteenth Census of the United States,* 1930, *Unemployment*, I, 798), and in 1934 relief costs in this county were only 87 cents per capita in contrast with $9.22 for the state average (*Brown School Survey*, 9). The entire tax duplicate of the county was $14,666,965 in 1933 (Ohio Auditor of State, *Annual Report*, 1934, 481), so it is apparent that most of the wealth is in agriculture. Nevertheless, there is a darker side to this picture. In 1929 over 22 percent of the farms were mortgaged $3,892,881 (Bureau of the Census, *Fifteenth Census of the United States,* 1930. *Agriculture*, II, pt. i, 468); in 1935, over 32 percent of the farming was done by tenants (*Brown School Survey*, 7); and the average farm income in 1935 was $736 in contrast with the state average of $1,122 (*ibid.*, 5).

For over half a century most of the commerce in Brown County moved down the banks of the Ohio River. In the early days this centered around Aberdeen. Traders and flatboat men returning from New Orleans by the overland route often continued their eastward journey from this point. After 1797 it was also the western terminus of the famous pioneer road known as Zane's Trace. (Fess, *op. cit.*, III, 278.) The first state road appropriation for Brown County was made in 1804 for a road to follow Zane's Trace, and in 1818 more funds were given. Three turnpike companies, organized in the thirties, also were of value to the county. (Beers, *Brown County*, 291-292.) The people of Brown County consistently opposed the canal schemes that became popular in Ohio in the twenties and thirties (Byron Williams, *History of Clermont and Brown Counties, Ohio*, Milford, Ohio, 1913, I, 395).

Of the two railroads in the county, one was incorporated in 1876 to be built from Cincinnati to Williamsburg. It was built on a three-foot gauge under the name of Cincinnati and Eastern. it was completed to Williamsburg in Clermont County in 1877, but missed practically all the old settlements in Brown. A road known as the Cincinnati and Portsmouth was chartered in 1873, and was in operation by 1881, but due to construction difficulties its extension to Georgetown was delayed for some years. In the meantime, the citizens of that city had undertaken to finance the Georgetown and Sardinia Railroad. Bonds were issued, and by 1882 the grade had been built to Sardinia. (Fess, *op. cit.,* III, 279.) To railroads in operation, the Ohio River deepened for navigation, and four United States and five state routes within its borders (*Brown School Survey*, 10), the county has more than adequate transportation facilities.

Comparatively few banking institutions were established in Brown County. In Georgetown the Penn and Phillips Bank operated from 1856 to 1878. In 1882 the First National Bank was organized in that village. (Beers, *Brown County*, 409.) Ripley's first bank was the Farmer's Branch of the State Bank of Ohio, established in 1847. The First National Bank was chartered in 1864, and the Farmers' Bank in 1865. (*Ibid.,*446.) Fayetteville also has one bank (Ohio Superintendent of Banks, *Annual Report*, 1930, 391).

Manufacturing has never assumed large proportions in the county. However, in the past certain industries have engaged in transitory prosperity. In 1848 there were 24 distilleries in the vicinity of Georgetown, and tanneries, flour mills, cooper's shops, and sawmills at one time were very numerous. At one time Ripley was the center for steamboat construction, particularly from 1820 to 1840. The father of Ulysses S. Grant owned a tannery in Georgetown, and the future president spent his boyhood in this village. (Beers, *Brown County*, 371-703, *passim.*)

At present, the major industries of Georgetown center around marble and granite, flour, shoes, grains, and tobacco; while Ripley has a shoe factory, foundry, sawmills, and tobacco warehouses (N. W. Ayer and Sons, *Directory of Newspapers and Periodicals*, Philadelphia, 1937, 716, 727). In the county in 1930 only 6.1 percent of the workers were engaged in manufacturing in contrast with 8.7 percent in trade and 7.1 percent in transportation (*Brown School Survey.* 8).

It is difficult to find exact information concerning the first efforts at education. It is said that a cabin for school purposes was erected in Lewis Township as early as 1802. In Huntington Township one of the oldest schools was built in 1805 or 1806. Teachers were paid by subscription for thirteen weeks at the rate of $1.50 to $2.00 per pupil, and made an average of $8.00 to $10.00 per month. In 1807 schools were built in Higginsport and in Eagle Township, and soon every township had schools in operation. In 1828 a college was founded in Union Township by Reverend John Rankin and continued until 1832. At that time he established a female seminary. In 1840 he started another college which continued until 1849. Black as well as white children could attend his schools. The Ohio Valley Academy was established at Decatur in 1862, but was short-lived. In 1860 Father Daly founded St. Patrick's Academy at Fayetteville. A boarding school for boys was maintained here, as was a parish school under the Sisters of Charity. (*Brown School Survey*, 3; Beers, *Brown County*, 382-398, *passim*; Edward A. Miller, "The History of Educational Legislation in Ohio from 1803 to 1850," *Ohio Archeological and Historical Quarterly*, XXVII, 1918, 117; W. W. Boyd, "Secondary Education in Ohio Previous to the Year 1840," *ibid.*, XXV, 1916, 121.) In 1935 there were 4,263 pupils enrolled in the county's schools, and the percentage of illiteracy in the county is only two percent (Bureau of Census, *Fifteenth Census of the United States,* 1930, *Population* III, pt. ii, 479).

Churches were organized early in the history of the county. In 1799 the Straight Creek Baptist Church was organized. In 1798 the Presbyterians held meetings, but did not organize until 1799. The Methodists were in the Miami Circuit, and Reverend Henry Smith was in charge of the circuit as early as the year 1799. (Beers, *Brown County*, 294-295; Rev. I.F. King, "Introduction of Methodism in Ohio," *Ohio Archeological and Historical Quarterly*, X, 1902, 188.) At the turn of the century a great Revival movement under the leadership of Reverend James McGready, a Presbyterian minister, swept through the county. It was not uncommon at the meetings for large numbers to fall to the floor and to lie unconscious; with hardly any signs of breathing or beating of the pulse. The "jerks" or convulsions were also common occurrences. This "New Light" revival swept through all the Presbyterian churches in southwestern Ohio, and influenced other sects as well. One of the results of this movement was the creation of the Christian church as a separate and distinct organization. Shaker missionaries from New York became interested in the revival and made converts in Brown County, among them being Belteshazzar Dragoo. (Beers, *Brown County*, 271-274; J. P. MacLean, "The Kentucky Revival and its Influence on the Miami Valley," *Ohio Archeological and Historical Quarterly*, XII, 1893, 242-286; Finley, *op. cit.*, 363-373.)

A Roman Catholic church was undertaken in 1823, a seminary was built in 1840, but in 1845 it was given over to the Ursuline Sisters, a colony of French nuns, led by Mother Julia Chatfield, an English lady. In September 1845 school was opened and it received the charter in 1846. (Beers, *Brown County*, 318-325. For an interesting study of the Ursuline Seminary and Sister Monica, *The Cross in the Wilderness*, New York, 1930, *passim.*) In 1926 there were 9,318 church members in the county: 2,304 of them belonging to the Catholic church, 1749 to the Methodist Episcopal, 1,336 to the Christian, 1,247 to the Disciples of Christ, and 905 to the Presbyterian (Bureau of the Census, *Census of Religious Bodies*, 1926, I, 656-657).

Politically, Brown County has always been strongly Democratic being Anti-Federalist or Jeffersonian Republican in the early years (Beers, *Brown County*, 311). It is a tribute to the patriotism of this county which opposed Lincoln in 1860. C. B. Galbreath, "Centennial Anniversary of the Birth of Ulysses S. Grant," *Ohio Archeological and Historical Quarterly*, XXXI, 1922, 283), that it sent 1,753 men to the Civil War (Beers, *Brown County*, 339), and gave a majority of its votes against Vallandingham in 1863 (*ibid.*, 316-317). The county also contributed heavily to the other wars (*ibid.*, 334-335).

Most of the newspapers of the county have been Democratic. In Georgetown the first paper was the *Benefactor* which was published about 1820 (*ibid.*, 395). In Ripley the first paper was the *Political Censor*, established about 1812 (*ibid.*, 422). The Castigator published in 1824 printed the anti-slavery tracts of Reverend Rankin which were later published in book form (John Rankin, *Letters on Slavery*, Ripley, Ohio, 1826). Other papers were established and abandoned in almost kaleidoscopic fashion. Some of their names were indeed unusual: thus, in 1843 appeared the *Freedom's Casket*, in 1845, the *Western Wreath*, in 1848 the *Taylor Battery*, and in 1852 the *Spiritual Era*. (Beers, *Brown County*, 396-399, 422-424.) In 1937 still in existence as weeklies were the Georgetown *News Democrat*, established in 1888 as a Democratic paper; the Ripley *Bee*, a Republican paper established in 1842; and the Sardinia *News*, an independent paper printed since 1905 (Ayer, *op. cit.*, 716, 727-728).

Ohio counties were laid out to fit the needs of an agricultural society of the nineteenth century. The last Ohio County was created in 1851 and there have been no changes in boundaries for over half a century. The counties now range in population from 10,000 to 1,2000,000. Approximately 70 of Ohio's 88 counties may be considered rural. R. E. Heiges, *The Office of Sheriff in the Rural Counties of Ohio*, Findlay, Ohio, 1933, 52.) The median population is approximately 30,000 but over half of the people live in eight large urban counties.

The county is a creation of the state for the execution of state policy and has such powers as the state confers upon it. It has, however, had to provide an ever-increasing number of local services similar to those rendered by municipalities and its legal status is there for changing. The county eventually may become relatively less the agent of the state and tend to approximate the municipal corporation in the character of its activities and in its legal status. (Report of Governor's Commission, *The Reorganization of County Government in Ohio*, 1934, 3, 28-29.)

The board of county commissioners is the central feature of the structure of county government. The functions of this board touch either directly or indirectly every other branch and department. The board is the agency in whose name actions for and against the county are brought. This board is empowered to determine certain policies for the conduct of county affairs such as adoption of the budget, establishment of services left optional by law, and the authorization of improvements. Thus in a limited sense it constitutes the legislative branch. The board also functions as the central administrative body although much of the administration, centered in other elective offices, is beyond its control. The county auditor was originally made secretary of the board and still functions as such in a majority of the counties. Later provisions of the law permitted the board to appoint its own clerk, thus removing this duty from the auditor. (*Ibid.*, 58-59.)

There are three types of financial functions performed by county officers and employees: tax administration, handling of the fiscal affairs of the county, and the trusteeship of funds held for individuals in court procedure. The principal financial authorities are the board of commissioners, the auditor, and the treasurer. The commissioners levy taxes, appropriate funds, and authorize payments. The auditor's primary duties are the keeping of accounts, the issuance of warrants, the valuation of real estate, and the preparation of the tax list. The treasurer collects taxes, receives and has custody of county moneys, and disburses upon warrant from the auditor. (*Ibid.*, 71.)

There are three strictly clerical officers whose work consists mainly of the preparation and custody of records: the recorder, the clerk of courts, and the judge of the probate court. All three have some part in the recording of documents and instruments affecting the title of property and of other documents presented for record. The last two have as their principal duty the keeping of court records; the clerk of courts serving both as clerk of the court of appeals and the common pleas court, and the probate court looking after its own records. (Report of Governor's Commission, *op. cit.*, 179.)

It is the duty of the recorder to copy, index, and file documents authorized to be recorded in his office. These consist almost entirely of chattel mortgages and instruments affecting the title to real estate (*ibid.*, 180). The system of recording is prescribed by Statute. With the exception of a few urban counties recording is done by typewriter with considerable use of printed forms. Thc photographic method of copying is now in use in Clark, Cuyahoga, Hamilton, Lucas, Montgomery, and Summit Counties.

The principal records of the clerk of courts are prescribed by statute. They include an appearance docket, an execution docket, a journal of the orders of the court, a complete record of proceedings, a system of indexes, and a file of original papers (51 O. L. 107). The clerk is responsible for a variety of non-judicial record work of which the filing and indexing of automobile bills of sale was a major item. The bill of sale law was repealed by an act effective January 1, 1938, requiring the clerk to issue a certificate of title and to file a duplicate of the certificate (G. C. sec. 6290-6). At present the clerk acts as the agent of the state for the sale of hunting and fishing licenses and also issues auctioneers' and ferry licenses.

The probate judge is by statute the clerk of his own court. The constitution permits the combination of the probate and common pleas courts in counties of less than 60,000 population. In this case the judge of common pleas becomes *ex officio* the clerk of the probate division and two separate offices are retained for keeping records. Such mergers now exist in three counties: Adams, Henry, and Wyandot. (Report of Governor's Commission, *op. cit.*, 182-183.)

Listed below, with amendments, are some notable provisions adopted at the conventions of 1851 and 1912 which affected the organization of county government:

> "Laws may be passed to secure to mechanics, artisans, laborers, subcontractors and material men, their just dues by direct lien upon the

property, upon which they have bestowed labor or for which they have furnished material" (Art. II, sec. 33. 1851). "All nominations for elective state, district, county and municipal offices shall be made at direct primary election or by petition as provided by law . . ." (Art. V, sec. 7. 11912). "The General Assembly shall provide by general law for the organization and government of counties, and may provide by general law alternative forms of county government. No alternative form shall become operative in any county until submitted to the electors thereof and approved by a majority of those voting . . .Municipalities and townships shall have authority, with the consent of the county, to transfer to the county any of their powers or to revoke the transfer of any such power, under regulations provided by general law, but the rights of initiative and referendum shall be secured to . . . every measure . . . giving or withdrawing such consent." (Art. X, sec. 1, amendment adopted 1933.) "Appointments and promotions in the civil service of the state, the several counties, and cities, shall be made according to merit and fitness, to be ascertained, as far as practicable, by competitive examinations" (Art. XV, sec. 10, 1912). "Elections for state and county officers shall be held on the first Tuesday after the first Monday in November in the even-numbered years" (Art. XVII, sec. 1, amendment adopted 1905).

The aim of the survey has been to make information available regarding the records which have accumulated over a period of more than 130 years. Survey workers have not made a study of the functions of the county offices with a view toward recommending any reorganization of county government but in the report of the Governor's Commission (*op. cit.*, 186-187) recommendations were made bearing upon the records system as follows:

1. County charters and optional forms of government should provide for a department of records and court service to take over the functions of the recorder and clerk of courts, the non-judicial record work of the probate court, and functions of sheriff as a court officer (see also Heiges, *op. cit.,* 55-66).
2. The issuance of licenses should be transferred from clerk of courts to department of finance.
3. Wider use should be made of the photographic process of recording in larger counties.

4. Legislation should be adopted permitting destruction of chattel mortgages and automobile bills of sale after they have ceased to have effect.
5. The requirements of the system of indexes of cases in the clerk's office should be eliminated from the code and only the index of pending suits and living judgments should be required.
6. Provisions should be made in the rules of the common pleas court for service of process by mail and that method should be brought into general use (see also Heiges, *op. cit.,*60-61).

Following the report of the governor's commission, a new law (116 O. L. 132-33) was passed in 1933 permitting any county to adopt a charter or an alternative form of government, as provided in section 3 of Article X of the Constitution of Ohio, if it does not interfere with or restrict in any manner a charter which has been adopted by any municipal government. The electors may establish by charter provision a civil service commission or personnel department. In April 1935 (116 O. L. 134) the legislature also provided that the electors of any county may establish by charter provision accounting department of health.

HOUSING, CARE, AND ACCESSIBILITY OF THE RECORDS

According to the act creating Brown County, the courts of the county were to be held at the house of Alexander Campbell in Ripley until a seat of justice could be established (16 O. L. 29-31). For several years the courts were held at Ripley, except for a term or two when they were held in a log structure at Bridgewater. After a bitter contest, Georgetown was made the county seat in 1821. The construction of a courthouse had already been begun in Ripley. A new one was filled in Georgetown in 1824 at a cost of $3,999,999. It served for 25 years. In 1849 the commissioners let the contracts for a new courthouse which was completed in 1851. This one is still in use. (Byron Williams, *History of Clermont and Brown Counties, Ohio*, 2 volumes, Milford, Ohio, 1913, I, 388-391; W. H. Beers and Co., comp., *History of Brown County, Ohio*, Chicago, 1883, 279-290.)

The county commissioners' office, consisting of one room, is located on the first floor in the northeast corner of the main portion of the courthouse. Only unbound records are filed in this office. The space is ample and accommodations are adequate for the use of the records by employees or the public. Other records of the commissioners are filed in the auditor's office or deposited in the basement and attic storerooms.

The recorder's office, located in the northwest corner of the first floor of the courthouse, consists of an office room and the only fireproof vault in the courthouse. Most of the recorder's bound and unbound records are housed in this vault which has become very crowded. There is no room for much-needed additional filing racks or cabinets. The office also is quite crowded and has inadequate accommodations for the use of the records.

The clerk of courts' office consists of one room which is the depository for the records of the clerk, the common pleas court, the court of appeals, and the jury commission, and is located on the second floor of the north wing of the courthouse. The space provided for this office is sufficient, but more racks are needed for filing bound records. Because of the lack of available equipment a large number of the clerk's volumes are kept in the sheriff's office and basement storeroom, making it inconvenient to use the records.

The probate court office, located on the first floor of the south wing, consists of a main office room with a rectangular room connecting the office with the main corridor. This latter room is used as a filing room for the records of the probate court, juvenile court, and children's home. Filing compartments are provided for bound volumes beneath the file box assemblies. The main office is equipped with file racks of the steel roller type, metal file boxes, and a steel safe 5 by 3 by 2.5 feet. All records in this office are in good condition. Ample space and adequate accommodations are provided for the use of the records. A large number of probate court records are located in the basement storeroom.

The prosecuting attorney's office, which consists of one room, is located on the south side of the first floor of the courthouse. There is ample space in the office as only a few current records are kept by the prosecuting attorney. Accommodations for the officials and for the public are adequate.

The treasurer's office, consisting of one room, is located on the first floor of the north wing of the courthouse. Two entrances to this office are provided, an outside entrance and one through a corridor between the auditor' and commissioners' offices. The office is equipped with steel roller racks for bound records and metal files for unbound records. There is also a fireproof steel safe 7 by 5 by 2.5 feet. The space provided is ample but additional filing equipment is badly needed for both bound and unbound records. Considering the limited amount of filing space the records are kept in an orderly arrangement and are in good condition. Some of the older records of this office are stored in the basement and others in the attic. Accommodations provided for the office employees and for the use of the records by the public are fair.

The auditor's office, which is the depository for the records of the county commissioners, the budget commission, and board of revision, as well as for the auditor's office proper, consists of one room located on the north side of the first floor. Bound records are filed on steel roller racks at the west end of the room, and beneath a counter table. Unbound records are kept in metal file boxes placed between windows along the north wall. The office is equipped with a small steel safe 5.5 by 3 by 2 feet. This office is very crowded, with no room for expansion, unless an addition is made. There is no room available for additional file racks and boxes, both of which are badly needed. The accommodations and conveniences for workers and for the public are fairly adequate. Considering the crowded conditions, the records are filed in a very orderly manner and are in good condition. Old records of this office are stored in the basement and in the attic.

The county board of education office is located on the second floor of the White and Loudon Building, Georgetown, Ohio. It consists of two rooms each approximately 14 by 20 feet. Lighting, both natural and artificial, is good. The space provided is ample for the needs of the office. Wooden shelving is provided for bound records, and cardboard files for unbound records. Accommodations for workers and for the public are satisfactory.

The county board of health office is located on the second floor of the Brown County Children's Home Building on Home Street, Georgetown, Ohio. The space provided is ample for the use of the records, one room measuring 16 by 18 feet. Facilities for filing and keeping records are poor. Accommodations for workers and for the public are poor.

Records of the county home are kept in the superintendent's office on the first floor of the administration building of the county home, located 1.5 miles west of Georgetown to the right of state route 125. The records are in good condition and conveniently located.

The children's home is located on Home Street, Georgetown, Ohio, but the few records, which are in good condition, are housed in the office of the probate court.

The county relief office, which consists of two rooms, is located on the second floor of the building at 107 North Appel Street, Georgetown, Ohio. The records are kept in the main room and are in good condition. Metal filing cabinets are provided for the records, all of which are unbound.

The office of the board of aid for the aged is located on the south side, on the first floor of the building which stands near the west entrance of the courthouse. It consists of one room which affords ample space for the needs of the office. All records are kept in this room. The filing equipment consists of two four-drawer metal filing cabinets each 54 by 26 by 18 inches. The records are in good condition. The accommodations and conveniences provided for the workers and for the public are adequate.

The office of board of elections is located on the first floor of the courthouse in the southwest corner room. The space provided is amble for the needs of this office. Most of the records are inbound volumes. Unbound records are kept in file boxes which measure 17 by 14 by 10 inches. Records are in good condition. The accommodations for users of the records are adequate. Some records of this office are stored in the basement.

The office of the engineer is located on the south side of the first floor in the southeast corner room of the courthouse. The space provided for this office is ample, but provisions for keeping maps and blueprints are lacking. The accommodations in the way of drafting and working equipment are fair. There are no provisions for filing found records. The records are in good condition.

The office of the agricultural agent is located on the first floor at 118 North Main Street, Georgetown, Ohio. It consists of one room which is somewhat crowded. Facilities for filing records are adequate; metal filing cabinets are provided. Accommodations for workers and for the public are only fair, owing to limited space.

The courthouse attic storeroom is located in the west end of the attic, and is reached by a winding stairway from the second floor. Ventilation and lighting are poor, and the room is very dusty; wooden shelving built around the walls provides space for the filing of the unbound records and about half of the bound records, the rest of the bound records are thrown in piles on the floor. Records of all the major county offices are stored here. No accommodations are provided for the convenience of those who find it necessary to search these old records. The records are not grouped as to the office or department, but placed on shelves promiscuously. Considering the adverse conditions the records are in fair condition.

The basement storeroom is located in the east end of the courthouse basement to the right of the stairs. The room has no ventilation, poor lighting, and is quite dusty. Wooden shelving for bound records is placed along the walls. The unbound records are kept in cardboard boxes. There are no tables, chairs, or other accommodations for those wishing to use the records. Old records of the probate court, clerk of courts, auditor, treasurer, commissioners, and recorder are stored here. The field workers of the Historical Records Survey separated and arranged the records in order according to the several offices. The records, for the most part, are in good condition.

Brown County, like other counties along the Ohio River, suffered from numerous floods, the most serious of which occurred in 1832, 1847, 1883, 1884, and 1913(J. C. Leggett, *The Flood in Ohio, February, 1884, Report of the Citizen's Relief Committee of Ripley, Ohio*, 1884, pamphlet). During the 1913 flood the water rose to 10 or 12 feet in most of Ripley's stores causing damage estimated at $100,000 (Ripley *Bee*, April 6, 1913; April 16, 1913). In spite of the seriousness of these floods, which caused a loss of hundreds of thousands of dollars' worth of property, there is no evidence that any of the county records have been destroyed by floods. Since 1824 when the county seat was removed to Georgetown, approximately 12 miles from the river, the county records have been, of course, out of the flood district.

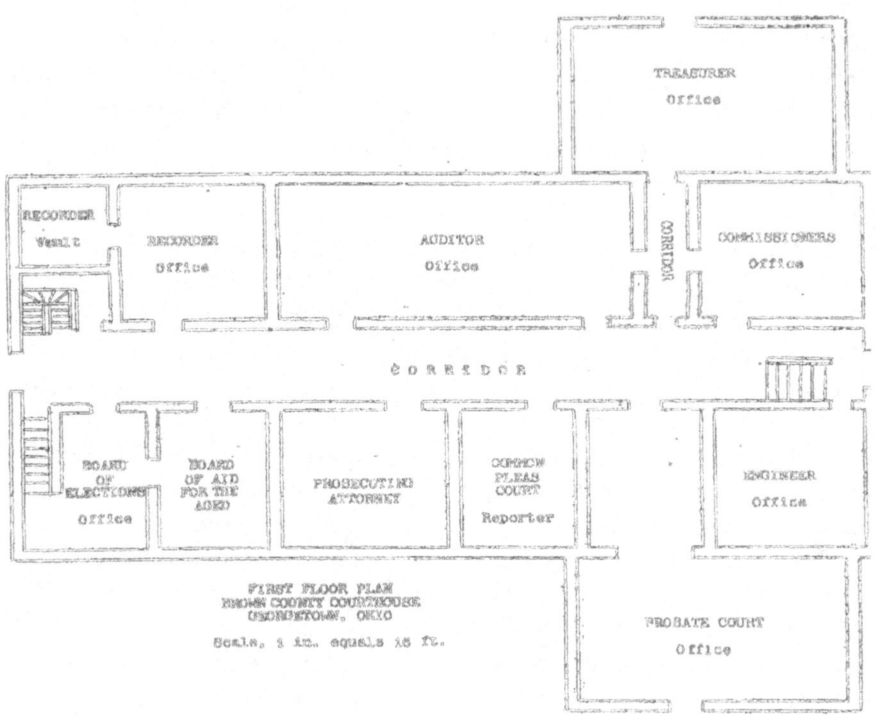

FIRST FLOOR PLAN
BROWN COUNTY COURTHOUSE
GEORGETOWN, OHIO

Scale, 1 in. equals 16 ft.

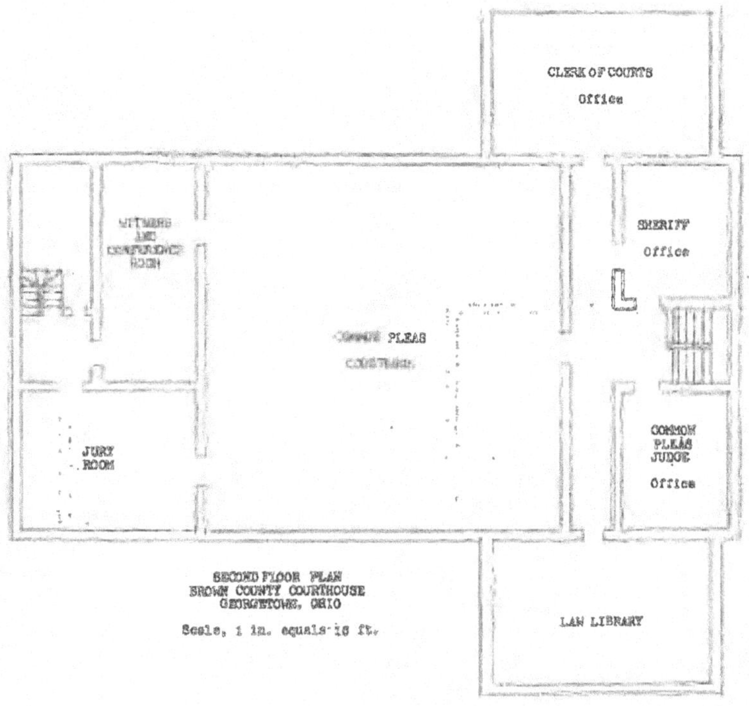

SECOND FLOOR PLAN
BROWN COUNTY COURTHOUSE
GEORGETOWN, OHIO

Scale, 1 in. equals 16 ft.

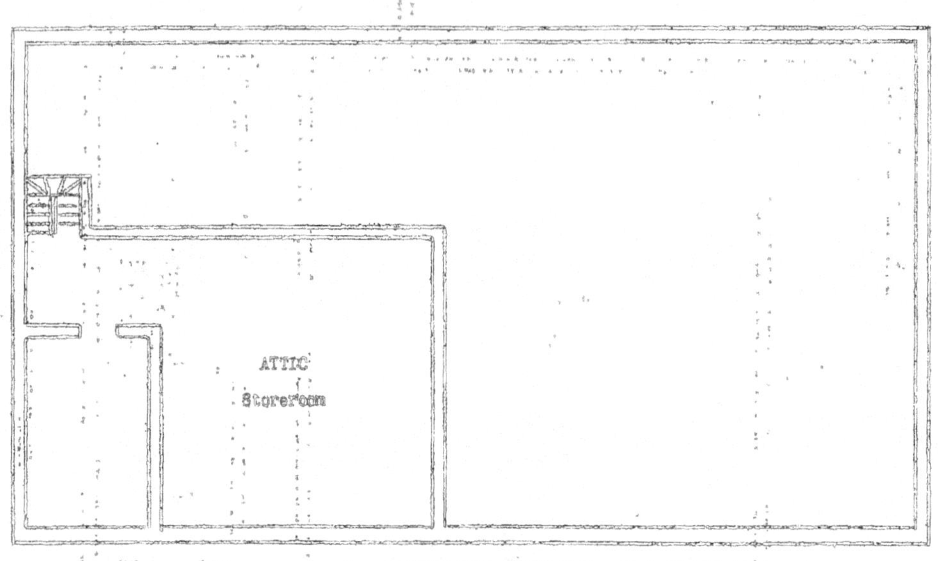

ATTIC FLOOR PLAN
BROWN COUNTY COURTHOUSE
GEORGETOWN, OHIO

Scale, 1 in. equals 16 ft.

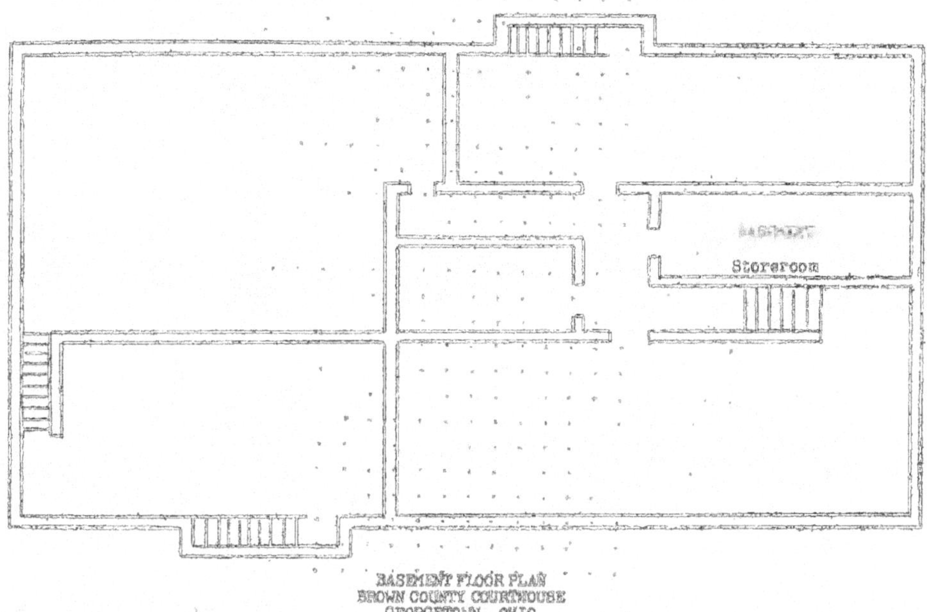

BASEMENT FLOOR PLAN
BROWN COUNTY COURTHOUSE
GEORGETOWN, OHIO

Scale, 1 in. equals 18 ft.

The local government system for the Northwest Territory comprising the present state of Ohio established the office of county commissioners. This office, created by the territorial act of 1792, consisted of two appointive commissioners who were directed to compile a tax list, levy taxes for the county, and draft plans for and supervise the construction of a "court-house, jail, pillory, whipping-post, and several stocks." (Theodore Calvin Pease, *Laws of the Northwest Territory 1788-1800, Ill. State Bar Assn., Law Ser.*, I, Springfield, 1925, 78).

The governmental system established in 1802, under the first constitution of Ohio, made no provision for the office and its existence is due entirely to statutory enactment. By an act of the legislature passed in 1804, the territorial office was re-created and was to be composed of three members elected for a three-year term (2 O. L. 150). Four years later the commissioners were made a corporate body invested with the power to sue and be sued (5 O. L. 97). They were required to keep a record of their proceedings; to assess taxes for the support of the county; appoint a county treasurer; and to supervise the construction of bridges (8 O. L. 48). They were paid on a per diem basis. Moreover, during the same period they were given the task of constructing courthouses, jails, and offices for the clerk of courts, court of common pleas, sheriff, auditor, and the treasurer (2 O. L. 154-157; 29 O. L. 316). Of these earlier duties the commissioners retain all but one; that of appointing a county treasurer. However, since 1831 they have been authorized to examine and compare the accounts of the county treasurer and county auditor and to examine the condition of county finances.

Besides the duties regarding construction and finance, the commissioners were given the task of constructing local highways when so authorized by the legislature. During the first thirty years of Ohio history the duties of the commissioners in this respect were local in nature. But as the system of road construction expanded they were given the additional duty of converting free turnpikes into state roads (44 O. L. 74). During the forties and fifties private companies were authorized by the legislature to construct plank roads (44 O. L. 126-127). When those companies were caught in the stringency of a financial depression in1857, the commissioners were authorized to purchase their holdings. If such transaction was made, the transfer signed by the president of the company was to be deposited with the county auditor. (54 O. L. 198). In the seventies the commissioners, although earlier subjected to regulatory measures by the legislature, were prohibited from levying taxes for roads to exceed three mills on the dollar on the taxable property in the county (69 O. L. 11). Later, in 1885, they were authorized to levy taxes not to exceed five mills on the dollar on all taxable property in the county for the maintenance of roads which had been damaged by excessive wear or were damaged from other causes (G. C. sec. 7419).

With the development of modern means of transportation, scientific principles were applied to road construction and maintenance. Although the county surveyor, now the county engineer, had in earlier years furnished the commissioners with estimates for bridge construction, it was not until the latter part of the nineteenth century that they were authorized to utilize his scientific knowledge in road construction. (78 O. L. 285; 98 O. L. 245-247). After the opening of the present century the surveyor was directed to appoint a maintenance engineer, with the consent of the commissioners, to supervise the repairing of improved roads in the county (108 O. L. pt. i, 497).

Although the county commissioners have never been closely associated with the administration of criminal justice, their earlier duties regarding the construction of county jails qualified them, in the earlier period, for additional duties in this respect. During the middle of the nineteenth century the commissioners of Cuyahoga County were authorized to employ persons on construction work who were confined in the county jails. (37 O. L. 54). While this provision was repealed by the criminal code adopted in 1853, other earlier functions applicable to all counties were continued. Since 1843 the commissioners have provided equipment and fixtures for places of incarceration, food and clothing for prisoners, and have appointed a jail physician. (41 O. L. 74; 87 O. L. 186). Since 1869 they have been authorized to offer a reward for the detection or apprehension of any person charged with a felony in the county. (66 O. L. 321). Since 1892 the commissioners in any county where there is no workhouse may, under certain conditions, release or parole an indigent person confined in the jail (89 O. L. 408; 113 O. L. 203). With the extension of modern crime into the rural areas in the form of small-town bank robbing, the commissioners were given the duty of furnishing motorcycles to the sheriff and his deputies in an attempt to compete with the high-powered equipment used by modern gangs. One of the latest functions in this respect is the contracting with radio stations for the broadcasting of descriptions of fleeing criminals (G. C. sec. 13431-1).

Besides providing for those who have violated the laws of the county, the commissioners were given the duty of caring for persons, who, because of poverty or physical or mental defects, became public charges. Since 1816 they have established and maintained "poor houses" (14 O. L. 477). Since 1908 the commissioners have been authorized to issue warrants for the relief of the blind in sums of from $100 to $400 per year (G. C. sec. 2969). Since 1913 they have been authorized, in any county containing a city which has an infirmary, to contract with the director of public safety for the care of the county's indigent. (G. C. sec. 2419-1). In 1933 the commissioners were designated as a board to administer the state law providing aid for the aged (115 O. L. pt. ii, 431-439). Two years later, in 1935, the commissioners were authorized to provide noninstitutional support, care, assistance, or relief for the indigent in the county and were authorized to establish a suitable agency or office for such purposes (116 O. L. 134).

In addition to furnishing financial aid to the civilian population the commissioners were authorized (1886) to levy a tax for the relief of indigent Union soldiers, sailors, or marines of the Civil War, or, if such veterans were deceased, for their dependents. (83 O. L. 232.) In 1919 the provisions of the original act were amended to include indigent veterans of the World War (108 O. L. pt. i, 633). The commissioners were authorized also, in 1884, to defray the funeral expenses of any honorably discharged soldier, sailor, or marine who died indigent. Ten years later, the provisions of the act were extended to include the mother, wife or widow of any soldier, sailor, or marine; and war nurses. (90 O. L. 177.)

The humanitarian duty of caring for the county's dependent and neglected children was delegated to the county commissioners. Since 1866 they have been authorized to establish and maintain children's homes. At the beginning of the present century, when the treatment of children was undergoing a remarkable change, they were authorized to place dependent and neglected children in private homes or institutions where they would receive food, clothing, and medical and dental treatment (109 O. L. 533). The development of the juvenile court system added new responsibilities. In order to completely segregate juvenile offenders from adults being tried in the regular criminal courts, the commissioners were authorized to provide a separate building, to be known as the "juvenile court."

The commissioners, by the authority conferred upon them to construct public buildings, were given duties regarding educational advancement. Since 1871 they have been authorized to accept bequests for the construction of county libraries, and since 1913 to issue bonds, after submitting such questions to the voters, for the construction of libraries, or to contract with existing libraries for the use of people in the county. (G. C. secs. 2454, 2434-1; 110 O. L. 242.) Moreover, during the same period they were authorized to provide and maintain civic centers in the county and to employ an expert director to supervise and administer them. (G. C. sec. 2457-4.)

Other duties not closely related to the original duties of the commissioners have been added from decade to decade. For example, in 1850 they were authorized to subscribe for one leading newspaper of each political party in the county and cause them to be bound and deposited with the county auditor as public archives. (48 O. L. 65.) The newspapers on file in the auditor's office have not been listed in this inventory as they are to be the subject of a separate report. An amendment to the original act, passed in 1923, provided for the preservation of such newspapers for a period of ten years, after which they may be removed to the Ohio State Archaeological and Historical Society. (110 O. L. 4.) They have been authorized also to promote historical research by appropriating annually a sum not to exceed $100 to defray the expenses of compiling and publishing historical data for historical societies not incorporated for profit (G. C. sec. 2457-1).

During the early years of the twentieth century the commissioners were given the duty of providing facilities for county sanitation, which, in previous years had been sadly neglected. In 1917, they were authorized to lay out, establish, and maintain one or more sewer districts within the county. Since 1917 no sewer or sewerage treatment works may be constructed outside of any incorporated municipality by any person, persons, firms, or corporations until the plans have been approved by the commissioners. (G. C. sec. 5502-1; 107 O. L. 440.)

Then, too, during the same period the commissioners were authorized to provide facilities for the treatment of tuberculosis. In 1913 they were empowered to appoint, with the approval of the state department of health, one or more instructing and visiting nurses to visit homes or places housing tubercular patients, and since 1917 have been authorized to establish tuberculosis dispensaries and provide by tax levies the necessary funds for their establishment and maintenance (G. C. sec. 3153, 3153-5). Meantime, they were instructed to cooperate with the commissioners of other counties for the establishment of a district tubercular hospital (100 O. L. 87).

Finally the county commissioners have acted in a supervisory capacity over other county officials. Since the middle of the nineteenth century they have been authorized to compare the annual reports and statements made to them by the prosecuting attorney, clerk of courts, sheriff, and treasurer; take measures to rectify errors, correct discrepancies, and record in their journal the results of such examinations. Such reports are filed with the county auditor who has custody of their official acts and proceedings. (G. C. sec. 2504; R. S. 886; 48 O. L. 66.) Moreover, in the latter part of the same century the commissioners were given their present duty of visiting hospitals, detention homes, private asylums, or any institution exercising a reformatory or correctional influence over individuals, and reporting on the sanitary conditions and the treatment of inmates. These reports, filed with the county prosecutor, are open to the inspection and examination of the public. (G. C. sec. 2499; 92 O. L. 212.)

The county commissioners offer a typical example of an office, which, designed primarily for an agricultural society, has expanded to meet the needs and requirements of modern society. At present the commissioners are elected for a four-year term (108 O. L. pt. ii, 1300).

Journals

1. COMMISSIONERS' JOURNAL

1843—. 19 volumes. Prior records missing.

Records and minutes of county commissioners' meetings showing all transactions pertaining to contracts for roads, turnpikes, and bridges; soldiers' relief records; and a record of all bills passed and ordered paid; also infirmary directors' reports of receipts and disbursements, 1872—. Contains: Bridge Reports, 1885—, entry 3; County Road Reports, 1888—, entry 6; Commissioners' Record of Road Bonds, 1895—, entry 7; Commissioners' Criminal Cost Docket, 1912—, Entry 9; Sheep Claim Record, 1892—, entry 12; Official Reports, 1906—, entry 14; Poundkeeper's Record, 1928—, entry 16; Soldiers' Burial Records, 1918—, entry 335. Chronologically arranged. 1843-1926, handwritten; 1927—, typed. Average 500 pages. 16 x 10 x 3.5. 1 volume, 1843-1853, Attic storeroom; 6 volumes, 1854-1892, Basement storeroom; 12 volumes, 1893—, Auditor's office.

For related records, see entries 4, 5, 8, and 278.

2. INDEX TO COMMISSIONERS' JOURNAL

1818—. 8 volumes.

Index to Commissioners' Journal showing names of contractors and creditors, and volume and page numbers of record. Alphabetically arranged under tabs by names of persons involved. Handwritten. Average 600 pages. 18 x 12 x 4. 4 volumes, 1818-1883, Basement storeroom; 4 volumes, 1884—, Auditor's office.

Bridge and Road Records
(See also entries 364-370)

3. BRIDGE REPORTS

1851-1884. 16 file boxes. 1855— in Commissioners' Journal, entry 1.
County surveyor's reports to county commissioners giving estimates on proposed new bridges and culverts and repairs to bridges and culverts on county roads; also inspection reports on completed new bridges. No systematic arrangement. No index. Handwritten. 11 x 5 x 4. Attic storeroom.

4. PIKE DIRECTORS' JOURNAL

1875-1915. 5 volumes.
Record of proceedings and minutes of meetings of board of pike directors and pike construction and repairs. This board consisted of county commissioners. Chronologically arranged. Alphabetically indexed by names of pikes. Handwritten. Average 380 pages. 16 x 11 x 2.5. Basement storeroom.

For subsequent road records, see entry 1.

5. FREE TURNPIKE LEDGER

1884-1917. 2 volumes. Discontinued.
Record of improvements and construction of free turnpikes in Brown County showing location of road, improvements or repairs made, and cost of project. Chronologically arranged. No index. Handwritten. Average 364 pages. 14 x 8 x 2.5. Basement storeroom.

For subsequent road records, see entry 1.

6. COUNTY ROAD REPORTS

1819-1887. 61 file boxes. 1888— in Commissioners' Journal, entry 1.
County surveyor's reports to county commissioners on surveys ordered of proposed new roads and changes in routes; also petitions from freeholders for new roads. No systematic arrangement. No index. Handwritten. 11 x 5 x 4. Attic storeroom.

7. COMMISSIONERS' RECORD OF ROAD BONDS

1867-1894. 4 volumes. 1895— in Commissioners' Journal, entry 1.

Record of bonds authorized and issued to finance road building and repairs. Chronologically arranged. No index. Average 400 pages. 16 x 9 x 3. 2 volumes, 1867-1879, Attic storeroom; 2 volumes, 1880-1894, Basement storeroom.

Business Administration of Office

8. COMMISSIONERS' DOCKET

1869—. 11 volumes.

Commissioners' docket of bills showing date, name of creditor, purpose, amount, and date paid. Chronologically arranged. No index. Handwritten. Average 375 pages. 18.33 x 17.25 x 2.67. 8 volumes, 1869-1901, Attic storeroom; 1 volume, 1902-1903, Basement storeroom; 2 volumes, Auditor's office.

For other records, see entries 1, 281, 282.

9. COMMISSIONERS' CRIMINAL COST DOCKET

1890-1911. 2 volumes. 1912— in Commissioners' Journal, entry 1.

Record copy of annual reports by clerk of courts to commissioners on cost of prosecuting criminal cases showing name of defendant, offense charged, court term, and itemized account of cost of prosecuting case. Chronologically arranged by dates of reports. Alphabetically indexed by names of defendants. Handwritten. Average 270 pages. 18 x 7 x 2. 1 volume, 1890-1897, Attic storeroom; 1 volume, 1898-1911, Basement storeroom.

10. INVOICES

1923—. 12 file boxes.

Invoices to county commissioners for equipment, material, and supplies, showing date, item, and amount. Chronologically arranged. No index. Typed on printed forms. Average 17.67 x 11.67 x 5.83 10 file boxes, 1923-1934, Basement storeroom; 2 file boxes, 1935—, Commissioners' office.

11. VOUCHERS

1920—. 36 file boxes.

Vouchers issued by county commissioners to county auditor for payment of bills allowed for services and material showing date, purpose, and amount. Chronologically arranged. No index. Handwritten on printed forms. Average 17.83 x 11.83 x 6. 33 file boxes, 1920-1934, Basement storeroom; 3 file boxes, 1935—, Commissioners' office.

12. SHEEP CLAIM RECORD

1878-1891. 1 volume. 1892— in Commissioners' Journal, entry 1.

Record of claims presented to county commissioners for payment of sheep which were killed or injured by dogs showing date filed, names of claimant and witnesses, number of sheep which were claimed killed or injured, and amount allowed. Chronologically arranged. No index. Handwritten. 400 pages. 18 x 11 x 3. Attic storeroom.

13. ANIMAL CLAIMS

1914—. 2 file boxes.

Original claims presented to county commissioners for payment of animals which were killed or injured by dogs. Chronologically arranged. No index. Handwritten. 17.25 x 11 x 5.5. 1 file box, 1914-1929, Basement storeroom; 1 file box, 1930—, Commissioners' office.

Miscellaneous

14. OFFICIAL REPORTS

1850-1905. 3 volumes. 1906— in Commissioners' Journal, entry 1.

Record copy of annual reports submitted to county commissioners by clerk of courts, the prosecuting attorney, the sheriff, and the treasurer, giving a detailed summary of receipts, disbursements, and balance of county funds for their respective offices; that for the clerk of courts includes a report of fines and costs assessed in criminal cases. Contains [Official Bonds], 1850-1857, entry 15. Chronologically arranged by dates of entries. 1 volume, 1850-1896, no index; 2 volumes, 1884-1905, alphabetically indexed by names of officials. Handwritten. Average 450 pages. 16 x 11 x 3.25. 1 volume, 1850-1896, Attic storeroom; 2 volumes, 1884-1905, Basement storeroom.

15. [OFFICIAL BONDS]

1850-1857. In official reports, entry 14.

Record of surety bonds given by county officials to insure that faithful performance of the duties to the county, showing names of officials and sureties, dates, title of office, amount of bond, and date of expiration.

For other records, see entries 76, 238, and 296.

16. POUNDKEEPER'S RECORD

1917-1927. 2 volumes. 1928— in Commissioners' Journal, entry 1.

Record of untagged dogs impounded by dog warden (sheriff or deputy) showing date picked up and impounded, description of dog, name of owner (if known), record of final disposition of dog; if claimed shows date redeemed and tag purchased, total costs, and license fee. Chronologically arranged by dates impounded. No index. Handwritten on printed forms. Average 100 pages. 15 x 10 x 1. Basement storeroom.

The office of county recorder, although not unknown as an early English institution for the registration of land titles, developed in colonial America, where, because of the mobility of the restless pioneers, changes in land titles were frequent and some system was needed to protect purchasers against previous encumbrances. Public land registers, established in most of the colonies during the colonial period and continued by the states following independence, served as a model of land registration for the territory of which the present state of Ohio was then a part. Thus the office of county recorder was established by an act of the Northwest Territory, August 1, 1795. This act, adopted from the Pennsylvania code, provided for the appointment by the governor of a recorder in each county whose principal duty was the recording of deeds (Pease, *op. cit.,* I, 197-199).

When Ohio entered the union in 1803 no constitutional provision was made for the continuance of the office, but the legislature during its first session passed an act providing for a recorder in each county to be appointed by the judges of the court of common pleas for a seven-year term (1 O. L. 136). The recorder continued to be an appointive officer until 1829, when, by an act of the legislature, he became elected for a three-year term (27 O. L. 65). The tenure of office remained at three years until the constitutional amendment on November 7, 1905, which provided for the election of all county officers in the even-numbered years (*Ohio Const.,* Art. XVII, sec. 2). The term of office was fixed at two years, and so continued until the amendment of 1933, which extended the tenure of the incumbent until January 1937, at which time the recorder, elected at the regular election in November 1936, began to serve a four-year term (115 O. L. 191).

The first county recorder was directed by statute to record "all deeds, mortgages and conveyances of lands and tenements," lying within his county, and also all instruments and writings required by law to be recorded (1 O. L. 137). In 1805 he was directed to record all plats and maps of newly laid-out villages and new subdivisions of towns and villages (3 O. L. 213-215). In 1835 he was permitted, when authorized by the county commissioners, to transcribe from the records of other counties all deeds, mortgages, and other instruments of writings for the sale or conveyance of lands, tenements, or hereditaments affecting land titles in his county (33 O. L. 8; 35 O. L. 10-11).

Since the establishment of the office many duties besides those of recording land titles have been added. The present practice of recording powers of attorney began in 1818 (16 O. L. 155-156). Although the mechanics of Cincinnati were authorized to file mechanics' liens with the recorder as early as 1823, it was not until 1843 that the privilege was extended to the laborers of Brown County (21 O. L. 8-10; 41 O. L. 66). Successive acts in 1865, 1872, 1881, 1884, 1904, and 1923 added new duties to the office in the recording of soldiers' discharges (62 O. L. 59), copies of certificates of compliance authorizing insurance companies not incorporated under the laws of Ohio to transact business in the state, and certified copies of renewal as granted by such companies to their agents (69 O. L. 32, 150; 97 O. L. 405), limited partnership agreements (78 O. L. 248), stallion keepers' liens (81 O. L. 43), oil and gas leases (85 O. L. 179), partition fence records (97 O. L. 140), and federal tax liens (110 O. L. 252). The recording of chattel mortgages and conditional sales began in 1846. Such instruments were to be deposited with the township clerk where the mortgagor was a resident. In all townships, however, in which the recorded maintained his office such instruments were to be deposited with him. (44 O. L. 61). Since 1906 chattel mortgages have been filed with the county recorder exclusively. It is provided that in order to be valid against subsequent mortgages, the chattel mortgages must be deposited with the county recorder of the county where the mortgagor resides at the time of its execution, and to retain its validity the mortgage must be renewed every three years. (G. C. sec. 8565). In 1936 the legislature passed an act authorizing the recorder to destroy such instruments six years after the time of refiling has expired (116 O. L. 324).

In the latter part of the nineteenth century an important extension of the method of recording land titles was provided by an act of the general assembly. The "Torrens System," as provided by the act of 1896 (92 O. L. 220), was declared unconstitutional by the supreme court of Ohio as being contrary to section 16 of the bill of rights of the state constitution (56 O. S. 575). The act of 1913, amended in 1913 and 1915 provides for the examination of land titles by the recorder and the issuance, if the title proves to be held in fee simple, of a certificate of title by the courts. The official certificate becomes a title of ownership and is indefeasible. However, in the event an interest is found in the land, after the issuance of the certificate, a claim is allowed to the legal claimant from a fund created for that purpose at the time of registration. (G. C. secs. 8572-34 - 8572-56; 106 O. L. 225; 115 O. L. 445-447).

This system, although adopted by a few counties, not including Brown, is not used as widely as it might be because of the difficulty of replacing the traditional complicated system.

The recorder, like other county officials, had been required in earlier years to keep records of the business of his office, but it was not until the middle of the nineteenth century that the legislature, looking forward to some uniformity in land registration, enacted measures prescribing the form and content of such records. Since 1850 the recorder has been required to keep a record of deeds in which is recorded all deeds, powers of attorney, and other instruments of writing for the unconditional sale of land, tenements, or hereditaments (48 O. L. 64). The same year saw the beginning of a record of mortgages in which was recorded all mortgages, powers of attorney, and other instruments of writing by which land, tenements, or hereditaments "shall or maybe mortgaged" or otherwise conditionally sold; and a record of plats in which was to be recorded all plats and maps of town lots and of subdivisions therefore, and other divisions or surveyed lands, and like regular succession according to the priority of the presentation (48 O. L. 64). Since 1851 the recorder has been required to keep a separate record of deeds and mortgages denominated respectfully as "Record of Deeds" and "Record of mortgages" (49 O. L. 103). The recorder of Brown County, however, introduced a separate mortgage record in 1833. Fourteen years later, in 1865, began a separate recording of leases in which the recorder was and is required to record all leases and powers of attorney for the execution of leases (62 O. L. 170). The present practice of keeping a daily register of deeds and a daily register of mortgages had its beginning in Brown County in 1892 although not required until 1896. In this record are entered in alphabetical order the names of the grantors and all deeds and mortgages affecting real estate. (92 O. L. 268).

Although indexes have been prepared in earlier years, the present system of indexing had its beginning in 1851 and took practically its present form in 1896 (49 O. L. 103; 92 O. L. 268; 102 O. L. 277). At the present the recorder, at the beginning of each day's business, is required to make and maintain a general alphabetical index, direct and reverse, of all names of both parties of all instruments recorded by him. The indexes show the kind of instruments, the date, the range, the township and section, the survey number and the number of acres, or the lot and sublot numbers and the parts thereof, of each tract or lot of land described in any such instrument of writing; the names of each grantor is entered in a direct index under the appropriate letter and followed on the same line by the name of the grantee; the name of each grantee is entered in a reverse index under the appropriate letter and followed on the same line by the name of the grantor (G. C. sec. 2764).

Since 1859 the county commissioners have been authorized to provide sectional indexes to the records of all real estate in the county, beginning with some designated year and continuing through a period of years as may be specified. (G. C. sec. 2766; 64 O. L. 256; 76 O. L. 49; 102 O. L. 289).

The present duties of the recorder do not differ, in the main, from those prescribed in the middle of the nineteenth century. His records, bound in large bulky volumes, are open to the inspection of the public and are transferred to his successor.

17. TRANSCRIBED RECORDS OF ADAMS COUNTY
1797-1818. 2 volumes.

Copy of records pertaining to that part of Brown County which had been a part of Adams County prior to 1818, listing land transactions, wills, tax records, judgments, and plats of towns. Chronologically arranged. Handwritten. Average 500 pages. 18 x 12 x 14. Recorder's vault.

For subsequent records, see entry 21.

18. INDEX TO TRANSCRIBED RECORDS, ADAMS COUNTY
1797-1818. 2 volumes.

Index to Transcribed Records of Adams County showing volume and page numbers of record. Alphabetically arranged by names of principals. Handwritten. Average 100 pages. 15 x 9 x .5. Recorder's vault.

19. TRANSCRIBED RECORDS OF CLERMONT COUNTY
1801-1818. 2 volumes.

Copy of records pertaining to that part of Brown County which had been a part of Clermont County prior to 1818, listing land transactions, patents, mortgages, and sheriff's sales. Chronologically arranged. Handwritten. Average 550 pages. 18 x 12 x 4. Recorder's vault.

For subsequent records, see entry 21.

20. INDEX TO TRANSCRIBED RECORD OF CLERMONT COUNTY
1801-1818. 1 volume.

Index to Transcribed Records of Clermont County showing volume and page numbers of record. Alphabetically arranged by names of principles. Handwritten. 200 pages. 15 x 8 x 1.5. Recorder's vault.

21. DEEDS
1818—. 136 volumes. (labeled alphabetically and chronologically). Title varies: 1818-1832, Deeds and Mortgages.

Exact copies of all deeds recorded in Brown County showing names of grantor and grantee, date of instrument and filing body of deed, signatures of principles, and seal; patent deeds showing name and address of patentee, name of article patented, patent number, date patent was approved and record filing, and signature of patentee; certificates of transfer showing name of original property owner and the property to whom title is transferred, description of property, date of original deed, date of title transfer, and date filed for record; sheriff's deeds; record of real estate devised by wills showing names of principals and estates, location and description of property, and date filed for record. Early volumes contain miscellaneous bonds and survey records. Contains: Lease Record, 1818-1964, entry 26; Mortgage Record, 1818-1832, entry 28; Power of Attorney, 1818-1824, entry 46; Articles of Agreements, 1812-1920, entry 57. Chronologically arranged by dates of filing. For index to sheriff's deeds, see entry 23. 1818-1900, Handwritten; 1901—, typed. Average 625 pages. 18 x 13 x 3.5. Recorder's vault.

For prior records, see entries 17 and 19.

22. GENERAL INDEX TO DEEDS
1818—, 12 volumes.

Index to Deeds showing names of grantor and grantee, mortgagor and mortgagee, date of filing, description of property, and volume and page numbers of record. Alphabetically arranged under tabs, direct, by names of grantors and reverse, by names of grantees. Handwritten. Average 500 pages. 18 x 13 x 3.5. Recorder's vault.

23. INDEX TO SHERIFF'S DEEDS
1823—. 1 volume.

Index to records of land sold at sheriff's sale showing names of purchaser and sheriff, and volume and page numbers of Deeds, entry 21. Alphabetically arranged under tabs by names of purchasers. Handwritten. 400 pages. 18 x 12 x 4. Recorder's vault.

24. DAILY CONVEYANCE REGISTER
1892—. 9 volumes.

Daily register of conveyances showing date, name of grantee and grantor, file number, quantity, consideration, and amount of fees. Alphabetically arranged by names of grantees and chronologically thereunder. No index. Handwritten. Average 400 pages. 18 x 14 x 3. 7 volumes, 1892-1926, Basement storeroom; 2 volumes, 1927—, Recorder's vault.

25. TRANSFER OF TAXABLE PROPERTY
1924-1927. 1 volume. Discontinued.

Record of notice of instruction to transfer property showing date of conveyance, names of grantor and grantee, description of tract, and volume and page numbers of Deeds, entry 21. Chronologically arranged. No index. Handwritten. 300 pages. 18 x 14 x 2.5. Recorder's vault.

Leases

26. TRANSFER OF TAXABLE PROPERTY
1865—. 5 volumes. 1818-1864 in Deeds, entry 21.

Record copy of leases and agreements showing names of parties and terms. Chronologically arranged. Alphabetically indexed by names of lessors. 1865-1900, Handwritten; 1901—, typed. Average 375 pages. 18 x 12 x 2.5. Recorder's vault.

27. STATE HIGHWAY EASEMENTS
1926—. 2 volumes.

Record of easements and perpetual leases for highway purposes showing name of property, location and extent of property, terms of easement or lease, and date of instrument and filing. Chronologically arranged. Alphabetically indexed by names of lessors. Typed on printed forms. Average 425 pages. 18 x 12 x 3. Recorder's office.

Mortgages

28. MORTGAGE RECORD

1833—. 63 volumes. 1818-1832 in Deeds, entry 21.

Record copy of real estate mortgages given as security showing names of mortgagor mortgagee, instrument number, description of property, amount of mortgage, dates of filing and cancellation, and acknowledgment of notary; also contains a record of releases, 1833-1891. Chronologically arranged. 1833-1907, handwritten; 1908—, typed. Average 500 pages. 18 x 13 x 3.5. Recorder's vault.

For subsequent records of releases, see entry 30.

29. GENERAL INDEX TO MORTGAGES

1833—. 9 volumes.

Direct and reverse index to Mortgage Record showing names of mortgagor and mortgagee, dates filed, date released, description of land, and volume and page numbers of record. Direct index on left-hand page and reverse on right-hand page. Alphabetically arranged, direct, by names of mortgagors and reverse, by names of mortgagees. Handwritten. Average 500 pages. 18 x 13 x 3.5. Recorder's vault.

30. CERTIFICATE OF DISCHARGE OF MORTGAGE

1892—. 2 volumes.

Record of certificate of discharge of mortgage giving names of mortgagor and mortgagee and dates of mortgage release. Chronologically arranged. Alphabetically indexed by names of mortgagees. 1892-1919, handwritten; 1920—, typed. Average 375 pages. 22 x 14 x 3. Recorder's office.

For prior records, see entry 28.

Liens

31. (Mechanics') LIEN RECORD

1845—. 3 volumes. No prior records.

Record of mechanics' liens charged against property for labor and material showing names of creditor and debtor, amount of claim, and date filed. Chronologically arranged. Alphabetically indexed by names of creditors; also separate index, 1920–, entry 32. 1845-1904, handwritten; 1905—, typed. Average 300 pages. 18 x 12 x 2. Recorder's office.

32. INDEX TO LIEN RECORDS

1920—. 2 volumes.

Index to (mechanics') Lien Record, entry 31, showing names of lienors and lienees, volume and page numbers of record, date of entry, filing number, description of property, lot and sublot numbers, townships, and tract. Alphabetically arranged by names of lienors. Handwritten on printed forms. Average 200 pages. 18 x 14 x 3. Recorder's office.

33. RAILROAD LIENS

1886—. 1 volume. Last entry 1903.

Record copy of liens against railroad companies in Brown County showing name of lien holder, name of railroad, and date. Chronologically arranged. Alphabetically indexed by names of creditors. Handwritten. 450 pages. 22 x 14 x 3.5. Recorder's vault.

34. EXCISE AND FRANCHISE TAX LIENS INDEX

1931—. 1 volume.

Index record of excise and franchise tax liens showing names of firms or corporations, date of filing, date discharge, amount of tax, and penalties. Alphabetically arranged under tabs by names of firms or corporations and chronologically thereunder. Handwritten on printed forms. 100 pages. 17 x 15 x 1. Recorder's office.

35. INDEX TO NOTICES OF LIENS AND DISCHARGE OF SURETY TO RECOGNIZANCES

1933—. 1 volume.

Index record showing names of sureties and defendant, description of real estate, amount of bail, and date of discharge. Alphabetically arranged by names of sureties. No index. Handwritten on printed forms. 250 pages. 16 x 20 x 2. Recorder's office.

Surveys and Plats

36. ORIGINAL SURVEYS

1787-1847. 1 volume.

Record copy of original surveys of military land grants made by Virginia to Revolutionary War soldiers and sailors. Chronologically arranged. Alphabetically indexed by names of grantees. Handwritten. 500 pages. 18 x 13 x 3.5. Recorder's vault.

37. PERPETUATION OF TESTIMONY, LANDS
1825—. 3 volumes.

Records of surveys made by county engineer showing sketches of surveys, boundary lines, and plats of towns and additions; also data on boundary lines and land contracts. Prepared by county engineer. Chronologically arranged. Handwritten and hand drawn. Scales vary. Average 410 pages. 22 x 14 x 3.5. Recorder's office.

38. PERPETUATION OF TESTIMONY INDEX
1825—. 1 volume.

Index to Perpetuation of Testimony, Lands, showing names of persons involved, town plat numbers, survey numbers, and volume and page numbers of record. Alphabetically arranged by names of landowners. Handwritten. 100 pages. 18 x 12 x 1. Recorder's vault.

39. ATLAS OF BROWN COUNTY
1876. 1 volume.

Historical data of Brown County townships including surveys and maps; town and village plats taken from actual surveys which were made by D. J. Lake and B. N. Griffing. Published by Lake, Griffing, and Stevenson, Cincinnati, Ohio. Alphabetical table of contents by name to townships and villages. Printed. Scales vary. 75 pages. 20 x 16 x 1. Recorder's office.

40. PARTITION FENCE RECORDS
1904—. 1 volume.

Record of partition fence lines established by township trustees showing names of contracting persons, term of agreements, and dates. Chronologically arranged. Alphabetical index by names of applicants. 1904-1919, handwritten; 1920—, typed. 300 pages. 18 x 10 x 2. Recorder's office.

Personal Property Transfers

41. CHATTEL MORTGAGE RECORD

1883-1931. 1 volume. Discontinued.

Record copies of mortgages secured by chattel or personal property showing names of mortgagors and mortgagees, and agreements. Chronologically arranged. Alphabetical index by names of mortgagors. Handwritten. 450 pages. 18 x 12 x 3.5. Recorder's vault.

42. CHATTEL MORTGAGES

1901—. 41 file boxes.

Original chattel mortgages showing names of mortgagor and mortgagee, number of mortgage, date of filing, amount, consideration, and listing of chattels. Numerically arranged by mortgage numbers. 1901-1919, handwritten on printed forms; 1920—, typed on printed forms. 13 x 18 x 5. 15 file boxes, 1901-1921, Basement storeroom; 26 file boxes, 1922—, Recorder's office.

43. CHATTEL MORTGAGE INDEX

1896—. 12 volumes.

Index record of chattel mortgages showing names of mortgagor and mortgagee, mortgage number, date filed, refiled or cancelled, and amount. Alphabetically arranged under tabs, direct, by names of mortgagor, and reverse, by names of mortgagees. Handwritten on printed forms. Average 500 pages. 18 x 14 x 3.5. Five volumes, 1896-1921, Basement storeroom; 7 volumes, 1922—, Recorder's vault.

Corporation and Traders' Records

44. CHURCH AND CORPORATION RECORD

1848—. 1 volume.

Record copy of articles of incorporation of churches, societies, and business concerns, showing name of church or corporation, names of incorporators, and date. Also record of incorporations cancelled by secretary of state. Chronologically arranged. Alphabetical index by names of corporations. Handwritten. 450 pages. 15 x 9 x 3.5. Recorder's vault.

45. PARTNERS' AND TRADERS' RECORD

1884-1886. 1 volume. Discontinued.

Record of partnerships showing names of partners, firm name and kind of business. Chronologically arranged. Alphabetical index by names of firms. Handwritten on printed forms. 580 pages. 18 x 10 x 4. Recorder's vault.

Grants of Authority

46. POWER OF ATTORNEY

1825—. 6 volumes. (1-6). 1818-1824 in Deeds, entry 21.

Record copy of power of attorney granted showing names of contracting persons and date. Contains [Indentures and Bills of Sale], 1825-1847, entry 59. Chronologically arranged. For index, 1825-1861, see entry 47; 1862—, alphabetical index by names of agents. 1825-1921, handwritten; 1922—, typed. Average 250 pages. 18 x 12 x 2. Recorder's vault.

47. INDEX TO POWER OF ATTORNEY

1825-1861. 2 volumes.

Index to volumes 1 and 2 of Power of Attorney, entry 46, showing names of persons involved and volume and page numbers of records. Alphabetically arranged by names of contracting persons. Handwritten. Condition poor. Average 150 pages. 16 x 10 x 1. Recorder's vault.

48. RECORD OF INSURANCE AGENTS' LICENSES AND RECORD OF COMPLIANCE

1930—. 1 file box. Prior records missing.

Record copies of licenses issued to insurance agents showing names of agents and companies, and record of compliance by insurance companies. Alphabetically arranged by names of companies or agents. No index. Typed on printed forms. 14 x 10 x 4.5. Recorder's vault.

Soldiers' Discharges

49. SOLDIERS' DISCHARGE RECORD

1862-1898. 1 volume.

Record copy of soldiers' discharges for Civil War period and subsequent enlistments on regular forms prescribed by United States War Department. Chronologically arranged. Handwritten on printed forms. 425 pages. 24 x 14 x 3.5. Recorder's vault.

For other discharge records, see entries 51-53.

50. INDEX TO SOLDIERS' DISCHARGE RECORD BOOK I

1862-1898. 1 volume.

Index to Soldiers' Discharge Record showing names of soldiers and volume and page numbers of record. Alphabetically arranged under tabs by names of soldiers. Handwritten. 50 pages. 18 x 8 x .5. Recorder's vault.

51. SOLDIERS' DISCHARGE RECORD

1863-1872. 1 volume.

Copy of soldiers' discharges showing names of soldiers and enlistment data. Contains [Squirrel Hunters], entry 54. Chronologically arranged. Alphabetical index by names of soldiers. Handwritten. 410 pages. 15 x 9 x 2.5. Recorder's vault.

For other discharge records, see entries 49, 52, and 53.

52. SOLDIERS' DISCHARGE RECORD

1898-1899. 1 volume.

Copy of discharge of soldiers enlisted for Spanish-American War, on regular forms. Chronologically arranged. Alphabetical index by names of soldiers. Handwritten on printed forms. 375 pages. 18 x 12 x 3. Recorder's office.

For other discharge records, see entries 49, 51, and 53.

53. SOLDIERS' DISCHARGE RECORD

1919—. 1 volume.

Record copy of discharges of soldiers serving in World War and subsequent enlistment made on the regular forms. Chronologically arranged. Alphabetical index by names of soldiers. Handwritten on printed forms. 450 pages. 18 x 12 x 4. Recorder's vault.

For other discharge records, see entries 49-52.

54. [SQUIRREL HUNTERS]

1863-1872. In Soldiers Discharge Record, entry 51.

Discharge record of Squirrel Hunters and copy of acknowledgment by Governor Todd of services rendered by this organization.

Business Administration of Office

55. CASH BOOK

1899-1902. 1 volume.

Record of cash received by county recorder listing name of payee, kind of instrument or service, amount of fee, amount accrued each month, and amount paid into county treasury. Chronologically arranged. No index. Handwritten. 100 pages. 20 x 14 x 3. Basement storeroom.

For other records, see entry 56.

56. RECORD OF FEES

1907—. 9 volumes,

Record of fees received by county recorder listing name of payee, kind of instrument or service, and total fees. Chronologically arranged. No index. Handwritten. Average 250 pages. 20 x 11 x 1.5. 6 volumes, 1907-1922, Basement storeroom; 3 volumes, 1923—, Recorder's vault.

For other records, see entry 55.

Miscellaneous

57. ARTICLES OF AGREEMENT

1921—. 1 volume. 1818-1920 in Deeds, entry 21.

Record of agreements of individuals and partners engaged in business in Brown County showing name of individual or firm, address, kind of business, articles of agreement, bill of sale, and contract. Chronologically arranged. Alphabetical index by names of firms or individuals. Typed. 350 pages. 22 x 14 x 2.5. Recorder's vault.

58. RECORD BOOK

1817-1819. 1 volume.

Record copy of indentures, bills of sale, and agreements, showing date of instrument, names of grantor and grantee or principals, description of property, terms of transaction, names of witnesses, date filed, and date recorded. Records 1817-1818 were originally recorded in Adams County but transferred to Brown County in 1818. Chronologically arranged by dates are recording. Alphabetical index by names of grantors and grantees. Handwritten. 389 pages. 14 x 8 x 3. Recorder's vault.

For other records, see entry 59.

59. [INDENTURES AND BILLS OF SALE]

1825-1847. In Power of Attorney, entry 46.

Copies of indentures and bills of sale showing names of grantors and grantees and term of agreements.

For other records, see entry 58.

The office of clerk of courts, an ancient English institution originating before the time of Edward I (Sir Frederick Pollock and Frederic William Maitland, *The History of English Law Before the Time of Edward I,* Cambridge, 1895 I, 184) was transplanted to America during the colonial period. The American Revolution made no radical change in the political heritage derived from England, and the office was continued by the states. The duties of the office were modified, however, because of a separation, in the newer states, of administrative and judicial functions, which under the English system had been combined.

The sections of the Ohio constitution of 1802 creating the judicial system for the state provided for the appointment of a clerk of courts by the judges of the court of common pleas. He was to serve a seven-year term, but was subject to removal by the appointing power for a breach of good behavior. (*Ohio Const. 1802,* Art. III, sec. 9). The constitution of 1851 made the office of clerk elective with a three-year term (*Ohio Const. 1851,* Art. IV, sec. 16). A constitutional amendment in 1905 provided that the term of all elective offices should be for an even number of years not exceeding four. In compliance with this amendment, the general assembly passed an act fixing the term of office of the clerk at two years (98 O. L. 273). The term remained at two years until 1935 when it was extended to four years (116 O. L. pt. ii, 184). The remuneration of the office was by fees until 1906 when the legislature prescribed a definite salary (98 O. L. 94, 117).

The duties of the clerk of courts, like those of other county officers are prescribed by statute. In 1853 a code of civil procedure was adopted summarizing the earlier duties and forming the basis for the present ones in most respects similar to those prescribed during the earlier years of the office. The clerk of courts was directed to issue all writs and orders for provisional remedies; endorse the date upon all papers filed in his office; keep the journal, record books, and papers appertaining to the court and record its proceedings, and keep at least five books to be called the appearance docket, the trial docket and a printed duplicate of the trial docket, the journal, the record, and the execution docket. (51 O. L. 107; 51 O. L. 158-159; 78 O. L. 108; 79 O. L. 115; 86 O. L. 174). The present practice of keeping an index, direct and reverse, to judgments began in Brown County in 1850 although not prescribed until 1866. (63 O. L. 10; 75 O. L. 103; 78 O. L. 88; 82 O. L. 39; 86 O. L. 26). In 1871, the clerk was made official custodian of the law reports and books furnished by the state for the use of the court and bar, and was made liable in the event of their destruction (68 O. L. 109).

Some of the duties of the clerk as defined by the civil code of 1853 are still effective, others have been added by subsequent legislation. Thus, for example, in 1858 the clerk was directed to receive notary commissions for record (55 O. L. 13; 93 O. L. 406; 115 O. L. 117). He was required, also, to receive for record special police commissions (1867), timber trade-marks (1883), partnership agreements (1894), copies of judgments of federal courts (1898), marks of ownerships [trade-marks] (1911), motor vehicle bills of sale (1921), and certificates of judgments to operate as a lien (1933) (64 O. L. 60; 80 O. L. 195; 91 O. L. 357; 92 O. L. 25; 93 O. L. 285; 102 O. L. 513-514; 109 O. L. 333; 116 O. L. 274; see also p. xxvii). On the other hand, many of the earlier duties of the clerk have been transferred to other departments of local government or have been abolished. The clerk issued marriage licenses and ministers' licenses until 1851, after that date they have been issued by the probate court. Moreover the clerk issued peddlers' licenses until the decade of the sixties, since that time they have been issued by the auditor (59 O. L. 67). These records were not found in the inventory. The practice of recording in the office of the clerk, the names of black or mulatto persons to be used as certificates of freedom was, of course, discontinued after the close of the War between the States in 1865.

In 1856 the clerk was directed by the legislature to preserve a list of birth, marriages, and deaths as returned to his office by the assessor, and to transmit on or before the first day of June annually a copy of such statistics to the secretary of state. From these county lists, the secretary of state prepared tabular statements showing the vital statistics in each county. The clerk received ten copies of the report, one of which he was required to preserve in his office. (53 O. L. 73-75). No record of vital statistics were found in the clerk's office. The clerk was relieved of the task of collecting and preserving vital statistics, when, in 1867, such powers and duties were vested in the probate judge (64 O. L. 63-64).

The clerk of courts was given other duties in addition to those of serving the court of common pleas and receiving documents for record. Since 1850 he has been required to report each year to the county commissioners all fines assessed by the county in criminal cases, together with the names of the parties to each case, and the amount of money he has paid to the treasurer (48 O. L. 66; 58 O. L. 69; 86 O. L. 239). Moreover, since 1867 he has been required to report annually to the secretary of state the number of crimes committed in his county, the number of pending cases, and the amount of fines collected (64 O. L. 17).

An act of 1927, amending the act of 1867, directed the clerk to report on any matters which the secretary of state might require, and to forward a duplicate copy of his report on crime in his county to the state board of clemency (112 O. L. 203). (The state board of clemency was abolished in 1931).

The county clerk of courts, like the prosecuting attorney, is one of the important persons in the judicial system. His significance and influence, however, were not recognized until recent years.

Jury Record

60. JURY BOOK

1892—. 6 volumes. Prior records missing.

Record of grand and petit jurors drawn for each term of court; also special venires listing date, number of days of jury service, mileage, total fees due, and date paid. Chronologically arranged. Alphabetical index by names of jurors. Handwritten. Average 275 pages. 15 x 11 x 2.5. 2 volumes, 1892-1904, 1914-1923, Basement storeroom; 4 volumes, 1905-1914, 1924—, Clerk of courts' office.

Motor Vehicles

61. MOTOR VEHICLE BILLS OF SALE

1921—. 100 file boxes.

Original bills of sale showing name of grantor grantee, date of sale, make of car, factory and engine numbers, model, and signatures of grantee and grantor; also contains sworn statements of ownership. Numerically arranged by bills of sale numbers. Typed on printed forms. 14 x 10 x 5. Clerk of courts' office.

62. INDEX TO MOTOR VEHICLE BILLS OF SALE

1921—. 4 volumes.

Index to Motor Vehicle Bills of Sale and sworn statements of ownership showing names of grantee and grantor, description of vehicle, and date of filing. Alphabetically arranged by names of owners and chronologically thereunder. Handwritten. Average 380 pages. 12 x 18 x 3. 1 volume, 1921-1923, Sheriff's office; 3 volumes, 1924—, Clerk of courts' office.

Licenses and Commissions

63. RECORD OF JUSTICE OF PEACE COMMISSIONS

1852—. 4 volumes.

Record copies of commissions issued by governor of Ohio on certificates of election of justices of peace; certificates of election and qualification of village mayors; and record of oaths sworn by the justice before the clerk of courts, showing date sworn, name of justice, name of clerk, and amount of bond posted. Chronologically arranged. Alphabetical index by names of officials. Handwritten on printed forms. Average 300 pages. 18 x 12 x 2. 2 volumes, 1852-1900, Basement storeroom; 2 volumes, 1901—, Clerk of courts' office.

64. RECORD OF NOTARY PUBLIC COMMISSIONS

1873—. 4 volumes. Prior records and 1908-1921, missing.

Copies of notary public commissions issued by governor of Ohio showing name of notary, date commission was issued, and date of expiration. Alphabetically arranged under tabs by initial letters and names of notaries and chronologically thereunder. Alphabetical index by names of notaries. Handwritten on printed forms. Average 295 pages. 15 x 9 x 2. 3 volumes, 1873-1907, Basement storeroom; 1 volume, Clerk of courts' office.

65. EMBALMERS' LICENSE RECORD

1907-1917, 1 volume. Last entry 1910. Discontinued as county record in 1917; subsequent records have been kept by the state board of embalmers.

Record copies of certificates of embalmers licenses issued showing number of license, and name and address of person to whom issued. Chronologically arranged. Alphabetical index by names of embalmers. Handwritten on printed forms. 250 pages. 16 x 9 x 1.5. Clerk of courts' office.

66. RECORD OF RAILROAD POLICE COMMISSIONS

1903—. 2 volumes. Last entry 1910. Prior records missing.

Record of railroad policemen commissioned by governor of Ohio to police railroad property of certain railroads in Brown County showing name of governor, name of appointee, date of appointment, and name of railroad company; also of oaths of appointees. Chronologically arranged. Alphabetical index by names of appointees. Handwritten on printed forms. Average 177 pages. 12 x 8 x 1.5. Basement storeroom.

67. HUNTERS' LICENSE RECORD
1913—. 4 volumes.

Record of licenses issued to hunt small game showing name, residence, description and occupation of applicant, and date. Alphabetically arranged by names of licensees. No index. Handwritten. 300 pages. 18 x 12 x 2. 3 volumes, 1912-1933, Basement storeroom; 1 volume, 1934—, Clerk of courts' office.

68. FISHING LICENSES
1926—. 1 volume. Prior records missing.

Record of licenses issued to fish with rod and reel showing applicants name, age, weight, height, occupation, personal description, and citizenship. Numerically arranged by license numbers. No index. Handwritten. 50 pages. 11 x 8 x .5. Clerk of courts' office.

69. REGISTER OF REAL ESTATE BROKERS AND SALESMEN
1935—. 1 volume.

Record of real estate brokers and salesmen receiving licenses to deal in real estate listing dates, names of employers, and license numbers. Alphabetically arranged by names of agents. No index. Typed. 200 pages. 15 x 9.5 x 1. Clerk of courts' office.

Naturalization
(See also entries 158-161)

70. DECLARATION OF INTENTION
1908—. 2 volumes.

Record of declarations of aliens of intention to become citizens of the United States showing name of applicant, personal description, name of native country, date and port of arrival, and signature of applicant. Chronologically arranged. Alphabetical index by names of aliens. Handwritten on printed forms. Average 200 pages. 16 x 11 x 1.25. Clerk of courts' office.

71. NATURALIZATION PETITIONS AND RECORD
1908—. 1 volume.
Record copy of naturalization petitions and citizenship granted to aliens; also oaths of allegiance showing names of alien and dates. Chronologically arranged. Alphabetical index by names of aliens. Handwritten on printed forms. 400 pages. 15 x 8 x 3. Clerk of courts' office.

Business Administration of Office

72. COST DOCKET
1879-1891. 1 volume.
Record copy of court costs in criminal cases showing case number, name of defendant, charge, and itemized statement of fees and costs. Chronologically arranged. Alphabetical index by names of defendants. Handwritten. 360 pages. 18 x 11 x 3. Sheriff's office.

For other records, see entry 73.

73. RECORD OF ACCRUED FEES AND COSTS
1899—. 4 volume.
Record of accrued fees and costs showing date accrued, case number, to whom charged, kind of action, docket number, amount of fees and cost, and date paid. Chronologically arranged. Alphabetical index by names of debtors. Handwritten. Average 400 pages. 20 x 14 x 3. 2 volumes, 1899-1911, Basement storeroom; 2 volumes, 1911—, Clerk of courts' office.

74. RECORD OF UNCLAIMED COST
1883—. 2 volumes.
Record of unclaimed court cost showing names of persons to whom due and by whom paid, case and docket numbers, amount, and date paid into county treasury by the clerk, and date certificate issued by clerk for recovery. Alphabetically arranged under tabs by names of creditors and chronologically thereunder. No index. Handwritten. Average 450 pages. 18 x 12 x 3.5. Clerk of courts' office.

75. CASH BOOKS

1920—. 9 volumes. Prior records missing.

Record of money received by the clerk of courts in court cases showing case number, title of case, kind of action, by whom paid, amount received, amount deposited and date deposited, to whom due, name of clerk of courts, name of sheriff, and witness fees. Chronologically arranged. For separate indexes to judgments, 1850—, see entries 78-81; for index, 1900—, see entry 82. Handwritten. Average 275 pages. 15.5 x 17 x 2. Clerk of courts' office.

Miscellaneous

76. RECORD OF BONDS

1821-1894. 1 volume.

Record copy of bonds executed by county officials for faithful performance of duty showing names of official, date, names of sureties, amount, and date of expiration. Chronologically arranged. No index. Handwritten. 360 pages. 18 x 11 x 3. Basement storeroom.

For other bond records, see entries 15, 238, and 296.

77. CORONER'S REPORTS

1869—. 8 file boxes. Prior records, 1885-1887, and 1905-1910, missing.

Coroner's reports to the clerk of courts of inquests held in case of sudden, accidental, and homicidal deaths. Chronologically arranged. No index. 1869-1924, handwritten on printed forms; 1925—, typed on printed forms. 11 x 5 x 4. 4 file boxes, 1869-1884, 1888-1904, Attic storeroom; 2 file boxes, 1911-1929, Basement storeroom; 2 file boxes, 1930—. Clerk of courts' office.

For other records, see entry 196.

The court of common pleas, like many other county institutions, originated in England during the reign of Henry II (George Burton Adams, *Constitutional History of England,* N. Y., 1921, 109, 134). Established in America during the colonial period, the office was continued by the states following the War of American Independence. The territorial act of 1788, establishing the American colonial policy in the newer west in respect to the judiciary, contained sections authorizing the establishment of a common pleas court to be composed of not less than three nor more than five members. These members, appointed and commissioned by the territory of governor, were giving jurisdiction in all civil matters. (Pease, *op. cit.,* 7).

The same act established in every county a primary court called the court of general quarter sessions of the peace to be composed of not more than five nor less than three justices of the peace appointed and commissioned by the governor (*Ibid.,* 4). This court, which had limited jurisdiction in criminal matters (*Ibid.,* 6), was not re-established by the constitution of 1802 hence was not in existence at the time of the organization of Brown County.

When a constitution was drafted for Ohio in 1802, preparatory to the entrance of the state into the union, provision was made for a continuation of the territorial common pleas (*Ohio Const. 1802,* Art. III, sec. 1). The articles of the constitution, regarding the judiciary, provided for a court of common pleas to be composed of a president and associate judges. The members of the court, appointed by joint ballot on both houses of the general assembly, were to hold court in three judicial districts into which the state was to be divided by legislative action. (*Ibid.,* Art. III sec. 8).

The court was assigned to common law and chancery jurisdiction in all cases that should be provided by law (*Ibid.,* Art. III, sec. 3). To the court was assigned jurisdiction in probate and testamentary matters and in the appointment of guardians. Moreover, the court of common pleas and supreme court were assigned original cognizance of criminal cases as might be provided by law. (*Ibid.,* Art. XXX, sec. 4). Appeals in civil cases might be made from the county commissioners, justices of the peace, and other inferior courts, to the court of common pleas (*Ibid.,* Art. III sec. 3). Finally, the court was authorized to appoint a clerk (*Ibid.,* Art. III sec. 9).

Since the constitution called for legislative action, an act interpreting the constitutional provisions was passed in 1803. Under this act the court was given original jurisdiction in all cases in law and equity, when the matter in dispute exceeded the jurisdiction of the justices of the peace, and was authorized to take original cognizance of all probate, testamentary, and guardianship matters, and in all criminal matters exceeding the jurisdiction of the justice of the peace, except in cases involving capital punishment (1 O. L. 39-40). A year later, in 1804, the jurisdiction of the court of chancery was restricted to cases where the sum involved was more than $500 (2 O. L. 261). In 1807 this restriction was removed, and the court of common pleas was given original jurisdiction in all cases cognizable by a court of chancery, subject to an appeal to the supreme court (5 O. L. 117).

In 1805 the court was authorized to appoint a county prosecuting attorney (3 O. L. 47). In 1806 the court of common pleas was assigned cognizance of original cases, wherein the punishment was capital, if the accused elected to be so tried (4 O. L. 57). The Chancery Act, adopted in 1824, conferred general chancery powers on the court (22 O. L. 75); and in 1843 it was given concurrent jurisdiction with the supreme court in cases of divorce and alimony (41 O. L. 94).

Significant changes were made in the composition of the court of common pleas and its jurisdiction during the middle of the nineteenth century. Under the constitution of 1851 the judges were made elective for a seven-year term. For the purpose of electing judges the state was divided into nine districts composed of three or more counties. Each district, in turn, was to be subdivided into three parts, in each of which one common pleas judge was to be elected. Court was to be held in every district or county with such jurisdiction as should be fixed by law. (*Ohio Const. 1851.* Art. IV, secs. 3, 4). Provision was made for the removal of judges by concurrent resolution of two thirds of the members elected in each house of the legislature (*Ibid.,* Art. IV, sec. 17).

Interpreting the constitutional provisions the legislature made provisions for judicial districts but left the jurisdiction of the court much the same as it had been in the earlier years of its existence (50 O. L. 70). However, with the re-establishment of the probate court by constitutional provision, the court of common pleas was denied jurisdiction in cases of probate, testamentary, and guardianship matters, but the judgments and final decrees of the probate court could be "reversed, vacated, or modified" on error proceedings by the court of common pleas (51 O. L. 145). A year later, in 1852, the court of common pleas was given original jurisdiction of all crimes and offenses except minor criminal cases the exclusive jurisdiction of which was invested in the justice of the peace or other minor courts (G. C. sec. 13422-5; 51 O. L. 474; 52 O. L. 73). In the same year the court of common pleas was given exclusive jurisdiction in divorce cases (51 O. L. 377).

Since 1906 the court of common pleas has had jurisdiction in naturalization proceedings. In that year the federal statute was amended to limit jurisdiction in the granting of naturalization to the United States district courts and state courts having a clerk, a seal, and jurisdiction in matters of law and equity in which the amount of controversy is unlimited (U. S. *Statutes at Large* XXXIV, 596).

At the opening of the twentieth century sweeping changes in the organization of the courts were made. The constitutional amendment of 1912 abolished the divisions and subdivisions provided by the constitution of 1851, and authorized the election of one or more common pleas judges in each county. (*Ohio Const.*, Art. IV, sec. 3). Ten years later, the selection of a chief justice of the court of common pleas was authorized. Under an act of March 13, 1923, in counties where there were two or more common pleas judges, they were authorized to designate one of their number as chief justice. The justice so designated by his colleagues was to serve in such capacity until the expiration of his term, after which time the office of chief justice was to be an elective one. This elective section of the act was nullified by the supreme court on the grounds that the creation of a new elective official was unconstitutional. Accordingly, in 1927, an amendment was passed eliminating the elective provision of the act.

With the increased number of issues presented to the court of common pleas, the problems of judicial administration have become greater. This problem was solved in part by the creation of a chief justice of the court of common pleas who has been given the duties of superintending the business of the court, classifying it, and distributing it among the judges. Besides the duties enumerated, the chief justice annually makes a report to the clerk of courts showing the work performed by the court and by each judge in the preceding calendar year. Moreover, he reports such other data as chief justice of the supreme court may require. (G. C. Sec. 1558).

In recent years attempts have been made to improve the efficiency of the court by imposing stricter qualifications upon those who seek election to the bench. In 1917 there was passed an act providing that a common pleas judge shall have been admitted to practice as an attorney and counselor-at-law for a period of six years preceding his election. (107 O. L. 164).

During the first three decades of Ohio history the movement for the extension of the popular election of public officers deprived the court of common pleas of the privilege of appointing the county recorder (1829), the county surveyor (1831), and the county prosecutor(1833) (27 O. L. 65; 29 O. L. 399; Salmon P. Chase, *The Statutes of Ohio and of the Northwest Territory,* Cincinnati, 1833-1835, III, 1935). The court continued to appoint a clerk of courts until 1851. In recent years, however, as new functions had been added to county government, the court has again been given a limited appointive power. Successive acts in 1886, 1891, 1913, 1914, in 1925, authorized the court to appoint a soldiers' and sailors' relief commission, a jury commission, an assessment commissioner, a conservancy district board, and a probation officer (83 O. L. 232; 88 O. L. 200; 103 O. L. 512; 104 O. L. 13-64; 111 O. L. 412). Other appointments, authorized in 1911, are that of a court interpreter and a criminal bailiff (G. C. sec. 1541). Since 1929 the court, in counties having a population in excess of 300,000, has been authorized to appoint one or more psychiatrists, psychologist, or other examiners or investigators who shall hold their office at the will of the court, and receive such compensation as the judge may determine, not exceeding the amount as may be appropriated by the county commissioners (G. C. sec. 1541; 113 O. L. 467).

The records of the court of common pleas are deposited for safekeeping with the clerk of courts, who is made liable for the destruction of all law reports and books furnished by the state for use of the court and the bar (68 O. L. 109).

Indexes

78. INDEX OF PENDING SUITS AND LIVING JUDGMENTS
[1898]—. 11 volumes.

Index record showing names of litigants, kind of action, case number, judgment number, volume and page numbers of Cash Book, entry 75, Appearance Docket, entry 84, and Execution Docket, entry 89. Alphabetically arranged under tabs by names of plaintiffs. Handwritten. Average 500 pages. 18 x 13 x 4. 3 volumes, no date, Basement storeroom 5 volumes, no date, and 3 volumes, 1920—, Clerk of courts' office.

79. JUDGMENT INDEX, REVERSE
1850—. 3 volumes. 1861-1919, missing.

Index showing names of litigants, date and amount of judgment, volume and page numbers of Cash Book, entry 75, Execution Docket, entry 89, Common Pleas Journal, entry 93, and Record of Common Pleas Court, entry 101; also remarks. Alphabetically arranged under tabs by names of defendants. Handwritten. Average 300 pages. 18 x 12 x 2.5. 1 volume, 1850-1860, Sheriff's office; 2 volumes, 1920—, Clerk of courts' office.

80. JUDGMENT INDEX, DIRECT
1850—. 4 volumes. 1871-1919, missing.

Index showing names of litigants, date and amount of judgment, volume and page numbers of Cash Book, entry 75, Execution Docket, entry 89, Common Pleas Journal, entry 93, and Record of Common Pleas Court, entry 101; also remarks. Alphabetically arranged under tabs by names of plaintiffs. Handwritten. Average 300 pages. 18 x 12 x 2.5. 2 volumes, 1850-1870, Sheriff's office; 2 volumes, 1920—, Clerk of courts' office.

81. GENERAL JUDGMENT INDEX
1901-1919. 1 volume. Discontinued.

Records names of litigants, cause of action, date and amount of judgment, volume and page numbers of Cash Book, entry 75, Execution Docket, entry 89, Common Pleas Journal, entry 93, and Record of Common Pleas Court, entry 101; also remarks. Alphabetically arranged under tabs by names of plaintiffs. Handwritten. 320 pages. 20 x 12 x 2.5. Sheriff's office.

82. GENERAL INDEX
1900—. 11 volumes.

Records names of litigants, date of filing original papers, and volume and page numbers of Cash Books, entry 75, and Record of Common Pleas Court, entry 101; also remarks. Alphabetically arranged by names of principles. Handwritten. Average 400 pages. 20 x 12 x 3. Clerk of courts' office.

83. CERTIFICATES OF JUDGMENT INDEX
1936—. 1 volume.
Index record of certificates issued in judgment decrees in which execution has not been ordered showing date of judgment, date of certificate, names of judgment debtor and creditor, judgment number, and amount of judgment. Chronologically arranged by dates of certificates. No index. Typed on printed forms. 480 pages. 18 x 12 x 2.

Dockets

84. APPEARANCE DOCKET
1853—. 34 volumes. 1868 and 1883, missing. Record initiated 1853.
Records date of hearing or trial, names of plaintiff and defendant, names of attorneys, cause of action, and sheriff's return. Contains State Appearance Docket, 1833-1874, entry 85. Chronologically arranged. Alphabetical index by names of plaintiffs showing names of defendants. Handwritten. Average 400 pages. 14 x 18 x 3. 16 volumes, 1853-1867, 1869-1882, 1884-1897, Sheriff's office; 18 volumes, 1898—, Clerk of courts' office.

85. STATE APPEARANCE DOCKET
1875—. 7 volumes. 1892-1905, missing. 1853-1874 in Appearance Docket, entry 84.
Records date of hearing or trial, criminal causes, name of defendant, offense charged, amount of bail, names of sureties and plea. Chronologically arranged. Alphabetical index by names of defendants. Handwritten. Average 425 pages. 10 x 12 x 3. 3 volumes, 1875-1891, Sheriff's office; 4 volumes, 1906—, Clerk of courts' office.

86. TRANSCRIPT LIEN AND EXECUTION DOCKET
1906—. 1 volume.
Record copy of transcripts in causes appealed from justice of peace courts to common pleas court showing date filed, date and amount of judgment, interest, itemized cost, and decisions and orders of common pleas court. Chronologically arranged. Alphabetical index by names of appellants. Handwritten. 380 pages. 18 x 12 x 3. Clerk of courts' office.

87. PRAECIPE DOCKET
1908—. 5 volumes.

Records date, number of case, names of parties to cause, and orders of clerk of courts to issue summonses and writs for witnesses and executions. Chronologically arranged. No index. Handwritten on printed forms. Average 480 pages. 14 x 9 x 3.5. 4 volumes, 1908-1912, 1920—, Clerk of courts' office; 1 volume, 1913-1920, Basement storeroom.

88. ISSUE DOCKET
1905—. 4 volumes.

Records of witnesses called to testify in court showing names of litigants, case number, kind of action, number of days in court, mileage due, and total fees due; also record of witnesses called to testify before grand jury. Chronologically arranged. Alphabetical index by names of witnesses. Handwritten. Average 525 pages. 20 x 14 x 4. 1 volume, 1905-1915, Basement storeroom; 1 volume, 1916-1936, Sheriff's office; 2 volumes, 1927—, Clerk of courts' office.

89. EXECUTION DOCKET
1838—. 30 volumes.

Record of execution on court orders showing amount of judgment and cost, description of property, and sheriff's return. Chronologically arranged. Alphabetical index by names of plaintiffs also separate indexes to judgments, 1850—, entry 78-81. Handwritten. Average 400 pages. 18 x 12 x 3. 15 volumes, 1838-1885, 1891-1898, Basement storeroom; 1 volume, 1886-1890, Sheriff's office; 14 volumes, 1899—,

90. MOTION AND DEMURRER DOCKET
1803—. 6 volumes.

Records names of litigants, case number, names of attorneys, date filed, motion demurrer, and orders of court. Chronologically arranged. Alphabetical index by names of plaintiffs. Handwritten. Average 230 pages. 16 x 11 x 2. 2 volumes, 1903-1910, 1921-1926, Basement storeroom; 4 volumes. 1911-1920, 1927—, Clerk of courts' office.

91. COURT DOCKET

1910—. 10 volumes.

Records date, case number, names of litigants and attorneys, kind of action, and court decisions. Chronologically arranged. Alphabetical index by names of plaintiffs. Handwritten. 420 pages. 18 x 12 x 3. Sheriff's office.

Records of Trials

92. JOURNAL OF ADMINISTRATION

1841-1850. 1 volume. Discontinued.

Daily record a court proceedings in probate matters showing names of litigants, case number, and action taken by the court. Chronologically arranged. Alphabetical index by names of decedents or wards. Handwritten. 500 pages. 14 x 9 x 3.5. Clerk of courts' office.

93. COMMON PLEAS JOURNAL

1821—. 79 volumes. Prior records, 1828-1829, and 1843, missing.

Journal entries of records and decisions in all causes filed in common pleas court showing names of plaintiffs and defendants, case numbers, and dates. Chronologically arranged. Alphabetical index by names of plaintiffs or defendants; also separate indexes to judgments, 1850—, entry 79-81. Handwritten. Average 450 pages. 18 x 12 x 3.5. 15 volumes, 1821-1827, 1830-1942, 1844-1845, 1852-1853, 1885-1888, Sheriff's office; 1 volume, 1846-1851, Basement storeroom; 63 volumes, 1854-1884, -1889—, Clerk of courts' office.

For other records, see entry 95.

94. ORIGINAL PAPERS

1865—. 762 file boxes (1865-1901, 525 file boxes not labeled; 1901—, 242 file boxes labeled by case numbers).

Original papers in criminal and civil cases, 1901—, 168 file boxes contains civil cases only; divorce and alimony records are filed in yellow envelopes; other civil cases in white envelopes. 1901—, 74 file boxes contain criminal cases only. 1865-1901, 520 file boxes, no systematic arrangement; 1901—, 242 file boxes, numerically arranged, by case numbers, and chronologically thereunder. No index. 1865-1901, handwritten on printed forms; 1901—, typed on printed forms. 14 x 10 x 5. Clerk of courts' office.

95. LAW RECORD (Old and New Series)

1818-1848. 8 volumes.

Opinions and decisions handed down by the common pleas court showing names of plaintiff and defendant, date, and name of presiding judge. Chronologically arranged. Alphabetical index by name of plaintiff's. Handwritten. Average 465 pages. 19 x 12 x 3.25. 3 volumes, 1818-1825, Basement storeroom; 5 volumes, 1826-1948, Sheriff's office.

For subsequent records, see entry 93.

96. TESTAMENTARY RECORD

1818-1840. 2 volumes. 1819-1820, 1822-1831, and 1841-1852, missing.

1853— in Final Record, entry 129.

Record of appointment of administrators and executors and settlements of estates. Chronologically arranged. Alphabetical index by names of decedents. Handwritten. Condition poor. 1 volume, 1818-1821, 98 pages. 12 x 8 x .5; 1 volume 1832-1840, 385 pages. 14 x 18 x 2.5. Sheriff's office.

97. CHANCERY RECORD

1820-1854. 10 volumes. Discontinued.

Complete record of all cases in chancery heard in common pleas court. Chronologically arranged. Alphabetical index by names of plaintiffs. Handwritten. Condition fair. Average 400 pages. 18 x 12 x 3. Sheriff's office.

98. PARTITION RECORD

1875—. 6 volumes. 1901-1914, missing.

Complete record of petitions to partition proceedings showing names of principals, date of petition, order of court, and costs assessed against each party. Chronologically arranged. Alphabetical index to by names of petitioners. 1875-1900, handwritten; 1915—, typed. Average 550 pages. 22 x 14 x 3.5. 3 volumes, 1875-1900, Basement storeroom; 1 volume, 1915-1920, Sheriff's office; 2 volumes, 1921—, Clerk of courts' office.

99. EXECUTION RECORDS

1879-1909. 3 volumes. 1890-1903, missing. Discontinued.

Record of journal entries in judgment proceedings showing sales ordered, case number, description of property, name of litigants, and amount of judgment.

Chronologically arranged. Alphabetical index by names of plaintiffs. Handwritten. Average 450 pages. 18 x 12 x 3.5. 1 volume, 1879-1885, Basement storeroom; 2 volumes, 1885-1889, 1904-1909, Sheriff's office.

100. STATE RECORD

1867-1894. 5 volumes. 1818-1866, 1895—, in Record of Common Pleas Court, entry 101.

Complete record of all criminal causes heard in common pleas court. Chronologically arranged. Alphabetical index by names of defendants. Handwritten. Average 600 pages. 18 x 11 x 3.5. Sheriff's office.

101. RECORD OF COMMON PLEAS COURT

1818—. 97 volumes.

Complete record of all causes coming before common pleas court. Contains State Record, 1818-1866, 1895—, entry 100. Chronologically arranged. Alphabetical index by names of plaintiffs or defendants; for index, 1919—, see entry 82; also separate indexes to judgments, 1850—, entry 79-81. 1818-1921, handwritten; 1922—, typed. Average 475 pages. 19 x 14 x 3.5. 4 volumes, 1818-1821, 1859-1861, 1888-1890, 1906-1908, Sheriff's office; 93 volumes, 1822-1858, 1862-1888, 1891-1905, 1909—, Clerk of courts' office.

The constitution under which state of Ohio operated for the first half century of its existence provided for a supreme court consisting of three judges appointed by a joint ballot of the legislature for a seven-year term. This court was required to hold sessions at least once a year in each county. (*Ohio Const. 1802,* Art. III, sec. 2). The number of judges, according to constitutional provisions, might be increased to four after a period of five years, in which case the judges were permitted to divide the state into two circuits. Accordingly, in 1808, the membership of the court was increased to four and the state was divided into the requisite number of circuits (6 O. L. 32). Two years later, in 1810, the membership of the court was reduced to three (8 O. L. 259); in 1824 it was again increased to four (22 O. L. 50).

By constitutional provision, this court was given original and appellate jurisdiction "both common law and chancery" cases, and in such cases as should be provided by law. Accordingly, by statutory provision, the court was assigned exclusive cognizance of all cases of divorce and alimony and concurrent jurisdiction of all civil cases both of law and equity where the title to land, or the matter in dispute exceeded $1,000; and appellate jurisdiction from the court of common pleas "in all cases respecting the title of land, or where the matter in controversy exceeds the value of one thousand dollars, and all cases where the proof or validity of wills or the right of administration shall be in question." (During the first half century of Ohio history the legislature granted decrees of divorce. Although the constitution of 1802 did not permit the legislature from exercising such jurisdiction, the supreme court prohibited the practice in 1848 (*Bingham* v. *Miller,* 17 O. 445). The constitution of 1851, Art. II, sec. 32, contains a prohibiting clause). Moreover the court was given original cognizance in the trial of capital offenses (1 O. L. 36-37). All cases where the title to land or freehold was a question were to be tried in the county where the land was situated. Furthermore the court was given appellate jurisdiction from the court of common pleas in all cases in which the court of common pleas had original jurisdiction (14 O. L. 310-354).

In 1831 the supreme court was directed to meet annually in the town of Columbus for the final adjudication of all such questions of law as may have been reserved in any county for decision. This session of the court, known as the court in bank, was required to have its decisions, in each case, reduced to writing, and transmitted to the clerk of the supreme court in each county in which such question was reserved. (29 O. L. 93-94). The clerk was directed to enter such decisions "on the journal of said court" and such proceedings were to be taken, as if such decisions had been made in the county (29 O. L. 93-94). Six years later, in 1837, an act was passed providing that the final judgments in the supreme court, held within any county within the state, could be re-examined and revised or affirmed in the court in bank upon a writ of error (35 O. L. 60-62).

This judicial arrangement continued until the adoption of the constitution of 1851, which provided a judicial system modeled upon the federal system existing at the time. The supreme court, as established in 1851, became for the first time in Ohio history, a reviewing court of last resort. At the same time the jurisdiction of the supreme court was restricted. In 1852 the court of common pleas, rather than the supreme court, was given original cognizance of all crimes and offenses, except minor criminal cases, the exclusive jurisdiction at which was invested in the justice of the peace and other minor courts (G. C. sec. 13422-5; 51 O. L. 474; 52 O. L. 72). The supreme court, which, between the years 1803 in 1843, had had original cognizance in divorced and alimony cases and after 1843 concurrent jurisdiction with the court of common pleas in such cases, was denied jurisdiction in 1852 (41 O. L. 49; 51 O. L. 377).

The opinions of the supreme court on circuit and the decisions of the court in bank, as transmitted to the clerk of the supreme court in each county, are in the office of the respective clerk of courts.

102. SUPREME COURT RECORD

1828-1832. 1 volume, Prior and subsequent records missing.

Complete record of all cases coming before supreme court meeting in circuit court in Brown County. Chronologically arranged. Alphabetical index by names of plaintiffs. Handwritten. 640 pages. 20 x 11 x 3.5. Sheriff's office.

Until 1851 the judicial power of the state of Ohio in matters of both law and equity was vested in the supreme court, the court of common pleas, and the justices' courts. During the first fifty years of Ohio history the supreme court served as a court of appeals, holding court in each county annually. When a new constitution was adopted in 1851 the judicial system was extended by the creation of district courts composed of one supreme court justice and several common pleas judges in the district. These courts were assigned original jurisdiction in the same matters as the supreme court, and such "appellate jurisdiction" as might be provided by law. (*Ohio Const. 1851,* Art. IV, secs. 5-6). Thus by constitutional provision the courts were assigned original cognizance in *quo warranto, mandamus, habeas corpus,* and *procedendo* (*ibid.,* Art. IV, sec. 2). In addition to this, in 1852 the legislature authorized the courts to issue writs of error, *certiorari, supersedeas, ne exeat,* and all other writs not specifically provided by statute, whenever such writs were necessary for the exercise of its jurisdiction. The same act gave the courts appellate jurisdiction from the court of common pleas in civil cases wherein the latter court had original jurisdiction. (50 O. L. 69).

For the purposes of the district courts the nine common pleas districts were apportioned into five judicial districts. A judge of the supreme court was designated to preside at the sessions of the district courts; in case no judge of the supreme court was present, as was often the case, the judge of the court of common pleas in whose subdivision court was being held was directed to preside. (50 O. L. 69).

The district courts failed to function properly. Evidence seems to indicate that the increasing numbers of cases coming before the supreme court made it difficult for the judges to attend the meetings of the district courts. Indeed, six years before the creation of the district courts, the supreme court dockets were overcrowded. In 1845 the legislature found it necessary to offer temporary relief by prohibiting appeals from the courts of common pleas to the supreme court (43 O. L. 80). A similar condition of overcrowding existed in the sixties; so that, in 1865, the supreme court justices were relieved of the duty of attending the meetings of the district courts for that particular year (62 O. L. 72). The judicial system had become slow and cumbersome. The courts declined rapidly after 1865 and were finally abolished.

Following the complete collapse of the district courts an amendment to the constitution, adopted in 1883, made provision for circuit courts. "The circuit courts," stated the amendment, "shall be the successor of the district courts, and all cases, judgments, records, and proceedings pending in said district court, in the several counties, of any district, shall be transferred to the circuit courts." (*Ohio Const.* Art. IV, sec. 6). The district courts, however, were to continue to function until the expiration of the terms of office of the district court judges then incumbent but were finally abolished in 1885 (82 O. L. 19). The circuit courts were assigned the same "original jurisdiction with the supreme court, and such appellate jurisdiction as maybe provided by law." The composition of the courts and the number of circuits was left to the discretion of the legislature. Accordingly, in 1884, an act was passed dividing the state into seven circuits, and providing for the election of three judges in each circuit (81 O. L. 170).

The circuit courts, in addition to the jurisdiction conferred upon them by the constitution (Art. IV, sec. 6), were authorized by the legislature to issue writs of *supersedeas* in any case, and all other writs not specifically provided by statute when they were necessary for the exercise of jurisdiction (81 O. L. 170). Moreover, the courts were authorized to make and publish, as they deemed expedient, rules of procedure in their respective circuits, not in conflict with the law or rules of the supreme court. The legislature directed that all cases taken to the circuit court were to be entered on the docket in the order in which they were commenced, received, or filed, and "be taken up and deposed of in the same order." However, cases in which persons were seeking relief from imprisonment or persons who were convicted of a felony; cases involving the validity of any tax levy or assessment; cases involving the constitutionality of a statute; and cases involving public right and proceedings in *quo warranto, mandmus, procedendo,* or *habeas corpus,* could be taken up in advance of their assignment or order on the docket. (21 O. L. 170). In 1913 the circuit courts were superseded by the courts of appeals (*Ohio Const.,* Art. IV, sec. 6).

The judicial system of Ohio was again slightly changed in 1912 when, by constitutional amendment the circuit courts were renamed courts of appeals. "The court of appeals shall continue the work of the respective circuit courts and all pending cases and proceedings in the circuit courts shall proceed to judgement and be determined by the respective courts of appeals." (*Ibid.,* Art. IV, sec. 6). The judges of the several circuit courts were designated as judges of the courts of appeals, and were directed to perform the duties thereof until the expiration of their terms of office. Vacancies caused by the expiration of terms of office of the judges were to be filled by the electors of the respective appellate districts. The term of office was fixed at six years.

The jurisdiction of the court of appeals remained much the same as that of the district court in 1851. However, the court was assigned original cognizance in writs of prohibition and appellate jurisdiction in the trial of chancery cases. (*Ohio Const*., Art. IV, sec. 6). Certain restrictions were imposed upon the court: "No judgment of a court of common pleas, a superior court or other court of record" shall be reversed except by "the concurrence of all the judges of the court of appeals" (*ibid*. Art. IV, sec. 6).

At present the court consists of three judges in each of the nine districts into which the state is divided, each of whom shall have been admitted to practice as an attorney-at-law in the state for a period of six years immediately preceding his election. One court of appeals judge is chosen every two years, and he holds office for six years beginning on the ninth day of February next after his election. The salary of the court of appeals judge, fixed it $6,000 per year in 1913, was increased to $8,000 in 1920 and so continues. (103 O. L. 418; 108 O. L. pt, ii, 1301). The judges hold at least one session of court annually in each county in the district (G. C. Sec. 1514).

District Court

103. APPEARANCE DOCKET

1855-1885. 2 volumes. Prior records missing.

Records names of plaintiff, defendant and attorneys, date of hearing or trial, cause of action, and case number. Chronologically arranged. Alphabetical index by names of plaintiffs. Handwritten. Average 450 pages. 14 x 8 x 3. Sheriff's office.

104. FINAL RECORD

1853-1884. 7 volumes. Prior records missing.

Complete record of district court proceedings. Chronologically arranged. Alphabetical index by names of plaintiffs. Handwritten. Average 500 pages. 24 x 14 x 3.5. 5 volumes, 1853-1867, 1875-1884, Basement storeroom; 2 volumes, 1868-1874, Sheriff's office.

Circuit Court

105. APPEARANCE DOCKET

1884-1913. 2 volumes.

Records case number, names of litigants and of attorney, kind of action, and date of trial. Chronologically arranged. Alphabetical index by names of plaintiffs. Handwritten. Average 420 pages. 18 x 12 x 3. Sheriff's office.

106. ISSUE DOCKET

1901-1913. 1 volume. Prior records missing.

Records of witnesses called to testify in causes before circuit court giving date, number days in court, mileage, and total fee due. Chronologically arranged. Alphabetical index by names of witnesses. Handwritten. 260 pages. 16 x 13 x 2. Sheriff's office.

107. RECORD OF CIRCUIT COURT

1884-1913. 5 volumes.

Complete record of all cases heard by circuit court. Chronologically arranged. Alphabetical index by names of plaintiffs. Handwritten. Average 450 pages. 18 x 12 x 3.5. Sheriff's office.

108. CIRCUIT COURT JOURNAL

1909-1912. 1 volume. Prior records missing.

Journal record of circuit court orders and decrees. Chronologically arranged. Alphabetical index by names of plaintiffs. Typed. 490 pages. 14 x 20 x 3.5. Sheriff's office.

Court of Appeals

109. APPEARANCE DOCKET

1913—. 1 volume.

Records date of trial, names of litigants and of attorneys, kind of action, and case number. Chronologically arranged. Alphabetical index by names of plaintiffs. Handwritten. 470 pages. 18 x 12 x 3. Clerk of courts' office.

110. APPEALS COURT RECORDS

1915—. 6 file boxes.

Copies of various legal documents from court of appeals including writs, subpoenas, and mandates. Chronologically arranged. No index. Typed on printed forms. 18 x 12 x 5. Clerk of courts' office.

111. JOURNAL

1913—. 2 volumes.

Record copy of all petitions, answers, affidavits, writs, mandates or other court orders, and decrees, showing names of litigants, title of action, case number, date filed. Chronologically arranged by dates filed. Alphabetical index by names of plaintiffs. 1913-1933, handwritten and typed; 1934—, typed. Average 550 pages. 22 x 14 x 4. Clerk of courts' office.

112. FINAL RECORD OF COURT OF APPEALS

1913—. 2 volumes.

Complete record of proceedings and final disposition of all cases filed in court of appeals showing case number, names of litigants, kind of action, date filed, and copy of bill of exceptions on appeal from lower court. Chronologically arranged by dates filed. Alphabetical index by names of plaintiffs. Typed. 350 pages. 22 x 14 x 2.5. Court's office.

The probate court, established by an act of the Northwest Territory on August 30, 1788, consisted of a probate judge with jurisdiction in probate, testamentary, and guardianship matters, and two judges of the court of common pleas, who sat with him and ruled on contested points, defective sentences, and final judgments (Pease, *op. cit.,* 9).

The judicial system established under the first constitution of Ohio in 1802 did not provide for a probate court but vested the court of common pleas with such powers as had been exercised by the court in the territorial period. The constitution of 1851 recreated the probate court and gave it original jurisdiction in "probate and testamentary matters, the appointment of administrators and guardians, the settlement of the accounts of executors, administrators, and guardians, and such jurisdiction in *habeas corpus,* . . . and for the sale of land by executors, the administrators, and guardians, and such other jurisdiction, . . . as may be provided by law" (*Ohio Const. 1851,* Art. IV, sec. 8). An amendment to the constitution, adopted in 1912, authorized the common pleas judge, when petitioned by ten percent of the qualified voters in counties having a population less than 60,000 to submit to the voters at any general election the question of combining the probate court and court of common pleas (*Ohio Const.,* Art. IV, sec. 7. See also p. xvii).

One of the primary functions of the court since its inception has been the settlement of estates. The civil code adopted in 1853 gave the court original jurisdiction in taking proof of wills, and granting letters testamentary, and in settling accounts of executors and administrators (51 O. L. 167). Until 1854 the court had jurisdiction in enforcing the payment of debts and legacies of deceased persons. While the court retains the original jurisdiction regarding estates, new duties have been added in recent years. With the development of inheritance tax laws in 1919 as a new means of taxation the probate court has been required to determine and assess the tax after the county auditor has appraised the descendent's estate (108 O. L. pt. i, 561).

By constitutional provision the probate court has original jurisdiction in granting marriage licenses (*Ohio Const.,* Art. IV, sec. 8). The court also issues licenses to ministers to solemnize marriages. The former provision was modified by an act adopted in 1931, which requires an elapse of at least five days between the time of application and that of the issuance of marriage licenses. However, power to suspend the operation of the act is vested in the probate judge. (14 O. L. 93).

Moreover, the probate courts in certain counties exclusive of Brown, were given concurrent jurisdiction with the court of common pleas and "divorce, alimony, foreclosure, and partition" cases. Thus, in 1894, the legislature conferred such jurisdiction upon the probate courts in Butler, Allen, Richland, Perry, Defiance, and Wood Counties (91 O. L. 791; 91 O. L. 799-800). The original act, subject to amendments in 1896, 1900, and 1904, which granted and denied such jurisdiction to the probate courts in certain counties, was repealed in 1911 (92 O. L. 643; 94 O. L. 137-138; 97 O. L. 113-114; 102 O. L. 100). In 1919 concurrent jurisdiction in such matters was reestablished in Pickaway, Licking, Richland, Perry, Defiance, Henry, and Coshocton Counties, and established in Fayette County (108 O. L. pt. i, 625). This jurisdiction was abolished in 1931 (114 O. L. 320).

The jurisdiction of the court extends to the state's unfortunates. The constitution of 1851 gave the court jurisdiction in making inquests respecting lunatics, insane persons, and idiots. The constitutional provision in this respect was interpreted by the civil code of 1853. In 1855 the court was granted jurisdiction in the appointment of guardians for minors, idiots, imbeciles, lunatics, and those incompetent by reason of advanced age; a year later the court was authorized to commit persons who were mentally incompetent to state institutions maintained for the care of such persons (53 O. L. 810. In recent years the court has been given jurisdiction in trial cases involving neglected, dependent, and delinquent children (see p. 68).

Since the middle of the nineteenth century the probate judge has been required to keep a record of vital statistics. In 1867 the duty of keeping a permanent record of birth and deaths, which, in 1856 had been conferred upon the clerk of courts, was transferred to the probate judge (64 O. L. 63-64). When, in 1908, a bureau of vital statistics under the direction of the secretary of state was created the probate judge was relieved temporarily of this task (99 O. L. 296-307). In 1921 the act of 1908 was amended so as to require the local registrars to transmit to the district health commissioner, who was directed to serve as a state deputy registrar of vital statistics, all certificates of birth and deaths received during the preceding month, and a copy of all certificates to the probate court. Although the General Code still requires the probate judge to keep a permanent record of birth and deaths and an index to such records (G. C. sec. 10501-15), none has been kept in Brown County since 1908.

Jurisdiction in naturalization proceedings was exercised by the probate court until 1906 when an amendment to the federal statute invested exclusive jurisdiction in naturalization matters in the United States district courts and all state courts a record having a seal, a clerk, and jurisdiction in actions at law and equity in which the amount in controversy was limited (*U. S. Statutes at Large,* XXXIV, pt. ii, 596. See also *State of Ohio* v. *George Metzger and Albert L. Irish,* 10 N. P., n. s., 97ff). The General Code still requires the probate judge to keep a naturalization record and an index to the records, but jurisdiction was transferred to the courts of common pleas.

During the early years of its existence the court was given limited criminal jurisdiction in cases in which the sentence did not impose capital punishment or punishment by imprisonment. By the code of civil procedure adopted in 1853 the judgments and final decrees of the probate court could be reviewed by the court of common pleas on error (51 O. L. 146). In 1857 the criminal jurisdiction of the probate court was transferred to the court of common pleas (54 O. L. 97), but later acts retained it in certain counties only. Thus, two years later the probate court of Brown County, among others was granted jurisdiction in all crimes in which the sentence did not impose capital punishment or imprisonment in a penitentiary (56 O. L. 300). This act was repealed in 1878 and the probate courts of certain counties, including Brown, was granted concurrent jurisdiction with the court of common pleas in all misdemeanors and proceedings to prevent crime (75 O. L. 960). The last vestige of criminal jurisdiction disappeared with the adoption of the probate code in 1931 (114 O. L. 475).

Miscellaneous duties, remotely related to probate and testamentary matters, have been added to legislative action. Since 1888 the court has been required to file a certified list of all unknown depositors as furnished by institutions or persons engage in lending money for profit (85 O. L. 65). In 1896 the probate court was given concurrent jurisdiction with the court of common pleas in the matter of changing the names of persons who desire it (92 O. L. 28), a matter in which the court of common pleas had exclusive cognizance from 1842 to 1896 (40 O. L. 28-29). Since 1896 the probate court has been required to file certificates of doctors and surgeons, and since 1916 the certificates of registered nurses which authorized them to practice their profession in the county (92 O. L. 46; 99 O. L. 499; 106 O. L. 193). Since 1913 the court has been vested with the power to grant injunctions (103 O. L. 427) and since 1915 has had concurrent jurisdiction with the court of common pleas in condemnation proceedings for roads (105 O. L. 583).

In like manner the appointive powers of the probate judge have been expanded. In addition to the authority to appoint administrators and guardians the act of 1861 authorize him to appoint one gauger and inspector of spirits, linseed, lard, and coal oil; one inspector of flour and meal; one inspector of beef, pork, lard, and butter; one inspector of sawyer lumber and shingles; and one inspector of salt (58 O. L. 105). Then, too, from 1908 to 1913 the probate judge was authorized to appoint a county blind relief commission (see p. 146) comprised of three members each of whom served a three-year term (99 O. L. 57; 103 O. L. 60). Since 1913 he has had authority to appoint members of the board of county visitors (103 O. L. 173-174, 853).

The probate judge, like other county officials, has been required by statute to keep a record of the business of his office. The present system of records, originating for the most part in 1853 and continued by the probate code of 1931, includes a criminal record, an administrative docket, a guardian's docket, a marriage record, a record of bonds, a naturalization record, and a permanent record of birth and deaths (51 O. L. 167; 52 O. L. 103; 72 O. L. 9; 114 O. L. 324).

The probate judge has the care and custody of the files, papers, books, and records belonging to the probate office and is ex officio clerk of the court. The probate code, adopted in 1931, directed the probate judge to preserve for future reference and examination of all pleadings, accounts, vouchers, and other papers in each estate, trust, assignment, guardianship, or other proceedings, such papers to be properly jacketed and tied together; he is required also to make proper entries and indexes omitted by his predecessor. Certificates of marriages, reports of births, and similar papers not a part of a case or proceeding are to be arranged and preserved separately in the order of dates in which they are filed. (114 O. L. 321-322).

At present the probate judge is elected for a four-year term (114 O. L. 320). In recent years there has been an attempt to raise the qualifications of those seeking election to this office. Accordingly, an amendment in 1935 to the probate code of 1931 restricted eligibility to the office to a practicing attorney or to a person who "*shall have previously served as probate judge immediately prior to his election*" (116 O. L. 481).

All records are located and the probate court office unless otherwise specified.

Calendars and Dockets

113. GENERAL INDEX

1880—. 1 volume.

Index to estate records showing case number, names of decedent, ward, and administrator, executor, guardian or assignor, and volume and page numbers of Civil Docket, entry 115, Administrative Docket, entry 119, and Guardian Docket, entry 120. Also indexes Probate Court Journal, entry 122, indirectly by case numbers. Alphabetically arranged by names of decedents, wards, or assignors. Handwritten. 650 pages. 20 x 12 x 4.5.

114. PROBATE COURT CALENDAR

1887—. 16 volumes.

Daily schedule of cases assigned showing names of principles and attorneys, case number, and volume and page numbers of Probate Court Journal, entry 122. Chronologically arranged. No index. Handwritten. Average 190 pages. 20 x 12 x 1.5.

115. CIVIL DOCKET

1853—. 7 volumes.

Record of proceedings of civil cases in probate court showing names of litigants and case numbers of original papers in Probate Files, entry 128. Chronologically arranged. Alphabetical index by names of plaintiffs; also separate index, 1880—, entry 113. Handwritten. Average 400 pages. 18 x 20 x 3.

116. CRIMINAL DOCKET

1878—. 2 volumes.

Record of proceedings of criminal cases heard in probate court showing names of defendant and case number of original papers in Probate Files, entry 128. Since 1931 records are of misdemeanors. Chronologically arranged. Alphabetical index by names of defendants. Handwritten. Average 480 pages. 18 x 12 x 3.5.

117. WITNESS DOCKET

1883-1918. 1 volume. Prior records missing. Discontinued.

Record of witnesses called to testify in cases before probate court giving names of parties involved, cause of action, days in court, mileage fee, and total fee due.

Chronologically arranged. Alphabetical index by names of witnesses. Handwritten. 450 pages. 16 x 10 x 3.5.

118. ADMINISTRATORS', EXECUTORS', AND GUARDIANS' DOCKET

1852-1859. 1 volume. 1860-1881, missing.

Record of appointments of administrators, executors, and guardians, showing name of decedent or ward, date, amount of bond, names of sureties, and volume and page numbers of Probate Court Journal, entry 122, and case number of original papers and Probate Files, entry 128. Contains: Administration Docket, entry 119; Guardians Docket, entry 120. Chronologically arranged. Alphabetical index by names of decedents or wards. Handwritten. 350 pages. 16 x 11 x 3. Basement storeroom.

119. ADMINISTRATION DOCKET

1882—. 3 volumes. 1852-1859 in Administrators', Executors', and Guardians' docket, entry 118.

Record of estates settled by administrator or executor showing name of decedent, date appointed, amount of bond, names of sureties, names of witnesses, volume and page numbers of Probate Court Journal, entry 122, and case number of original papers in Probate Files, entry 128. Chronologically arranged. Alphabetical index by names of decedents; also separate index, entry 113. Handwritten. Average 350 pages. 32 x 16 x 3.

120. GUARDIAN DOCKET

1882—. 3 volumes. 1852-1859 in Administrators', Executors', and Guardians' docket, entry 118.

Record of appointments of guardians for minors or irresponsible persons showing date, amount of bond, names of sureties name of ward, volume and page numbers of Probate Court Journal, entry 122, and case numbers of original papers in Probate Files, entry 128. Chronologically arranged. Alphabetical index by names of wards; also separate index, entry 113. Handwritten. Average 440 pages. 20 x 14 x 3.5.

121. SETTLEMENT CALENDAR
1872-1934. 2 volumes. Discontinued.

Records case number, name of decedent, ward, or assignor, name of administrator, executor, guardian, or trustee, docket and page numbers, date inventory filed, date account filed, when due, notices issued, and remarks. Alphabetically arranged by names of decedents, wards, or assignors. No index. Handwritten. Average 475 pages. 21 x 18 x 3.5. 1 volume, 1872-1896, Basement storeroom; 1 volume, 1897-1934, Probate courts' office.

Court Proceedings

122. PROBATE COURT JOURNAL
1853—. 47 volumes.

Journal entry record of all proceedings in this court showing term of court in which case was heard, docket number, and case number of original papers in Probate Files, entry 128; also names of plaintiffs and defendant. Contains Criminal Journal, 1871—, entry 124. Chronologically arranged. For index, 1855-1887, see entry 123; 1888—, alphabetical index by names of principles; also separate indexes, entries 118-120; 1887—, entry 114. 1853-1928, handwritten; 1929—, typed. Average 350 pages. 18 x 20 x 2.5.

123. INDEX TO JOURNAL
1853-1887. 3 volumes. Discontinued.

Index to Probate Court Journal, entry 122, showing names of principals in cases handled by this court, volume and page numbers of record, and kind of action. Alphabetically arranged by names of principals. Handwritten. Average 350 pages. 16 x 11 x 3.

124. CRIMINAL JOURNAL
1850-1870. 2 volumes. 1871— in Probate Court Journal, entry 122.

Record and journal of all proceedings in criminal cases, chronologically arranged. Alphabetical index by names of defendants. Handwritten. Average 100 pages. 12 x 8 x 1. Basement storeroom.

125. CRIMINAL RECORD

1879-1924. 3 volumes. 1853-1878 in final Record, entry 129; discontinued. Complete record of all criminal cases heard in this court, chronologically arranged. Alphabetical index by names of defendants. Handwritten. Average 425 pages. 18 x 12 x 3.5.

126. ADMINISTRATORS' RECORD

1847-1852. 1 volume. 1853— in Final Record entry 129. Record of court proceedings in settlement of estates by administrator showing inventory record, sales account filed, and final settlement. This is an administration record of common pleas court. Chronologically arranged. Alphabetical index by names of decedents. Handwritten. 300 pages. 16 x 11 x 2.5. Basement storeroom.

127. ADMINISTRATORS' AND EXECUTORS' RECORD

1837-1851. 1 volume. 1853— in Final record, entry 129. Record of appointments of administrators and executors and proceedings in settlement of estates; also final settlement record. This is a record of common pleas court covering the settlement of estates before the probate court was created. Chronologically arranged. Alphabetical index by names of decedents. Handwritten. Condition fair. 350 pages. 14 x 8 x 2.5. Basement storeroom.

128. PROBATE FILES

1852—. 1,173 file boxes (labeled by case numbers). Original papers in all cases in probate court including copies of wills, settlement of estate papers, affidavits pertaining to estate probated, proof of publication, final statements; also records of appointments of administrators, executors, and guardians, and miscellaneous cost bills. Records show title of case, names of persons involved, and case number. Numerically arranged by case numbers. For indexes, see entries 115, 116, 118-120, 122, 131, 154, 156, and 188. 1852-1928, handwritten; 1929—, typed. 887 cardboard file boxes, 8 x 5 x 4; 286 metal file boxes, 14 x 10 x 5.

129. FINAL RECORD

1853—. 37 volumes. Complete record of proceedings in matters filed in probate court showing case number, names of parties involved, kind of action, copy of petition setting forth grounds of suit or affidavit of information in criminal cases, date filed, testimony and evidence admitted, court orders, and decrees. Contains: Testamentary Record, entry 96; Criminal Record, 1853-1878, entry 125; Administrators' Record, entry 126; Administrators' and Executors' Record, entry 127; Final Record of Assignments, 1853-1885, entry 153. Chronologically arranged by dates of filing. Alphabetical index by names of plaintiffs. 1853-1928, handwritten; 1929—, typed. Average 450 pages. 20 x 14 x 3.

130. SEARCH WARRANT RECORD
1922-1935. 1 volume. Discontinued.
Record copies of search warrants issued by probate judge authorizing search of premises for intoxicating liquor or manufacturing equipment. Chronologically arranged. No index. 1922-1928, handwritten on printed forms; 1929—, typed on printed forms. 100 pages. 14 x 10 x 1.

Wills

131. WILL RECORD
1818—. 21 volumes.
Record copies of original wills or testaments entered for probate. Wills filed before probate court was created have been transcribed from common pleas records making a complete record since the county was created. Shows case numbers of original papers in Probate Files, entry 128. Chronologically arranged. 1818-1927, handwritten; 1928—, typed. Average 450 pages. 16 x 11 x 3.5.

132. INDEX TO WILLS
1818—. 2 volumes.
Index to Will Record showing date of will, name of testator, names of witnesses, name of executor, and volume and page numbers of records. Alphabetically arranged by names of testators. Handwritten. Average 300 pages. 18 x 10 x 2.

Estates

Appointments, Bonds, and Letters

133. NOTICE RECORD
1866—. 5 volumes.
Record of administrators, executors, guardians, and trustees, appointed by probate court, with proofs of publications sworn to before notary public and clipped copy of newspaper advertisement. Alphabetically arranged by names of decedents and wards. No index. Handwritten on printed forms. Average 450 pages. 17 x 10 x 3.5. 1 volume, 1866-1881, Basement storeroom; 4 volumes, 1882—, Probate court office.

134. ADMINISTRATORS' AND EXECUTORS' APPOINTMENTS, BONDS AND LETTERS
1905-1915. 1 volume.
Record of appointment of administrators and executors; also copies of bonds given by administrators and executors showing amount and names of sureties. Chronologically arranged. Alphabetical index by names of decedents. Handwritten on printed forms. 375 pages. 15 x 9 x 3. Basement storeroom.

For other records of bonds, see entries 135-138.

135. BOND RECORD
1852-1864. 2 volumes.
Record copies of bonds filed by administrator, executors, and guardians, showing amount and names of sureties. Chronologically arranged. Alphabetical index by names of decedents and wards. Handwritten on printed forms. Average 600 pages. 16 x 11 x 4.5. Basement storeroom.

For other records, see entries 134 and 136-139.

136. ADMINISTRATORS' BOND RECORD
1855—. 11 volumes.
Record copies of bonds filed by administrator showing amount and names of sureties. Chronologically arranged. Alphabetical index by names of decedents. Handwritten on printed forms. Average 450 pages. 15 x 9 x 3.5. 10 volumes, 1855-1876, Probate court office; 1 volume, 1877-1885, Basement storeroom.

For other bond records, see entries 134, 135, and 137.

137. ADMINISTRATORS' BOND RECORD WILL ANNEXED
1869-1886. 1 volume.

Record copies of bonds filed by administrators with wills annexed showing amount and names of sureties. Chronologically arranged. Alphabetical index by names of decedents. Handwritten on printed forms. 395 pages. 14 x 10 x 3. Basement storeroom.

For other records, see entries 134-136.

138. EXECUTORS' BOND RECORD
1855—. 9 volumes.

Record copies of bonds filed by executors showing amount and names of sureties. Chronologically arranged. Alphabetical index by names of decedents. Handwritten. Average 400 pages. 15 x 9 x 3. 1 volume, 1855-1886, Basement storeroom; 8 volumes, 1887—, Probate court office.

For other records, see entries 134 and 135.

139. GUARDIANS' BOND RECORD
1866—. 7 volumes.

Record copies of bonds filed by guardians showing amount and names of sureties. Chronologically arranged. Alphabetical index by names of wards. Handwritten. Average 380 pages. 15 x 9 x 3. 1 volume, 1866-1884, Basement storeroom; 6 volumes, 1885—, Probate court office.

For prior records, see entry 135.

Inventories, Sale Bills, and Schedules of Debt

140. INDEX TO RECORD OF INVENTORIES AND SALE BILLS
1853—. 40 volumes.

Inventories and appraisement of property, both real and personal, and settlement of estates; also record of sale of property. Chronologically arranged. 1853-1938, handwritten on printed forms; 1929—, typed on printed forms. Average 425 pages. 18 x 12 x 3.5.

159. NATURALIZATION RECORD

1880-1906. 1 volume. Last entry 1901.

Record copies of certificates granting citizenship to aliens on filing of final papers. Chronologically arranged. Alphabetical index by names of aliens. Handwritten on printed forms. 400 pages. 15 x 8 x 3.

160. NATURALIZATION RECORD, MINORS'

1880-1906. 1 volume. Last entry 1898.

Declaration of intention by aliens entering United States before reaching legal age to become citizens. Contains [Final Record], 1880-1898, entry 161. Chronologically arranged. Alphabetical index by names of aliens. Handwritten on printed forms. 420 pages. 15 x 8 x 3.

161. [FINAL RECORD]

1880-1898. In Naturalization Record, minors, entry 160.

Record of citizenship granted to aliens in Brown County showing name of applicant, affidavits of supporting witnesses, and date citizenship granted.

Vital Statistics

Births and Deaths (See also entries 319-321)

162. BIRTH RECORDS

1857-1908. 4 volumes. Discontinued as a county record; subsequent records kept by the state bureau of vital statistics.

Record of births showing names of child and parents, date, place of birth, and attending physician or midwife. Chronologically arranged. Handwritten. Average 200 pages. 14 x 8 x 1.5.

163. INDEX TO BIRTH RECORDS

1857-1908. 1 volume.

Index to birth records showing names of infants and parents, and volume and page numbers of record. Alphabetically arranged by names of infants. Handwritten. 200 pages. 12 x 9 x1.5.

164. DEATH RECORDS

1857-1908. 3 volumes. Discontinued as a county record; subsequent records kept by the state bureau of vital statistics.

Record of death as reported to probate court showing name of decedent, date and cause of death, and residence. Chronologically arranged. Handwritten. Average 200 pages. 14 x 8 x 1.5.

165. INDEX TO DEATH RECORDS

1857-1908. 1 volume.

Index to Death Records showing names of decedents and volume and page numbers of record. Alphabetically arranged by names of decedents. Handwritten. 200 pages. 12 x 9 x 1.5.

Marriages

166. MARRIAGE LICENSE RECORD

1818—. 34 volumes.

Record of licenses to marry with copies of certificates by minister or magistrates performing ceremonies. Record of marriage banns are found in back of each volume. Chronologically arranged. 1818-1862, handwritten; 1863—, handwritten on printed forms. Average 300 pages. 12 x 9 x 2.

167. INDEX TO MARRIAGE LICENSE RECORD

1818—. 3 volumes.

Index to Marriage License Record showing name of contracting parties and volume and page numbers of record. Alphabetically arranged by names of contracting parties. Handwritten. Average 250 pages. 12 x 9 x 2.

168. MARRIAGE RECORD

1822-1935. 2 volumes. Discontinued.

Record of personal appearances in probate court of person seeking marriage licenses showing names of principles and minister or magistrate, date, place of marriage. Chronologically arranged by dates of marriage certificates. No index. Handwritten. Condition fair. Average 140 pages. 14 x 8 x 1.5. Basement storeroom.

169. MARRIAGE RECORD, JOURNAL
1931—. 1 volume.
Record of request for waiver of time limit before marriage license is issued. Chronologically arranged. Alphabetical index by names of contracting parties. Handwritten on printed forms. 300 pages. 18 x 12 x 2.

170. CONSENTS
1854-1870. 1 file box.
Consents and requests in cases of minors from parent or guardian of one or both contracting parties for issuance of marriage license. Chronologically arranged. No index. Handwritten. 8 x 5 x 4.

171. MARRIAGE RETURNS
1825—. 42 file boxes (labeled chronological).
Certificates of marriages filed by ministers and magistrates showing names of contracting parties, signature of minister or magistrate, and date and place of marriage. Chronologically arranged. No index. 1825-1854, handwritten; 1855—, handwritten on printed forms. 8 x 5 x 4.

Licenses

172. MINISTERS' LICENSES
1852—. 2 volumes.
Record of licenses issued to ministers to perform marriages showing name of minister, date and place of ordination, and date files for record of court. Chronologically arranged. Alphabetical index by names of ministers. Handwritten. Average 300 pages. 14 x 9+ x 2.5. 1 volume, 1852-1868, Basement storeroom; 1 volume, 1869—, Probate court office.

173. PHYSICIANS' AND LIMITED PRACTITIONERS' LICENSES
1855—. 1 volume.
Record of physicians and surgeons admitted to practice medicine and record of persons licensed to a limited practice. Chronologically arranged. Alphabetical index but names of licensees. Handwritten. 200 pages. 14 x 9 x 1.5.

174. RECORD OF REGISTERED NURSES

1916—. 1 volume.

Record of graduate nurses and of certificates issued to nurses showing name, address, and date of certificate. Alphabetically arranged by names of nurses. No index. Handwritten on printed forms. 200 pages. 18 x 12 x 1.

Business Administration of Office

175. CITATION COST BILL

1867-1878. 2 volumes. Discontinued.

Itemized bills and costs due probate court in citation orders. Chronologically arranged. Alphabetical index by names of principles. Handwritten. Average 98 pages. 12 x 9 x .5. Basement storeroom.

176. CIVIL CAUSES COST BILL

1867-1870. 1 volume. Discontinued.

Record of cost due probate court from civil causes. Chronologically arranged. Alphabetical index by names of plaintiffs or principles. Handwritten. 98 pages. 12 x 10 x .5. Basement storeroom.

177. CRIMINAL COST BILL RECORD

1888-1903. 1 volume. Discontinued.

Cost due probate court from criminal causes. Contains Lunacy Inquest Cost Bills, entry 157. Chronologically arranged. Alphabetical index by names of defendants. Handwritten. 350 pages. 18 x 12 x 2.5. Basement storeroom.

178. COST BOOK

1852-1926. 16 volumes. Discontinued. 1861-1871, missing.

Record of cost in probate court causes giving date, case number, to whom charged, type of cause, and date paid. Alphabetically arranged by names of debtors. No index. Average 300 pages. 17 x 8 x 2.5. 10 volumes, 1852-1860, 1872-1898, Basement storeroom; 6 volumes, 1899-1926, Probate court office.

179. CASH BOOK

1907—. 9 volumes.

Record of receipts into probate court showing case number, names of payer and payee, volume and page numbers of Record of Accrued Fees, entry 180, and amount. Chronologically arranged. No index. Handwritten. Average 275 pages. 18 x 12 x 2.

180. RECORD OF ACCRUED FEES

1907—. 5 volumes.

Record of fees accrued in probate court causes showing date, case number, to whom charged, amount due from county juvenile court and for transcripts, date paid, and volume and page numbers of Cash Book, entry 179. Chronologically arranged. No index. Handwritten. Average 300 pages. 18 x 12 x 2.

181. COST BILL, PATENT RIGHT

1868-1869. 1 volume. Discontinued.

Itemized cost bill due probate court for license to vend patent rights. Chronologically arranged. Alphabetical index by names of patentees. Handwritten. 245 pages. 8 x 9 x 1.5. Basement storeroom.

Miscellaneous

182. PATENT RECORD

1868-1869. 1 volume.

Affidavits to patent rights issued by United States commissioner of patents with description of articles patented. Chronologically arranged. Alphabetical index by names of patentees. Handwritten on printed forms. 457 pages. 15 x 9 x 3.5. Basement storeroom.

183. EXAMINERS' REPORTS

1879-1900. 1 volume.

Reports to probate judge by examiners on the financial condition of county offices. Chronologically arranged. No index. Handwritten on printed forms. 300 pages. 14 x 8 x 2. Attic storeroom.

For other records, see entry 239.

184. UNCLAIMED DEPOSITS

1889-1903. 1 volume. Discontinued.

Reports of unclaimed deposits of unknown depositors filed in probate court by banks showing amounts and dates of deposits. Alphabetically arranged by names of banks. No index. Handwritten on printed forms. 300 pages. 18 x 14 x 2. Attic storeroom.

185. LIQUOR DEALERS' BONDS

1882-. 1 volume. Kept for this year only.

Record copies of bonds filed by individuals or partnerships to retail intoxicating liquor giving amount and names of sureties. Chronologically arranged. Alphabetical index by names of retailers. Handwritten on printed forms. 320 pages. 18 x 12 x 2.5. Basement storeroom.

186. MISCELLANEOUS BONDS

1888—. 2 volumes.

Record of special bonds filed in probate court including additional guardians' bonds and administrators' bonds showing names of person bonded and of sureties, also amount of bond. Chronologically arranged. Alphabetical index by names of principles. Handwritten. 415 pages. 15 x 9 x 3.

187. MISCELLANEOUS RECORD

1892-1916. 1 volume. Discontinued.

Record of miscellaneous matters filed in probate court as *habeas corpus* proceedings, condemnation proceedings in acquiring lands for public roads, highways and streets, and injunction proceedings, showing names of litigants, kind of action, record hearing, court orders, and decrees. Chronologically arranged by dates of filing. Alphabetical index by names of plaintiffs. Handwritten. 570 pages. 18 x 12 x 3.5.

The juvenile court, though of uncertain origins, has been generally recognized as an American contribution to the administration of social justice. The establishment of such courts was the logical outcome of the practical philosophy of enlightened public men that child offenders against the law, or conventional social standards, should not be treated as criminals, but as unfortunates needing the help, supervision, and protection of the state (Mariam Van Waters, *Youth in Conflict,* N. Y., 1925, 147, 159, 161). Although the first separate court in the United States for the trial of juvenile offenders was established in 1899, in Chicago, Cook County, Illinois, by an act of the legislature of that state, the juvenile court was an institution of gradual growth. The Illinois experiment gave impetus to the children's movement in the middle west. (Edwin H. Sutherland, *Principles of Criminology,* Chicago, 1934, 270-272).

The Ohio legislature was not slow in seeing the advance of the Illinois experiment, and accordingly, in 1902, an act was passed creating the juvenile court in Cuyahoga County. Under this act all counties having a population over 380,000 and an insolvency court were authorized, under an extension of the jurisdiction of this court, to establish children's courts. The stipulation of this act excluded Brown County. It gave the court jurisdiction of the trial of cases involving delinquent and neglected children; defined the term "delinquent, dependent, and neglected"; authorize the appointment of a probation officer, and made it his duty to investigate the facts of cases coming before the court, and to take charge of the offender before and after trial. The clerk of the juvenile court was directed to keep a journal in which were to be recorded the minutes of the case. The judge was to serve for a period of five years. (95 O. L. 785). The term remained at five years until 1935 when it was extended to six years. (116 O. L. pt. ii, 157).

Two years later after the establishment of the Cuyahoga County juvenile court, the assembly provided by statute for the establishment of juvenile courts in the rural counties of the state which, because of the lack of population, were unable to create the newer agencies under the provision of the act of 1902. Under the act of 1904 the judges of the court of common pleas, probate court, and where established, the insolvency courts, wherein three or more judges held court concurrently, were authorized to appoint one of their members as "juvenile judge." The court was given original jurisdiction in all cases involving neglected, dependent, and delinquent children under the age of sixteen years; and all children, who have been scheduled in the past for trial in a justice of the peace or police court were in the future to be tried before a juvenile judge. As under the act of 1902, the judge was authorized to appoint a probation officer, and the clerk of courts was directed to keep a journal of the minutes of each case. (97 O. L. 561). In 1908 the court was given jurisdiction in cases involving minors under seventeen years of age, and such children as were brought before the juvenile judge were to become wards of the court until they had attained the age of twenty-one years. The county commissioners were authorized to provide by lease or purchase, a "detention home" where neglected or dependent children might be detained pending the final disposition of their cases. The clerk of courts was directed to keep not only a journal, but also an appearance docket containing all orders, judgments, and findings of the court. It provided also for case studies to be made by the probation officer (99 O. L. 196). The age jurisdiction of the court was increased to eighteen in 1913 (103 O. L. 877).

While provisions were being made for the establishment of juvenile courts, the legislature gave the court jurisdiction in cases involving adults who committed crimes against children or contributed to the delinquency of dependent children. Thus in 1906 it was made a misdemeanor to contribute to the delinquency of a child under seventeen years of age (98 O. L. 314). Two years later the "lack of parental care" was defined and it was made a misdemeanor to fail to support a minor, or to cause him to engage in begging (99 O. L. 196). In 1913 "proper parental care" was defined by statute (103 O. L. 870).

Marked progress has been made in the medical treatment of juveniles. While the act of 1913 authorized the juvenile judge to submit any child sentenced to an institution for correction to a mental test, the act of 1929 authorized him to submit any child coming before the court to a mental and physical test to be made by a physician or psychiatrist (103 O. L. 872; 113 O. L. 471). To further the scientific handling of children, the county commissioners were authorized, in the same year, to lease or construct a separate building to be known as the "juvenile court" which should be appropriately constructed, arranged, furnished, and maintain for the convenient and effective transaction of the business of the court, including adequate facilities to be used as laboratories, dispensaries, or clinics for the scientific use of specialists attached to the court (113 O. L. 470).

One of the guiding principles of the court has been to make its "custody and discipline" of children approximate as nearly as possible that which should be given by their parents. In the cases involving neglected or dependent children, not sentenced to state institutions, it has been the policy of judges to assign children to private homes, and make arrangements for their adoption. Many other functions have been taken over by the juvenile court such as administrating mothers' pensions (103 O. L. 877).

The juvenile court of Cuyahoga County is the only independent juvenile court in the state. There are seven other juvenile courts in Ohio attached to the court of domestic relations. In Brown County, as in all other counties where there is no independent juvenile court or no court of domestic relations, the probate judge serves as judge of the juvenile court (G. C. Sec. 1639-7).

188. JUVENILE JOURNAL
1908— . 2 volumes.

Record entry of proceedings in juvenile cases showing case number of original papers in Probate Files, entry 128. Chronologically arranged. Alphabetical index by names of juveniles. Handwritten. Average 300 pages. 16 x 11 x 2.5.

189. JUVENILE RECORDS
1906—. 2 volumes.

Complete record of proceedings in juvenile division of probate court in which minors are involved. Chronologically arranged. Alphabetical index by names of defendants. 1906-1927, handwritten; 1928—, typed. Average 300 pages. 18 x 12 x 2.5.

In 1891 the judges of the court of common pleas in counties having a population of not less than 33,000 nor more than 50,000 were authorized to appoint four residents of the county to serve as a jury commission for a term of one year. The limitations of this act excluded Brown County. It was the duty of this commission to determine the qualifications and fitness of persons to be selected as jurors (88 O. L. 200). Three years later, in 1894, the provisions of the act were extended to Brown County and all other counties in the state except Cuyahoga, Franklin, Hamilton, Lucas, Montgomery, and Mahoning (91 O. L. 176). In 1902 the statute was amended to include all counties (96 O. L. 3). In 1913 the number of jury commissioners in each county was reduced to two (103 O. L. 512; 105 O. L. 106).

The jury code, which became effective August 2, 1931, provided for a jury commission of the same number and same qualifications previously provided for, to hold office at the pleasure of the court, and to meet and select prospective jurors both grand and petit, for the ensuing year from a list provided by the board of elections (114 O. L. 193-213). At the beginning of each jury year the commissioners are required to make up a new and complete jury list, known as the annual jury list, arranged alphabetically by precincts, districts, and townships, recording the name, occupation, business address, and residence of each prospective juror, and to prepare an index to this list. A duplicate list is certified by the commissioners and filed in the office of the clerk of court of common pleas. (114 O. L. 205).

The jury commissioners select prospective jurors for civil and criminal cases as well as for the grand jury. It selects jurors for the probate court, juvenile court, and other minor courts. All records are located in the clerk of courts office.

190. JOURNAL

1932—. 1 volume. Prior records missing.

Record of minutes of meetings of jury commission showing certified list of electors eligible for jury duty; also grand and petit venires drawn each session. Chronologically arranged. No index. Typed. 500 pages. 12 x 10 x 2.

191. MISCELLANEOUS

1932—. 1 file box. Prior records missing.

Copies of appointments to serve on commission and certified copies of orders by common pleas judge to draw jury venires giving date and number to be drawn, also signatures of judge, clerk of courts, and sheriff. Chronologically arranged. No index. Typed on printed forms. 14 x 11 x 5.

The grand jury, sometimes called the palladium of English liberty, has as its function the preliminary examination of persons charged with a capital or other infamous crime. The right, guaranteed by the federal constitution, to an examination by a grand jury, is recognized in the provisions of the Ohio constitution of 1802 and 1851 and in the amendments of 1912 (*Ohio Const. 1851,* Art, I, sec. 10).

The present system, which does not differ in detail from that inaugurated in the early days of the state's history, the grand jury is composed of fifteen members, resident electors of the county having "the qualifications of jurors" (G. C. sec. 13436-2). It is the duty of the grand jury "to inquire of and present all offenses committed in the county and for which it was empaneled and sworn" (G. C. sec. 13436-5). The proceedings of the grand jury are secret and each juror is required to take an oath to preserve such secrecy. Moreover, no grand juror may be required to reveal the way he or other grand jurors voted (G. C. sec. 13436-16).

The grand jurors are aided in their investigations by the county prosecuting attorney who since 1869 has been authorized by statute to present evidence before this body and compel the attendance of witnesses against whom he may institute contempt proceedings if they refuse to testify. (See p. 76). The prosecuting attorney must leave the room before the jurors begin the expression of the views or before a poll is taken. The courts have decreed, however, that the mere presence of the prosecuting attorney in the room during the deliberations is "not sufficient to sustain a plea in abatement" (see *State* v. *Stichenoth* 8 N. P., n. s., 297-338). Since 1902 the official court stenographer of the county, may take shorthand notes of testimony, and furnish a transcript to the prosecuting attorney, at his request. This reporter, like the prosecuting attorney and his assistants, is required to retire from the jury room before the grand jury begins its deliberations. (G. C. sec. 13436-8).

At least twelve of the fifteen jurors must concur in finding an indictment (G. C. 13236-17). Indictments found by the grand jury are presented by the foreman to the court and are filed with the clerk of courts (G. C. sec. 13436-21). No grand juror or officer of the court is permitted to disclose that a person has been indicted before such indictment is filed and the case is docketed (G. C. sec. 13436-15). Any incarcerated person charged with an indictable offense who has not been indicted during the term of court at which he is held to answer is discharged. (G. C. sec. 13436-23).

Since 1869 it has been the duty of the grand jury to visit the county jail once at each term of court at which they may be in attendance, examine its state and condition and inquire into the discipline and treatment of prisoners, and return a written report to the court (G. C. sec. 13436-20).

The majority of contemporary opinion holds that the grand jury, although still defended as a safeguard against needless oppressive prosecution, seems to be of little usefulness in the administration of modern criminal justice. It is argued that the grand jury not only delays the prosecution of criminal offenses but makes it impossible to place responsibility for neglect of duty, and is, in many instances, a rubber stamp for the opinions of the county prosecuting attorney.

The grand jury keeps no permanent records. For records in other officers, see entries 60, 190, and 193.

PETIT JURY

The petit jury, like the grand jury, had its origin in England during the reign of Henry II (George Burton Adams, *Constitutional History of England*, N. Y. 1921, 116). The right of trial by jury, guaranteed by the federal constitution, was included in each of the Ohio constitutions. At any trial, in any court, for the violation of a statute of the state of Ohio, or any ordinance of any municipality, except in cases where the penalty involved does not exceed a fine of fifty dollars, the accused is entitled to a trial by jury (G. C. sec. 13443).

Except in the method of selecting prospective jurors, the petit jury has remained unchanged for over 134 years. At each session of the court the jury commission (see p. 72) selects not less than fifty nor more than seventy-five names for jury service. A venire is issued to the county sheriff for the persons whose names are so drawn to appear on the day fixed for trial. (G. C. sec. 13443-1). From the persons so summoned a jury of twelve is empaneled. The county prosecuting attorney and the defense counsel may, in capital cases, peremptorily challenged six of the jurors. In other cases, four peremptory challenges are allowed. (G. C. secs. 13443-4, 13443-6). Other challenges, alternately made, may be made for reasons prescribed by statute (G. C. sec. 13443-8).

When the case is submitted, the jury may decide the question before it in court, or retire to deliberate. Upon return the jury members, in charge of an officer at a convenient place, must be kept together until they agree upon a verdict or are discharged by the court. The court may be permit them to separate at night. (G. C. sec. 11420-3). If the jurors disagree as to testimony, or desire to be further instructed on the law in the case, they may request the officer in charge to conduct them to the court for additional information (G. C. sec. 11420-6). In civil actions a jury renders a verdict upon the conclusion of three-fourths or more of its members. This verdict, in writing, is signed by each juror concurring therein (G. C. sec. 11420-9).

Under the criminal code adopted in 1929, the accused may waive his right to a jury trial in favor of a trial by a judge. This procedure, although criticized by some, is considered by others to be a logical step in the administration of criminal justice in a modern state.

No separate records are kept by the petit jury. For records in other officers, see entries 60 and 193.

The office of county prosecuting attorney, unlike the sheriff and coroner, is relatively one of the newer agencies in the administration of criminal justice. Established in America by the English during the colonial period, it offers a striking difference in the development of American criminal procedure as contrasted with English procedure where criminal prosecutions were usually instituted by private person. As developed in recent years, the office of the prosecuting attorney has become one of the state's most important agencies in its defense against modern crime.

The acts of the Northwest Territory placed the responsibility for criminal prosecutions upon the attorney general, who, in turn, appointed and commissioned persons to prosecute cases in their respective counties.

While the acts of the Northwest Territory outlined the local institutions for the newer states, the constitution of Ohio contained no provision for a prosecutor, leaving its creation to the discretion of the legislature. In 1803, during the first session of the legislature, an act was passed authorizing the supreme court to appoint in each county an attorney to prosecute cases in behalf of the state (1 O. L. 50). Two years later, the appointing power was vested in the court of common pleas (3 O. L. 47). The office remained an appointive one until 1833 when the electorate of the county was directed to choose a prosecutor in each county for a two-year term (31 O. L. 13-14; Chase *op. cit.,* III, 1935). The act of 1852 left the office elective and the term unchanged, but in 1881 the term of office was set at three years and in 1906 it was reduced to two years (78 O. L. 260; 98 O. L. 271-272).

Under the present system the prosecuting attorney is elected for a four-year term. He is required to give bond of not less than one thousand dollars conditioned for the faithful performance of the duties of his office. If the office becomes vacant the court of common pleas is authorized to appoint a successor. (G. C. sec. 2912).

The county prosecuting attorney is authorized to appoint clerks, assistants, and stenographers and to fix their salaries subject to the approval of the county commissioners. Since 1911 he has been authorized to appoint a secret service agent or officer whose duty it is to aid him in the collection of evidence to be used in the trial of criminal cases and in matters of a criminal nature. The compensation of such an officer is determined by the court of common pleas. (G. C. secs. 2914, 2915-1).

Most important among the duties of prosecuting attorney are those connected with criminal prosecutions. Differing little from those of the early days of the office, these duties include the prosecution on behalf of the state of all complaints, suits, and controversies in which state is a party, and such other suits, matters, and controversies as he is directed by law to prosecute within or without his county, in the probate court, court of common pleas, and court of appeals. In conjunction with the attorney general, he prosecutes cases in the supreme court which originated in his county. (G. C. sec. 2916).

In felony cases, when a complaint is made to the prosecuting attorney, he is required to examine the evidence and determine if it is sufficient for prosecution. If he decides in the affirmative, he prepares the evidence for presentation to the grand jury. (see p. 74). If this body returns an indictment the prosecutor prepares to present the evidence in trial court. The court of common pleas may appoint an attorney to assist the prosecuting attorney in criminal cases (G. C. sec. 2818). In the case of conviction, the prosecutor causes execution to be issued for the fines or cost and pays into the county treasury all monies so received (G. C. sec. 2916). Without reference to the grand jury the prosecuting attorney may initiate prosecutions in misdemeanors cases in the court of common pleas by information (G. C. Sec. 13437-34). After prostitution is inaugurated, he may eliminate the case without trial by means of the *nolle prosequi.* Although he is prohibited from enlisting the *nolle prosequi* without leave of the court on good cause shown, his requests are usually granted. (G. C. Sec. 13437-32). After prosecution has begun, it remains with the prosecuting attorney whether the case shall be pressed and steps taken that will lead to conviction.

Besides prosecution in criminal cases, the prosecuting attorney also acts in civil matters. He may bring suit in the name of the state when he is convinced that public money is being misapplied or is being illegally withheld or withdrawn from the county treasury. Moreover, he may bring suit against persons violating the obligations of contracts at which the county is a party or when county property is being used or occupied illegally. (G. C. sec. 2921).

In addition to these, other duties have been prescribed by statute. On the request of the judge having jurisdiction over juvenile cases, he must prosecute individuals for committing crimes against children (G. C. sec. 1664). Furthermore, when directed by the court of common pleas, he must prosecute persons for keeping a house of prostitution (G. C. secs. 6212-5, 6212-7). At the investigation of the secretary of state, he must prosecute any officer who refuses to furnish gratuitously statistical information for the use of that office (G. C. sec. 174).

The prosecuting attorney has also served in an advisory capacity since 1906 (98 O. L. 160-161). He acts as an advisor to all county boards and officials and to township officers who may require his opinion in writing on matters connected with their official duties (G. C. sec. 2917). In addition to this, he prepares official bonds for all county officers (G. C. sec. 2920).

The prosecuting attorney is required to make annually a report to the county commissioners stating the number of criminal prosecutions completed, the name or names of the party or parties to each, and the amount collected in fines and costs, and the amount forfeited (G. C. sec. 2926). Moreover, on the demand of the attorney general he must make an annual report on forms provided by the state on all criminal actions prosecuted by indictment in his county (G. C. sec. 2925; 78 O. L. 120; 90 O. L. 225).

Current records of the prosecuting attorney were the only ones that could be found in Brown County. These are all located in the office of the prosecuting attorney.

192. PROSECUTOR'S JOURNAL

January 4, 1937—. 1 volume.

Record of criminal cases showing information and evidence, grand jury action, and trial records. Chronologically arranged. Alphabetical index by names of defendants. Typed. 275 pages. 18 x 12 x 2.

193. JURY AND WITNESS JOURNAL

January 4, 1937—. 1 volume.

Records names of grand and petit jurors; also names of grand jury and trial witnesses. Chronologically arranged. No index. Typed. 275 pages. 18 x 12 x 2.

194. AFFIDAVITS

January 4, 1937—. 1 bundle.

Signed statements concerning current cases and investigations. Chronologically arranged. No index. Typed on printed forms. 15 x 7 x 2. Desk drawer.

195. PROSECUTOR'S MEMORANDUM

JANUARY 4, 1937—. 1 volume.

Record of miscellaneous matters brought to attention of county prosecuting attorney. Chronologically arranged. No index. Handwritten. 150 pages. 15 x 9 x 1.

The office of coroner, next to that of sheriff the oldest county office in America, had its inception in England during the latter part of the twelfth century when the coroner kept a record of the activities in the county, especially regarding criminal justice. At the end of the thirteenth century it was his duty to make inquests whenever there was a sudden death in the shire, and the results were recorded in the coroner's rolls and presented to the justices when they made their eyre. (Sir Frederick Pollock and Frederic William Maitland. *The History of English Law Before the Time of Edward I,* Cambridge, 1895, I, 519, 571; II, 588, 641).

This office, transplanted to America during the colonial period, was continued by the states, and was adopted by the territory of which the state of Ohio was then a part. An ordinance of the Northwest Territory published in 1788 authorized the governor to appoint a coroner in each county within the territory. This act, together with a supplementary act of 1795 adopted from the Massachusetts code, fixed the power and duties of the coroner. He was empowered to do any act which, by previous legislation had been delegated to the sheriff; and was given the ancient duty of English coroners in holding preliminary investigations over the bodies of all persons found within his county, who were believed to have died by violence or casualty. (Pease, *op. cit.,* I, 24-25, 272-275).

The Ohio constitution of 1802 continued the historic office, making it elective for a two-year term (*Ohio Const. 1802,* Art. VI, sec. 1). A statute of 1805 defined the duties and authority of the coroner which, in the main were comparable with those prescribed in the territorial code, except that he was denied the privilege of concurrent jurisdiction with the sheriff (3 O. L. 156-161). The act further provided that the coroner should receive his remuneration from fees; and that if the office of sheriff were to become vacant the coroner was to execute temporarily the duties of the sheriff (3 O. L. 158-161). The latter provision remain active until its abrogation in 1887 (84 O. L. 208-210).

The constitution of 1851 and the constitutional amendments of 1912 left the duties of the coroner unchanged and it was not until recent years when he became an aid in the scientific detection of crime that laws have been passed which materially affected his office. By the legislative act of 1921 in all counties having a population of 100,000 or more only licensed physicians were eligible to the office, and at the same time the coroner was made official custodian of the morgue (109 O. L. 43-44).

In 1927 an act was passed, apparently designed to attract more highly trained physicians, which set the salary of the coroner at $6,000 per year in all counties having a population of 400,000 or more, and authorized him to appoint one stenographer, a secretary, and three assistant custodians of the morgue (112 O. L. 204-205). Two years later, in counties having a population of 400,000 or more, the coroner was empowered to appoint a pathologist to serve as deputy coroner whose duties are to make chemical tests and to conduct autopsies (113 O. L. 497).

In 1936 the tenure of office of the coroner was extended from two to four years (G. C. sec. 2823).

196. CORONER'S RECORD

1913-1915. 1 volume.

Coroner's record of inquest held in cases of accidental, sudden, or homicidal deaths; also record of injuries impaneled for inquest duty and sheriff's or deputy sheriff's returns on coroner's writs. Chronologically arranged. Alphabetical index by names of decedents. Handwritten. 310 pages. 15 x 8 x 2.5. Basement storeroom.

For reports to clerk of courts, see entry 77.

The office of county sheriff, one of the oldest elective offices in America, had its inception in the Anglo-Saxon period of English history (Adams, *op. cit.,* 17+19; W. A. Morris, "The Office of Sheriff in the Anglo-Saxon Period," *English Historical Review,* XXXI, 1916, 19-40). This ancient institution was introduced into the American colonies modified form and continued by the states created after independence. (For a comparative study of the sheriff in England and Chesapeake colonies, see Cyrus Harreld Kerraker, *The Seventeenth-Century Sheriff,* Chapel Hill, 1930). The office assumed a new significance in the latter part of the eighteenth century when they flood of colonists swept across the Alleghenies to establish homes in the Northwest Territory organized by congress and 1787. In the remoter West the pioneers, far removed from the orderly legal processes and courts of the east, was subjected to the mechanization of the lawless elements evidence in every new community. In 1792 the governor and judges of the territory adopted an act providing for the appointment by the governor of a sheriff in each county, defining his duties: to keep and preserve the peace, and suppress affrays, routs, riots, unlawful assemblies, and insurrections; to apprehend, and confined in jail all felons and traders; to return persons who, having committed a crime in his county, and have taken refuge in another; to attend upon the court of common pleas in the court of appeals during their sessions, and to execute all warrants, writs, and processes directed to him by the proper and local authority. (Pease, *op. cit.,* I, 8).

When Ohio entered the union as a state in 1803 the office of sheriff was continued by constitutional provision, and was made elective for a two-year term (*Ohio Const. 1802,* Art, VI, sec. 1). Although it did not specifically provide for the office, the constitution of 1851 stated that no person should be eligible to the office for more than four in any period of six years (*Ohio Const. 1851,* Art X, sec. 3). This provision was repealed by an amendment in 1933 authorizing any county to adopt a charter form of government. The term of office remained at two years until 1936, when it was extended to four years. (116 O. L. pt. ii, 1st. secs. H. 603). The sheriff received his remuneration from fees until 1906 when a definite salary was specified by the legislature (3 O. L. 49-51; 33 O. L. 18; 35 O. L. 53; 52 O. L. 86). The salary for each sheriff was based on the population of his county according to the last federal census next preceding his election (98 O. L. 86).

The duties of the sheriff were and are prescribed by statute. During the legislative session of 1805 the general assembly passed an act defining the duties of the sheriff, which was in all respects similar to the provisions inherited from the territorial code (3 O. L. 156-158). In the same year the sheriff was designated as the county's executioner, and was bound to carry out sentences of death when imposed by the courts upon those convicted of murder. Hanging was the legal method for the infliction of the death penalty (Chase, *op. cit.,* I, 97-101, 109, 442-443). Public executions, the general rule during the earlier years, were abolished in 1844 (42 O. L. 71). In 1886 the sheriff's duties in this respect were delegated to the warden of the Ohio Penitentiary (83 O. L. 145).

As in England the sheriff, during the earlier years of his office, was required to notify the electors of his county of the time and place of holding elections. He was required to furnish the ballot boxes at the expense of the county, hold special elections when so directed by the governor, and deliver the poll books to the secretary of state (O. L. 88-89; 3 O. L. 331-332). Since 1891 these duties have been taken over by the board of elections (see p. 149).

An act of 1831, repealing the act of 1805, redefined the duties of the sheriff as a conservator of the peace in his county and as an executive agent of the courts (29 O. L. 112). The present duties of the sheriff in this respect are survivals from the provisions of this act (29 O. L. 112-113; 82 O. L. 26). In the execution of his duties, as prescribed by law, he was again empowered to summon to his aid such persons as he deemed necessary to perform his lawful duty in the apprehension of criminals (29 O. L. 112-113). Thus the *posse comitatus* was at his disposal as it is today. In 1818 the sheriff had been authorized to appoint, with the consent of the court of common pleas, one or more deputies who, like himself, were required to give bond for the faithful performance of the duties of their office. The sheriff was made responsible for the neglect of duty or misconduct in office. (29 O. L. 410).

Not only was the sheriff charged with the duty of apprehending law violators, but he was made responsible for their safekeeping. As early as 1803 he was also made official custodian of the county jail (3 O. L. 157). Although the early statutes directed the county commissioners to provide dungeons for the incarceration of prisoners, the act of 1847 directed the sheriff to exercise reasonable care for the preservation of the life, health, and welfare of those committed to his care. He was and is authorized to transport prisoners to other counties for safekeeping (3 O. L. 157; 29 O. L. 112-113; 93 O. L. 131). In 1910 provision was made for the removal of the sheriff by the governor if he were proved guilty of negligence in not affording a prisoner adequate protection from mob violence (101 O. L. 109).

Although the sheriff is still regarded as the chief peace officer in the county, many of his earlier duties in this respect have been absorbed by the development of other agencies of law enforcement, notably the state highway patrol. On the other hand, the powers of the sheriff to suppress affrays, riots, and unlawful assemblies become specifically important in times of strikes or threatened riots. On a properly issued warrant he may arrest any person charged with the probability of doing injury to another person or the property of another (G. C. sec. 13463). Moreover, since 1921 the sheriff has forwarded to the bureau of criminal identification all fingerprints of persons arrested for a felony (110 O. L. 5; 109 O. L. 585), and since 1913 has been authorized to arrest any prisoner violating his parole (103 O. L. 405).

As an executive agent of the court the sheriff still executes all writs, warrants, and other processes directed to him by lawful authority; he attends the court of common pleas and court of appeals during their sessions, and, when required, the probate court (29 O. L. 112, 316: 82 O. L. 26).

The sheriff was and is required by law to keep a record of the business of his office. The present practice of keeping a foreign execution docket began in 1838 (36 O. L. 18; 57 O. L. 6; 84 O. L. 208-209). Since 1842 the sheriff has kept a cash book (40 O. L. 25; 65 O. L. 115; 84 O. L. 2081 86 O. L. 239), and since 1843 a jail register (41 O. L. 74). Indexes, direct and reverse, to the foreign execution docket were prescribed by the legislature in 1925 (111 O. L. 31). Since 1843 he has been required annually to transmit the jail register, in certified copies, to the clerk of courts, the county auditor, and the secretary of state (41 O. L. 74). Since 1850 he has been required, on the first Monday of September in each year, to submit to the county commissioners a certified statement of all fines and costs collected during the year and the amount of fees collected and paid to the clerk of courts of common pleas (G. C. sec. 2504; 48 O. L. 66).

The sheriff's records are public property and open to the inspection of the public. They are transferred together with all effects appertaining to the office of his successor.

Court Orders

197. FOREIGN SUMMONS DOCKET

1879—. 4 volumes. Prior records missing.

Records names of county and court of origin, kind of writ, names of litigants, kind of action, case number, names of attorneys, date writ received, date writ served, sheriff's fees, and amount deposited for fees. Chronologically arranged. Alphabetical index by names of plaintiffs. Handwritten. Average 470 pages. 16 x 11 x 3.5. 2 volumes, 1879-1912, Basement storeroom; 2 volumes, 1913—, Sheriff's office.

198. FOREIGN EXECUTION DOCKET

1872—. 4 volumes. Prior records missing.

Records names of parties to case, county and court of origin, case number, kind of case, date writ received, date to be returned, names of attorneys, amount of judgment and interest, amount of original cost, amount increased on this writ, and total cost. Chronologically arranged. Alphabetical index by names of plaintiffs. Handwritten. Average 240 pages. 16 x 11 x 2. 2 volumes, 1872-1900, Basement storeroom; 2 volumes, 1901—, Sheriff's office.

Business Administration of Office

199. CASH BOOK

1869—. 11 volumes. Prior records missing.

Records case number, dates, by whom paid, to whom due, kind of case, total sheriff's fee, court costs, judgments and sales, and date payment receipt. Chronologically arranged. Alphabetical index by names of payers. Handwritten. Average 275 pages. 17 x 13 x 2. 3 volumes, 1869-1904, Basement storeroom; 8 volumes, 1905—, Sheriff's office.

200. RECORD OF ACCRUED FEES

1885—. 8 volumes. 1899-1906, missing.

Records date, case number, cause, to whom charged, total fees, civil, criminal and foreign writs, probate and juvenile court, and date paid. 1885-1921, alphabetically arranged by names of debtors; 1922—, chronologically arranged. 1885-1921, no index; 1922—, alphabetical index by names of debtors.

Handwritten and typed. Average 245 pages. 18 x 12 x 1.5. 3 volumes, 1885-1898, Basement storeroom; 5 volumes, 1908—, Sheriff's office.

201. UNCLAIMED MONEY RECORD
1910—. 1 volume.
Records date, amount, name of payee, for what, date paid into county treasury, and date certificate issued to payee for recovery. Alphabetically arranged by names of payees. No index. Handwritten. 325 pages. 14 x 8 x 2.5. Sheriff's office.

Miscellaneous

202. PARTITION RECORD
1876—. 2 VOLUMES.
Sheriff's record of petition to partition case listing names of litigants, description of real estate involved, amount appraised for, amount sold for, amount of each share, and date proceeds distributed. Chronologically arranged. Alphabetical index by names of plaintiffs. Handwritten. Average 225 pages. 18 x 13 x 1.75. 1 volume, 1876-1888, Basement storeroom; 1 volume, 1930—, Sheriff's office.

203. JAIL REGISTER
1869—. 3 volumes. Prior records missing.
Sheriff's jail record listing name of prisoner, residence, color, why committed to jail, commitment number, by whose authority committed, description of prisoner, length of sentence, date discharged, by whose authority discharged, and sheriff's fees. Alphabetically arranged by names of prisoners. No index. Handwritten. Average 250 pages. 18 x 12 x 2. 2 volumes, 1869-1927, Sheriff's office; 1 volume, 1928—, Jail office.

The office of county treasurer was established by an act of the Northwest Territory in 1792 and continued by the state of Ohio (Pease *Op. cit.,* 68-69). Although the constitution of 1802 made no provision for the Office county treasurer, it was created by the legislative act of 1803 (1 O. L. 98). The treasurer, appointed by the associate judges in 1803 and by the county commissioners in 1804, was required to take an oath and give bond for the faithful performance of the duties of his office, and was subject to removal by the appointing power (1 O. L. 98; 2 O. L. 154). The treasurer remained an appointive official until 1827 when the office became an elective one by popular vote in the county (25 O. L. 25-32). Although it did not specifically create the office, the constitution of 1851 stated that no person should hold the office of treasurer for more than four years in any six (*Ohio Const. 1851,* Art. X, sec. 3). This provision was repealed in 1933 as an amendment authorizing any county to adopt a charter form of government. Interpreting the constitutional provision, the legislature fixed the term of office at two years in 1859 (56 O. L. 105). The term of office continued at two years until 1935 when it was extended to four years (116 O. L. pt. ii, 1st, s. sess. H. 603). Until 1906 the county treasurer received his remuneration from fees; since that date his salary has been determined by law according to the population of the county (98 O. L. 89).

The duties of the treasurer were defined by statute in the earlier period and specified in detail by the act of 1827 and 1831 repealing previous acts. The provision of the latter act, although subject to amendment and repeal, furnished the basis for subsequent legislation and laid the basis for the present duties of the treasurer, which do not differ greatly from those prescribed by the earlier statutes.

In 1803 the treasurer was given his present duty of giving public notice of the tax duplicate. On receiving from the county auditor a duplicate of the taxes assessed upon the property of the county, the treasurer prepares and post notices in three places in each township including the place in which elections are held; and inserts the notice for six consecutive weeks in the newspapers having the greatest circulation in the county (1 O. L. 98; 29 O. L. 291; 52 O. L. 124). He receives money in payment of taxes levied for the county, for the state, and for other purposes, and gives the payer a receipt (G. C. sec. 2650; 29 O. L. 292; 76 O. L. 70; 85 O. L. 327). And the earlier years of the office the treasurer was required to give announcement of the time he would be in the respective townships of the county and in his office at the seat of justice to receive tax collections. Since 1858 the treasurer has been authorized to prescribe the semiannual payment of taxes or assessments levied upon real estate or upon delinquent real estate taxes or assignments (55 O. L. 62; 56 O. L. 101). Moreover, since 1908 the commissioners have been authorized to extend the time of paying taxes for not more than thirty days after the time fixed by law (99 O. L. 435; 114 O. L. 730; 115 O. L. pt. ii, 226).

After each semiannual collection of taxes, the treasurer is required to report to the auditor showing the amount of taxes received in each taxing district in the county since the last settlement. Since 1908 the semiannual settlements have been made under the heads of liquor, cigarette, inheritance, and delinquent personal, road, and general taxes. The treasurer keeps his accounts in books which enable him to compile such reports (G. C. Sec. 2643; 29 O. L. 296; 97 O. L. 458).

After the taxes are collected and immediately following each settlement with the county auditor, the county treasurer, upon the presentation of the proper warrant from the auditor, pays to the township treasurer, city or village treasurer, the treasurer of the school district, or treasurer of any "legally constituted board authorized by law to receive the funds or proceeds of any special tax levy," or other officer delegated with authority to receive such funds, all money in the county belonging to such boards and subdivisions (G. C. Sec. 2689; R. S. 1122; 56 O. L. 101). In addition, after the treasurer has made each settlement with the county auditor, he is required to pay to the state treasurer, on warrant from the state auditor, the full amount of all sums" found by the latter to belong to the state (56 O. L. 101; 114 O. L. 732).

Another function of the county treasurer, which had its inception in the earlier years of the office, is the collection of delinquent taxes. It was and is his duty to assess a penalty on the tax duplicate for nonpayment of tax–which penalty when collected, is paid to the treasurer's fund. If the treasurer is unable to collect the delinquent taxes, he is authorized to apply to the clerk of court of common pleas who serves notice to show cause why such taxes were not paid. The court may enter a rule against the delinquent taxpayer for the payment and cost and enforce it by attachment. (G. C. sec. 2660; 56 O. L. 175; 99 O. L. 435).

During the last decade provision has been made whereby delinquent taxes, assessments, and penalties charged on the tax duplicate against any entry of real estate may be paid in installments during the five consecutive semiannual taxpaying periods, "whether such real estate has been certified as delinquent or not (G. C. sec. 2672; 114 O. L. 827). The Whittemore Act, passed as an emergency measure in 1933, provided for the collection of installments, without interest or penalty, of delinquent real estate taxes and assessments, personal property, and classified property taxes. Anyone electing to pay such delinquent real property taxes and assessments in installments pursuant to this act may, at any installment period, pay the entire unpaid balance of the principal sum and such delinquent taxes and assessments, in which event no interest shall be charged or collected on the amount so paid. (115 O. L. 161-164; 116 O. L. pt. ii, 14-21; 116 O. L. 261-267). In some counties more populous than Brown, the treasurer maintains a separate bureau for the collection of delinquent taxes.

The county treasurer has charge of the funds collected by taxes, and also other funds belonging to the county. Although earlier acts made provision for storage vaults in the county treasury for county deposits, the commissioners have been authorized, since 1894, to receive sealed bids for the deposit accounting funds; and the banks or trust companies offering the highest rates of interest are selected as the county depositories (91 O. L. 403; 102 O. L. 60; 115 O. L. pt. ii, 215).

The treasurer is required to keep an account current with the county auditor–a practice which originated in 1831. Each day the treasurer makes a statement to the county auditor for the previous day's business showing the amount of taxes received on auditor's drafts, the amount received from other sources, together with the amount of money deposited in the depository, the total amount paid out by check and by cash, and the balance in the treasury. (G. C. Sec. 2642; 97 O. L. 458).

The treasurer, as well as sheriff, prosecuting attorney, and clerk of courts, is required to report annually to the county commissioners (G. C. sec. 2504). Since 1874 the county auditor and county commissioners have been required to make a thorough examination of all books, vouchers, accounts, moneys, bonds, securities, and other property in the treasury at least every six months (G. C. sec. 2699; R. S. 1129; 71 O. L. 137). Besides being under the supervision of the county commissioners and county auditor, the treasurer is subject to the supervision of the state auditor. In 1902 an act was passed providing for a uniform system of accounting and auditing for all public offices in the state, under the direction of a bureau of inspection in the office of the state auditor, and for the annual examination of finances of all public offices. (G. C. sec. 2641; 114 O. L. 728; R. S. 1084).

The treasurer is a member of the budget commission, the county board of revision, and serves as a trustee of the sinking fund (G. C. sec. 5625-19; G. C. sec. 5580; see also pp. 117, 118, and 121). Since the inception of the office the treasurer has been official custodian of the bonds furnished to the state by the county auditor, county commissioners, county sheriff, and other officials. Since 1869 he has been required to record and preserve a record of the deputies appointed and removed by the county auditor (G. C. sec. 2563; 66 O. L. 35).

Like other county officials, the treasurer is required at the expiration of his term to turn over to his successor all books, papers, moneys, and records appertaining to his office (G. C. sec. 2639).

All records are located in the treasurer's office unless otherwise specified.

Tax Records
(See also entries 245-269)

Tax Duplicates (See also entries 248-252)

204. TREASURER'S DUPLICATES
1861—. 752 volumes. 1862-1863, 1865-1886, 1891, 1893, 1913, 1915, and 1917, missing.

Record showing tract and receipt numbers, name of owner, description of land, quantity, value, semiannual and total taxes. Contains additions and deductions, 1861-1920, entry 207. One volume each year in each township and county. Alphabetically arranged by names of taxpayers. No index. Handwritten on printed forms. Average 80 pages. 18 x 14 x .75. 416 volumes, 1861, 1864, 1887-1890, 1892, 1894-1912, Attic storeroom; 192 volumes, 1914, 1916, 1918-1927, Basement storeroom; 144 volumes, 1928—, Treasurer's office.

205. LIQUOR DUPLICATE
1891-1902. 1 volume. Discontinued.

Treasurer's duplicate of assessments on liquor dealers showing name, location and description of premise on which sold, name of property owner, amount of assessment, and amount of refund of unused portion of asset (if any). Alphabetically arranged by names of dealers. No index. Handwritten. 162 pages. 20 x 16 x 1. Attic storeroom.

206. CLASSIFIED TAX DUPLICATE
1932—. 1 volume.

Duplicates of classified tax including investments, accounts, and other intangibles give name of owner and amount assessed. Alphabetically arranged by names of taxpayers. No index. Handwritten on printed forms. 204 pages. 20 x 18 x 1.5.

207. ADDITIONS AND DEDUCTIONS

1921—. 2 volumes. 1861-1920 in Treasurer's Duplicates, entry 204.
Record of additions to tax duplicates for improvements to property or error on previous assessment; also deductions for tax duplicate for devaluation of property after assessment or error on previous assessment. Additions in front of each volume; deductions in back of each volume. Chronologically arranged. No index. Handwritten. Average 200 pages. 20 x 18 x 1.5. 1 volume, 1921-1933, Basement storeroom; 1 volume, 1934—, Treasurer's office.

For concurrent records, see entry 254.

Tax Collections and Receipts

208. SPECIAL ASSESSMENT RECEIPTS

1905-1912. 2 volumes. 1906 and 1919 missing.
Duplicate receipts for special paving assessments for village of Georgetown. Alphabetically arranged by names of taxpayers. No index. Handwritten on printed forms. Average 150 pages. 16 x 12 x 1.5. Attic storeroom.

209. EXCISE AND COSMETIC TAX RECORDS

1932-1935. 2 file boxes. Discontinued.
Record of excise and cosmetic taxes paid into treasury showing date paid and name of payer. Chronologically arranged. No index. Handwritten on printed forms. 11 x 5 x 4.

210. INVENTORY AND SALES TAX RECEIPTS

1935—. 1 volume.
Daily record of sales and tax stamps sold indicating denomination, amount on hand, and amount received from state. Chronologically arranged. No index. Handwritten. 125 pages. 20 x 16 x 1.

211. TREASURER'S INHERITANCE TAX CHARGES

1921—. 1 volume.
Record of inheritance taxes due listing name of person owing tax, case number, date tax accrued, amount as fixed by court, interest, total amount due, and date paid; also township or municipality. Chronologically arranged. Alphabetical index by names of decedents. Handwritten. 375 pages. 12 x 12 x 3.

212. RECORD OF TAX COLLECTIONS

1905-1915. 4 volumes. 1908-1912, missing.

Treasurer's record of taxes collected showing name of taxpayer, receipt number, dog tax, road, special and general paid, and total amount; also total for each district. Alphabetically arranged by names of taxing districts and alphabetical thereunder by names of taxpayers. No index. Handwritten. Average 500 pages. 18 x 12 x 4. 2 volumes, 1904-1907, Attic storeroom; 2 volumes, 1913-1915, Basement storeroom.

For other records of tax collections, see entry 223.

213. TAX RECEIPTS

1891—. 656 volumes. 1897-1900 and 1913, missing.

Stubs of county treasurer's official receipts for taxes paid showing name of tax district, name of taxpayer, and amount paid which includes special assessments and penalties. Alphabetically arranged by names of taxing districts and alphabetical thereunder by names of taxpayers. No index. Handwritten on printed forms. Average 150 pages. 17 x 15 x 1.5. 304 volumes, 1891-1896, 1901-1912, 1914, Attic storeroom; 176 volumes, 1915-1925, Basement storeroom; 175 volumes, 1926—, Treasurer's office.

214. DELINQUENT TAX RECEIPTS

1920-1932. 1 volume. 1933— in Treasurer's Personal and Classified Delinquent Records, entry 215.

Treasurer's duplicate receipts for delinquent tax paid listing name, property value, amount of tax, penalty, and total amount paid. Chronologically arranged. No index. Handwritten on printed forms. 250 pages. 18 x 11 x 2.5. Basement storeroom.

215. TREASURER'S PERSONAL AND CLASSIFIED DELINQUENT RECEIPTS

1933—. 1 volume.

Treasurer's duplicate receipts for delinquent personal and classified taxes paid listing names, township, date, value, and amount of tax. Contains Delinquent Tax Receipts, entry 214. Chronologically arranged. No index. Handwritten on printed forms. 200 pages. 18 x 15 x 2.

Delinquent Taxes (See also entries 261-269)

216. TREASURER'S DELINQUENT TAX DUPLICATE
1906-1901. 1 volume. 1911-1919, missing. 1920— in Treasurer's Cumulative Delinquent Duplicate, entry 218.

Duplicate of delinquent real estate taxes listing name of taxpayer, entry number, original owner, quantity, value, tax, penalty, and total due. Alphabetically arranged by names of taxpayers. No index. Handwritten. 476 pages. 20 x 14 x 3.5. Basement storeroom.

217. TREASURER'S DELINQUENT PERSONAL TAX DUPLICATE
1898-1911. 8 volumes. 1899-1900 and 1912-1919, missing. 1920— in Treasurer's Cumulative Delinquent Personal Tax Duplicate, entry 219.

Duplicate of delinquent personal taxes listing name of taxpayer, valuation, road tax, dog tax, amount of tax due, penalty, and total due. Alphabetically arranged under tabs by names of taxing districts, and alphabetical thereunder by names of taxpayers. No index. Handwritten. Average 300 pages. 16 x 11 x 3. 7 volumes, 1898, 1901-1909, Attic storeroom; 1 volume, 1910-1911, Basement storeroom.

218. TREASURER'S CUMULATIVE DELINQUENT DUPLICATE
1920—. 2 volumes.

Duplicate of accumulated real taxes listing name, year entered, tax district, value, and total amount including penalties. Contains Treasurer's Delinquent Tax Duplicate, entry 216. Arranged under tabs by names of townships and alphabetical thereunder by names of taxpayers. No index. Handwritten and typed. Average 350 pages. 12 x 14 x 2.5.

219. TREASURER'S CUMULATIVE DELINQUENT PERSONAL TAX DUPLICATE
1920—. 1 volume.

Duplicate of accumulated personal taxes listing name, year entered, tax district, value, total amount of tax including penalties, and volume and page numbers of Personal Tax List, entry 257. Contains Treasurer's Delinquent Personal Tax Duplicate, entry 217. Alphabetically arranged under tabs by names of taxing districts and alphabetical thereunder by names of taxpayers. No index. Handwritten and typed. 350 pages. 12 x 14 x 2.5.

220. UNDERTAKINGS, COUNTY TREASURER
1933—. 1 volume.
Treasurer's record of payment of delinquent real taxes under the provision of the Whittemore law showing tax district, name of property owner, property value, total amount of delinquencies, amount of annual installments, dates paid, and balance due. Chronologically arranged. No index. Typed. 375 pages. 18 x 17 x 3.

221. TREASURER'S QUADRENNIAL DELINQUENT LAND CERTIFICATES
1922—. 1 volume.
Treasurer's record of auditor's certification each four years of land on which the taxes are delinquent giving amount of taxes, penalties, interest, and fees due. Alphabetically arranged by names of taxing districts and alphabetical thereunder by names of taxpayers. No index. Typed on printed forms. 200 pages. (Loose-leaf) 17 x 14 x 2.

Business Administration of Office

222. TREASURER'S RECEIPTS AND EXPENDITURES
1884-1890. 1 volume.
Treasurer's record of sundry receipts and expenditures listed names of payer and payee, amount, and for what purpose. Chronologically arranged. No index. Handwritten. 350 pages. 24 x 16 x 3. Basement storeroom.

223. TREASURER'S CASH BOOK
1887—. 18 volumes. 1899-1901, missing.
Treasurer's daily record of collections and disbursements showing total collections and disbursements and depository record. Contains: Treasurer's Record of Fees, 1924—, entry 236; [Bids for County Funds] 1894—, entry 241. Chronologically arranged. No index. Handwritten. Average 300 pages. 18 x 12 x 2. 4 volumes, 1887-1898, 1902-1904, Attic storeroom; 12 volumes, 1905-1930, Basement storeroom; 2 volumes, 1931—, Treasurer's office.

For other records of tax collections, see entry 212.

224. RECEIPTS
1923—. 9 volumes.
Carbon copies of receipts given by county treasurer listing date, name, purpose, name of fund, and amount. Chronologically arranged. No index. Handwritten. Average 300 pages. 15 x 8 x 3.

225. TREASURER'S LEDGER
1883—. 8 volumes. 1906-1909, missing.
Treasurer's record of various funds showing credit, debit, and balance of each fund. Alphabetically arranged under tabs by names of funds and chronological thereunder. Handwritten. Average 700 pages. 18 x 16 x 5. 4 volumes, 1883-1905, Attic storeroom; 4 volumes, 1910—, Treasurer's office.

226. DAILY CASH BALANCE
1904—. 12 volumes. Record initiated 1904.
Record of daily statements of receipts, disbursements, and balances, showing date and amount credited to general cash in county treasury and to personal, delinquent, road, general, cigarette, liquor, and inheritance taxes. Chronologically arranged. No index. Handwritten. Average 360 pages. 18 x 12 x 2.5. 2 volumes, 1904-1910, Attic storeroom; 8 volumes, 1911-1931, Basement storeroom; 2 volumes, 1932—, Treasurer's office.

227. TREASURER'S JOURNAL OF WARRANTS REDEEMED
1909—. 10 volumes.
Treasurer's record of warrants and vouchers redeemed showing date, name of person to whom issued, purpose, warrant number, amount, and name of fund. Chronologically arranged. No index. Handwritten. Average 350 pages. 18 x 12 x 3. 4 volumes, 1909-1921, Attic storeroom; 2 volumes, 1922-1927, Basement storeroom; 4 volumes, 1928—, Treasurer's office.

228. TREASURER'S JOURNAL, COURT WARRANTS REDEEMED
1921—. 1 volume.
Treasurer's record of court warrants redeemed showing date, name of person to whom issued, warrant or voucher number, name of court, amount, and why issued. Chronologically arranged. No index. Handwritten. 340 pages. 18 x 12 x 2.5.

229. TREASURER'S ACCOUNTS

1898-1904. 1 volume.

Treasurer's record of disbursements listing order number, to whom paid, purpose, amount, and fund. Chronologically arranged. No index. Handwritten. 640 pages. 24 x 16 x 5. Basement storeroom.

230. FEE AND SALARY LEDGER

1902-1907. 1 volume.

Record of fees paid into county treasury by each county official and of salary allowance paid out by treasurer. Chronologically arranged. No index. Handwritten. 400 pages. 16 x 11 x 3. Attic storeroom.

For subsequent records of fees, see entry 236.

231. TREASURER'S BOOK OF ACCOUNTS

1895-1899. 1 volume.

Treasurer's accounts with incorporated villages in Brown County showing receipts and expenditures of various funds. Alphabetically arranged by names of villages and chronologically thereunder. No index. Handwritten. 340 pages. 16 x 11 x 2.5. Attic storeroom.

232. TREASURER'S BLOTTER

1896—. 9 volumes. 1907-1908, missing.

Record of calculations of all income for each fund for fiscal year. Chronologically arranged. No index. Handwritten. Average 500 pages. 15 x 10 x 4. 2 volumes, 1896-1906, Attic storeroom; 5 volumes, 1907-1926, Basement storeroom; 2 volumes, 1927—, Treasurer's office.

233. TREASURER'S DAILY STATEMENTS

1921-1931. 1 volume. Discontinued.

Daily record of treasurer's transactions showing debt, credit, debit balance, and credit balance. Chronologically arranged. No index. Handwritten. 400 pages. 18 x 14 x 4. Basement storeroom.

234. TREASURER'S SETTLEMENT RECORD

1894—. 7 volumes.

Treasurer's record of semiannual settlement with each taxing district.

Chronologically arranged. No index. Handwritten on printed forms. Average 450 pages. 15 x 8.5 x 3.5. 2 volumes, 1894-1908, Attic storeroom; 3 volumes, 1909-1927, Basement storeroom; 2 volumes, 1928—, Treasurer's office.

235. TREASURER'S DAILY DISTRIBUTION OF MOTOR VEHICLE LICENSE FEES

1925-1927, 1 volume. Discontinued.

Record of distribution of license fees to townships and taxing districts showing amount and dates of distribution. Chronologically arranged. No index. Handwritten. 375 pages. 10 x 11 x 3. Basement storeroom.

236. TREASURER'S RECORD OF FEES

1907-1923. 1 volume. 1924— in Treasurer's Cash Book, entry 223.

Record of fees paid into county treasury listing date, by whom paid, settlements, penalties, sundries, and total paid. Chronologically arranged. No index. Handwritten. 340 pages. 15 x 10 x 2.5. Basement storeroom.

Bonds

237. TOWNSHIP CLERKS' BOND RECORD

1913—. 2 volumes. Prior records missing.

Record of bonds executed by township clerks showing names of clerks and sureties, amount, and approval by township trustees. Chronologically arranged. Alphabetical index by names of clerks. Handwritten. Average 220 pages. 18 x 12 x 1.5. 1 volume, 1913-1923, Basement storeroom; 1 volume, 1924—, Treasurer's office.

238. OFFICIAL BOND RECORD

1914—. 2 volumes. Prior records missing.

Record of bonds of elected county officials showing amount of bond, signatures, names of witnesses, name of office, and approval by county commissioners. Chronologically arranged. Alphabetical index by names of officials. Handwritten. Average 240 pages. 16 x 11 x 1.5. 1 volume, 1914-1923, Basement storeroom; 1 volume, 1924—, Treasurer's office.

For other records, see entries 15, 76, and 296.

Miscellaneous

239. TREASURER'S RECORD OF INSPECTORS' REPORTS

1898-1906. 1 volume. Discontinued.

State examiners' reports on condition of county office finances together with recommendations. Chronologically arranged. No index. Handwritten. 156 pages. 18 x 12 x 1. Basement storeroom.

For other records, see entry 183.

240. RECORD OF APPOINTMENTS

1869—. 1 volume.

Record of deputies appointed and removed by the county auditor showing date of appointment and removal, name and address of appointee, and remarks. Chronologically arranged by dates of entries. No index. 300 pages. 18 x 14 x 2.5.

241. [BID FOR COUNTY FUNDS]

1894—. In Treasurer's Cash Book, entry 223.

Record of bids by various depositories for county funds showing name of banks, date, and amount of interest bid for active funds and amount of interest bid for inactive funds.

The first Ohio constitution, in 1802, did not provide for the office of county auditor and it was not until 1820 that the general assembly by joint resolution appointed an auditor in each county for a one-year term (18 O. L. 70). In 1821 the office became elective and the term was fixed at one year (19 O. L. 116). In 1831 the term was set at two years, in 1877 at three years, in 1906 reduced to two years, and in 1919 extended to four years (29 O. L. 280; 74 O. L. 381; 98 O. L. 271; 108 O. L. pt. ii, 1294).

The county auditor is required to take oath and give bond for faithful performance of the duties of his office; to preserve all copies of entries, surveys, extracts, and other documents transmitted to his office from the state auditor; and to transfer to his successor all books, records, maps, and other papers pertaining to his office (19 O. L. 116; R. S. 1033; G. C. secs. 2559, 2582). With the approval of the county commissioners he is authorized to appoint deputies, for whose official acts he and his sureties are held liable; the record of these appointments which has been required to be filed with the county treasurer since 1869 (55 O. L. 20; 66 O. L. 35; G. C. sec, 2563) was not located in the inventory of the Brown County treasurer's office. If the office of county auditor falls vacant, the county commissioners are authorized to appoint a successor (29 O. L. 280-291; 67 O. L. 103).

The first auditor in each county was required to list all lands in his county subject to taxation. From this list and one submitted to him by the county commissioners and one from the state auditor, the county auditor was directed to make a tax duplicate to be kept in a book for that purpose, and to give a copy of the list to the tax collector. (18 O. L. 70). The auditor was also directed to compile from the treasurer's duplicate a list of lands on which taxes were delinquent, and if such lands are sold for taxes to grant a deed to the purchaser (18 O. L. 70; 19 O. L. 116).

Subsequent legislation expanded and itemized the duties of the auditor regarding taxation; with modifications to meet modern requirements these duties have continued much as they were during the earlier years of his office. During the 1840s the office of county assessor was abolished and provision was made for township assessors whose duty it was to list all taxable property and make a return to the auditor (39 O. L. 22-25). Since 1874 the auditor is required by statute to keep a book in which he lists additions to and deductions from the amount of the tax assessment (71 O. L. 30). In 1915 he was made chief assessing officer of the county (106 O. L. 246).

The county auditor has served as a member and the secretary of the county budget commission since its beginning in 1911, his duties including keeping full and accurate records of the proceedings of that body. For the purpose of adjusting the tax rates and fixing the amount to be levied each year the commissioners are governed by the amount of taxable property as shown on the auditor's tax list for the current year. He submits to the commissioners the annual tax budget given him by each taxing authority of each subdivision, together with an estimate of any state levy prepared by the state auditor, and such other information as a budget commission may request or the state tax commission require. (G. C. sec. 5625-19; 112 O. L. 339).

Tax settlements had been made annually until 1859 when the auditor was required to make semiannual settlement with the treasurer to ascertain the amount of taxes the treasurer is to stand charged. (G. C. sec. 2596; 56 O. L. 132; 78 O. L. 226). Since 1904 liquor, cigarette, and inheritance taxes have constituted separate funds. All other taxes are credited to the general fund. (97 O. L. 457).

Since 1831 the county auditor has kept an account current with the county treasurer showing the payments of moneys into the treasury, listing the date, by whom paid, and on what fund. On receiving the treasurer's daily statement the auditor enters on his account current the amount shown as a charge to the treasurer. (29 O. L. 280-291; 67 O. L. 103). Another important function of the county auditor is the approval before payment of bills and other claims against the county. Since 1831 he is authorized to issue, on presentation of the proper voucher, all warrants on the county treasurer for moneys payable from the county treasury; and to preserve all warrants, showing the number, date of issue, amount for which drawn, in whose favorite, and from what fund (G. C. Sec. 2570; R. S. 1024; 29 O. L. 280-291; 67 O. L. 103). County money due the state is paid on warrant of the state auditor. Since 1904 a bill or voucher for payment from any fund controlled by the county commissioners or board of county infirmary directors is filed with the county auditor and entered in a book for that purpose at least five days before its approval for payment by the commissioners, and when approved the date is entered opposite the claim (97 O. L. 25; 108 O. L. pt. i, 272).

Besides approving bills and claims against the county, the auditor in 1835 was given the duty of certifying all moneys, except collections on the tax duplicate, into the county treasury, specifying by whom paid and the fund to which such payment is credited. Such money he charges to the treasurer and keeps a duplicate copy of the statement in his office. Since 1835 all costs collected in penitentiary cases which have been or are to be paid to the state have been certified into the treasury as belonging to the state. (33 O. L. 44; 67 O. L. 103).

In 1902 the legislature provided for a system of uniform accounting and auditing of all public offices, and for the annual examination of their finances, under the director of a bureau of inspection in the office of the state auditor (95 O. L. 511-515). Since 1904 the county auditor is required to report to the commissioners on the state of county finances; on the first business day of each month he prepares in duplicate a statement of county finances for the preceding month, compares it with the treasurer's balance, and submits it to the commissioners who post one copy of it in the auditor's office for thirty days for public inspection (97 O. L. 457).

During the development of the office additional duties in great diversity have been delegated to the county auditor. Since 1833 he has been authorized to discharge prisoners jailed for nonpayment of fine or amercement due the county when in his opinion payment is not collectible (G. C. Sec. 2576; 31 O. L. 18; 67 O. L. 103). In 1838 an act was passed making him county superintendent of schools. He was relieved of this duty in 1848 when a county superintendent of schools was authorized in each county (see p. 123). Since 1846 he has served as a sealer of weights and measures, is responsible for the preservation of the copies of the original standards delivered to his office, and enforces in his county all state laws regulating weights and measures (G. C. sec. 2615; 44 O. L. 55; 58 O. L. 78; 101 O. L. 234). In 1861 he was authorized to report to the state auditor statistics concerning the deaf, dumb, blind, insane, and idiots in his county, with the names and addresses of their parents or guardians (58 O. L. 40). Eight years later, in 1869, he was authorized to report to the same officer statistics concerning livestock in his county as returned to his office by assessors, and an abstract of the funded indebtedness of his county, and of each township, city, village, and school district (G. C. sec. 2604). In 1862 he was authorized to issue peddlers' licenses to persons who filed a statement of stock and trade in conformity with the law requiring the listing of such stock for taxation, and since 1917 he issues dog licenses (59 O. L. 67; 79 O. L. 96; 107 O. L. 535).

Since 1824 the county auditor has served as clerk to the county commissioners, his duties including keeping an accurate record of their proceedings and preserving all documents, books, records, maps, and papers which might be required to be filed in his office (G. C. sec. 2566; 22 O. L. 269). Since 1850 he has been official custodian of the reports submitted to the commissioners by the prosecuting attorney, the clerk of courts, the sheriff, and the treasurer; these reports are recorded by the auditor in books kept especially for the purpose (G. C. sec. 2504; R. S. 886; 48 O. L. 66).

The county auditor is a member of the county board of revision established in 1825, and served as a trustee and a secretary of the board of the sinking fund trustees established in 1919 (see pp. 117 and 121).

In recent years there has been increasing criticism of the office of county auditor. The chief complaint is the duplication of the work of the office of the county treasurer, the daily registers of the two offices being similar in all respects.

Property Transfers
(See also entries 17-40)

242. AUDITOR'S TRANSFER RECORD
1821—. 94 volumes.
Auditor's record of land transfers showing name of owner, date of transfer, entry number, name of original proprietor, quantity, value, and to whom transferred. Alphabetically arranged by names of townships and alphabetical thereunder by names of property owners. No index. 1821-1900, handwritten; 1901—, typed. Average 400 pages. 18 x 12 x 3. 1 volume, 1821-1825, Basement storeroom; 93 volumes, 1826—, Auditor's office.

243. RECORD OF AUDITOR'S DEEDS
1826—. 4 volumes.
Record of deeds executed by county auditor for land sold for delinquent taxes giving description of tract, name of owner and purchaser, and amount sold for. Chronologically arranged. Alphabetical index by names of owners. Handwritten. Average 280 pages. 15 x 9 x 2. 1 volume, 1826-1961, Attic storeroom; 1 volume, 1862-1881, Basement storeroom; 2 volumes, 1882—, Auditor's office

Plats

244. PLATS
1801—. 1 volume. Last entry 1926.
Plats of each village or addition to villages in county showing location and amount of land. Prepared by county engineer. No systematic arrangement. Alphabetical

index by names of villages and additions. Hand drawn and handwritten; black and white. Scales vary. Approximately 200 pages. 22 x 32 x 1.5. Auditor's office.

Tax Records
(See also entries 204-210)

Appraisements and Assessments

245. RAILROAD APPRAISEMENT RECORD
1891-1910. 2 volumes. Discontinued.

Record of proceedings of board of appraisers and assessors in appraising railroad property. Chronologically arranged. No index. Handwritten. Average 150 pages. 22 x 14 x 1. Basement storeroom.

246. REAPPRAISEMENT RECORD
1931. 16 volumes. Prior records missing.

Auditors real estate appraisement record listing name of owner, description of tract, quantity, and appraised value. There is one volume for each township. Arranged by taxing districts and alphabetical thereunder by names of property owners. Handwritten and typed. Average 90 pages. 17 x 14 x .75. Auditor's office.

247. ROAD ASSESSMENTS
1920—. 3 volumes.

Auditor's record of assessments on real estate for highway improvements listing name of owner, description of land, amount assessed, interest, date due, and total amount due. Chronologically arranged. Alphabetical index by names of taxpayers. Handwritten. Average 300 pages. 24 x 16 x 2. Auditor's office.

Tax Duplicates (See also entries 204-207)

248. AUDITOR'S DUPLICATES
1832—. 145 volumes. Prior records, 1833-1845, 1847, 1850-1852, 1870 and 1891-1895, missing.

Duplicate of taxes assessed on real estate listing name of owner, entry number, name of original owner, original quantity, water courses (shown on all duplicates to 1915), number of acres, value, and amount of assessed; also personal property duplicates, 1832-1933. Contains Auditors Delinquent Personal Duplicate, 1923-1932, entry 263. Alphabetically arranged by taxing districts and alphabetical thereunder by names of property owners. No index. 1832-1921, handwritten; 1922—, typed. 1832 and 1846, 2 volumes, condition fair. Average 425 pages. 17 x 13 x 3.25. 81 volumes, 1852, 1846, 1848-1849, 1853-1869, 1871-1890, 1896-1909, Attic storeroom; 8 volumes, 1910-1913, Basement storeroom; 56 volumes, 1914—, Auditor's office.

249. AUDITOR'S LIQUOR TRAFFIC DUPLICATES
1883-1903. 3 volumes. Discontinued.

Auditor's duplicates of tax assessed against liquor dealers listing name of dealer, location and description of real estate, owner of premises, amount of assessment or tax, and date. Chronologically arranged. No index. Handwritten. Average 125 pages. 20 x 14 x .75. 1 volume, 1883-1890, Attic storeroom; 2 volumes, 1891-1903, Basement storeroom.

250. AUDITOR'S CIGARETTE DUPLICATE
1920—. 1 volume.

Auditor's duplicate licenses to retail dealers to traffic in cigarettes showing name of dealer, address, description of property, owner of property, date, amount of assessment, date of expiration, and license number. Chronologically arranged. No index. Handwritten on printed forms. 275 pages. 18 x 12 x 2. Auditor's office.

251. PAVEMENT ASSESSMENT DUPLICATE
1904—. 1 volume.

Auditor's duplicate of assessments against abutting property for share of payment cost listing name of owner, lots number, quantity, description, foot frontage, amount assessed, interest, and installment payments. Alphabetically arranged by names of taxing districts and alphabetical thereunder by names of property owners. No index. Handwritten. 292 pages. 18 x 16 x 2. Auditor's office.

252. AUDITOR'S EXEMPT REAL AND PERSONAL PROPERTY DUPLICATE
1929—. 1 volume. Prior records missing.

Auditor's duplicate of tax exempt property such as church, school, county, and municipal property, and charitable institutions, showing name of owner, number of lot or survey, quantity, value, and description. Alphabetically arranged by names of owners. No index. Typed. 200 pages. 14 x 17 x 1.5. Auditor's office.

Tax Rates, Additions, and Deductions

253. TAXES AND RATES

1903-1921. 1 volume. Discontinued.

Record of tax rate levied in each tax district in county and rate levied as to county, state, and special funds, showing total rate in mills. Chronologically arranged. No index. Handwritten on printed forms. 316 pages. 16 x 9 x 2.5. Basement storeroom.

254. ADDITIONS AND DEDUCTIONS

1881—. 4 volumes. Prior records, 1903-1904, and 1922-1934, missing.

Auditor's record of additions to tax duplicate on account of improvement on property or error on previous duplicate, and deductions from tax duplicate on account of loss of building or other damages or error on previous duplicate. Alphabetically arranged under tabs by names of taxing districts. No index. Handwritten. Average 350 pages. 16 x 9 x 2.5. 2 volumes, 1881-1902, Attic storeroom; 1 volume, 1905-1921, Basement storeroom; 1 volume, 1935—, Auditor's office.

For concurrent records, see entry 207.

Tax List

255. AUDITOR'S GENERAL TAX LIST

1932—. 2 volumes.

Records name of taxpayer, value of property, location, description, amount of assessed, advanced payment, tax due, and tax unpaid. Alphabetically arranged by names of taxing districts and alphabetical thereunder by names of taxpayers. No index. Typed. Average 350 pages. 18 x 17 x 2.5. Auditor's office.

256. AUDITOR'S TAX LIST, REAL PROPERTY

1915—. 51 volumes.

Auditor's record of real estate subject to tax giving name of owner, description of property, valuation of land, and valuation of improvements. Alphabetically arranged by names of taxing districts and alphabetical thereunder by names of property owners. No index. Typed. Average 400 pages. 15 x 18 x 3. Auditor's office.

257. PERSONAL TAX LIST
1914—. 21 volumes.

Auditor's tax listing of personal property subject to tax showing name of taxpayer, kind of property, valuation, rate, amount assessed, penalty, and date of payment. Alphabetically arranged by names of taxing districts and alphabetical thereunder by names of property owners. No index. Typed. Average 380 pages. 18 x 15 x 3. 16 volumes, 1914-1930, Basement storeroom; 5 volumes, 1931—, Auditor's office.

258. AUDITOR'S CLASSIFIED TAX LIST
1928—. 6 volumes.

Auditor's list of classified personal property showing assessment certificate number, taxpayer's name, address, production investment, nonproductive investment, credits, money and other taxable intangibles, total tax for year, advanced payment, and balance. Alphabetically arranged by names of taxing districts and alphabetical thereunder by names of property owners. No index. Typed. Average 300 pages. 17.5 x 15 x 2.5. Auditor's office.

Tax Returns

259. PERSONAL TAX RETURNS
1924—. 299 volumes.

Itemized list of personal property returns as listed and valued by owner. Alphabetically arranged by names of property owners. No index. Handwritten on printed forms. Average 375 pages, (loose leaf). 10 x 15 x 4.5. 184 volumes, 1924-1931, Basement storeroom; 115 volumes, 1932—, Auditor's office.

260. AUDITOR'S INHERITANCE TAX RECORD
1915—. 2 volumes.

Auditor's record of inheritance taxes as determined by probate court showing case number, name of administrator or executor, kind of property, value, rate amount of tax, interest, and total due. Chronologically arranged. No index. Handwritten on printed forms. Average 144 pages. 18 x 12 x 1. 1 volume, 1915-1923, Basement storeroom; 1 volume, 1924—, Auditor's office.

Delinquent Taxes (See also entries 216-210)

261. DELINQUENT TAX RECORD
1830—. 8 volumes. Prior records, 1861-1881, 1885-1910, 1916-1917, and 1921-1929, missing.

Auditor's record of tax delinquencies on real estate showing name of owner, entry number, original owner, quantity, value, amount delinquent, penalty, and total amount due. Alphabetically arranged by names of property owners. No index. 1830-1920, handwritten; 1930—, typed. Average 225 pages. 18 x 14 x 2.5. 5 volumes, 1836-1960, 1882-1884, 1911-1915, 1918-1920, Basement storeroom; 3 volumes, 1830-1925, 1930—, Auditor's office.

262. AUDITORS DELINQUENT REAL DUPLICATE
1934—. 1 volume.

Auditor's record of real estate tax delinquencies listing town and village lots, name of owner, lot number, description, quantity, valuation, amount delinquent, penalty, and total amount due. Alphabetically arranged by names of villages and alphabetical thereunder by names of property owners. No index. Handwritten. 350 pages. 17 x 14 x 2.5. Auditor's office.

263. AUDITOR'S DELINQUENT PERSONAL DUPLICATE
1886-1922. 15 volumes. 1901-1902 and 1904-1905, missing. 1923-1932 in Auditor's Duplicate, entry 248.

Auditor's record of taxes unpaid on personal property showing name of taxpayer, valuation, tax due, penalty, total due, and amount paid. Alphabetically arranged under tabs by names of taxing districts and alphabetical thereunder by names of property owners. No index. Handwritten. Average 275 pages. 16 x 11 x 2. 11 volumes, 1886-1900, 1903, 1910, Attic storeroom; 4 volumes, 1906-1909, 1911-1922, Basement storeroom.

For other records, see entry 264.

264. AUDITOR'S CUMULATIVE DELINQUENT TAX LIST
1933—. 1 volume.

Auditor's record of accumulated delinquent taxes other than upon real estate showing year, tax district, volume and page numbers of Personal Tax List, entry 257, amount of tax and penalties due. Alphabetically arranged by names of taxing districts and chronologically thereunder. No index. Typed. 250 pages. 10 x 12.5 x 2. Auditor's office.

For other records, see entry 263.

265. UNDERTAKINGS, COUNTY AUDITOR

1936—. 1 volume.

Auditor's record of delinquent taxes and assessments charged and partial payment made. Alphabetically arranged by names of taxing districts and alphabetical thereunder by names of property owners. No index. Typed. 250 pages. 17 x 16 x 2. Auditor's office.

266. DELINQUENT LAND SALES

1822-1918. 5 volumes. 1837-1872, missing.

Record of land sold for delinquent taxes showing name of owner, entry number, original quantity, original owner, description of tract, value, taxes, penalties, and costs due, purchaser, and amount of sale. 1822-1836, chronologically arranged; 1873-1917, alphabetically arranged by names of townships and alphabetical thereunder by names of property owners. No index. Handwritten. Condition fair. Average 400 pages. 18 x 12 x 3.25. 1 volume, 1822-1936, Attic storeroom; 4 volumes, 1873-1918, Basement storeroom.

267. DELINQUENT LAND TAX CERTIFICATE

1918—. 1 volume.

Record of certified delinquent land taxes showing name of owner, description of property, value, taxes, assessments, and penalties. Chronologically arranged and alphabetically thereunder by names of property owners. No index. Handwritten and typed. 425 pages. 14 x 18 x 3.5. Auditor's office.

268. AUDITOR'S QUADRENNIAL DELINQUENT LAND CERTIFICATES

1922—. 1 volume. Last entry 1930.

Auditor's quadrennial certification of delinquent land tax showing general taxes and penalties with interest; also special assessments and penalty with interest and total amount due. Alphabetically arranged by names of property owners. No index. Typed. 395 pages. 14 x 18 x 3.5.. Auditor's office.

269. AUDITOR'S TRIENNIAL DELINQUENT LAND TAX CERTIFICATE
1936—. 1 volume.

Auditor's triennial certification of delinquent land tax showing general and special assessments delinquent with penalties and interest and total amount due. Alphabetically arranged by names of taxing districts and alphabetical thereunder by names of property owners. No index. Handwritten. 325 pages. 14 x 18 x 2.5. Auditor's office.

Settlement Records

270. SETTLEMENT WITH TOWNSHIP TREASURERS
1882-1894. 1 volume.

Auditor's record of annual settlement with township treasurers. Chronologically arranged. Alphabetical index by names of townships. Handwritten. 390 pages. 15 x 9 x 3. Basement storeroom.

For other records, see entry 271.

271. SETTLEMENT RECORD, TOWNSHIPS AND VILLAGES
1873—. 9 volumes. 1893-1897, missing.

Auditor's record of disbursements of funds to various townships and villages in county. Alphabetically arranged under tabs by names of villages and townships and chronologically thereunder. No index. Handwritten. Average 500 pages. 18 x 14 x 4. 1 volume, 1898-1902, Attic storeroom; 5 volumes, 1873-1892, 1903-1922, Basement storeroom; 3 volumes, 1923—, Auditor's office.

For other township settlement records, see entry 270.

272. SCHOOL FUND SETTLEMENT
1903—. 5 volumes.

Auditor's record of disbursements of funds to various school districts in county. Arranged under tabs by names of school districts and chronologically thereunder. No index. Handwritten. Average 450 pages. 18 x 14 x 3.5. 3 volumes, 1903-1928, Basement storeroom; 2 volumes, 1929—, Auditor's office.

273. CIGARETTE SETTLEMENT

1927—. 1 volume.

Auditor's record of distribution of cigarette license fees to the various tax districts showing name of tax district, date, and amount distributed to each tax district. Chronologically arranged by dates of distributions. No index. Typed. 250 pages. 19 x 12 x 1.75. Auditor's office.

274. SETTLEMENT RECORD, MOTOR VEHICLE LICENSE FEES

1925—. 2 volumes.

Auditor's record of distribution of motor vehicle license fees to various subdivisions in county showing amount to each. Chronologically arranged. No index. Handwritten. 250 pages. 12 x 17 x 2.5. 1 volume, 1925-1931, Basement storeroom; 1 volume, 1932—, Auditor's office.

Business Administration of Office

General Accounts

275. AUDITOR'S LEDGER

1854—. 10 volumes. Prior records, 1874-1881, and 1921-1923, missing.

Auditor's daily record of transactions showing nature of transaction, credit, debit, balance, and name of fund. Chronologically arranged. No index. 1854-1931, handwritten; 1932—, typed. Average 450 pages. 18 x 12 x 3.5. 2 volumes, 1854-1973, 1893-1903, Attic storeroom 7 volumes, 1882-1920, 1924-1931, Basement storeroom; 1 volume, 1932—, Auditor's office.

276. AUDITOR'S RECORD OF FEES

1911—. 4 volumes. Prior records missing.

Auditor's record of fees received showing name a pair, name a service, and total fee. Chronologically arranged. No index. Handwritten. Average 290 pages. 16 x 11 x 2. 2 volumes, 1911-1923, Basement storeroom; 2 volumes, 1924—, Auditor's office.

277. APPROPRIATION LEDGER

1928—. 4 volumes.

Auditor's record of appropriations to various funds with record of warrants drawn against funds. Alphabetically arranged under tabs by names of funds. No index. Handwritten. Average 500 pages. 12 x 14 x 4.5. Auditor's office.

Special Accounts

278. RECORD OF SOLDIERS' RELIEF
1887—. 2 volumes.

Auditor's record of relief to indigent soldiers, or to soldiers' widows and minor children. Chronologically arranged. No index. Handwritten. Average 335 pages. 18 x 12 x 2.5. 1 volume, 1887-1906, Basement storeroom; 1 volume, 1907—, Auditor's office.

For other records, see entry 1.

279. SHEEP CLAIM RECORD
1892—. 1 volume.

Auditor's record of claims granted for sheep killed or injured by dogs showing name of claimant, date claim allowed, amount allowed, and warrant number. Chronologically arranged. No index. Handwritten. 398 pages. 16 x 11 x 3. Auditor's office.

280. MOTHERS' PENSION RECORD
1915—. 1 volume.

Auditor's record of mothers' pension account showing award granted and warrants number. Chronologically arranged. No index. Handwritten. 300 pages. 18 x 12 x 2.5. Auditor's office.

Bills and Orders

281. AUDITOR'S DOCKET OF BILLS FILED
1904—. 4 volumes.

Auditor's record of bills presented for payment and filed listing date, name of creditor, purpose, date approved, amount, date paid, and warrant number. Chronologically arranged. No index. Handwritten. Average 500 pages. 18 x 12 x 4. Auditor's office.

For other records, see entry 8 and 282.

282. AUDITOR'S DOCKET, COMMISSIONERS' BILLS
1902—. 4 volumes.

Auditor's record of bills filed with county commissioners listing date, purpose, date approved, amount, date paid, and warrant number. Chronologically arranged. No index. Handwritten. Average 450 pages. 18 x 12 x 3.5. 2 volumes, 1902-1921, Basement storeroom; 2 volumes, 1922—, Auditor's office.

For other records, see entries 8, 281, and 288.

283. ORDER BOOK
1832-1869. 2 volumes. 1843-1860, missing.

Record of orders issued on county treasurer by county auditor showing order number, to whom issued, purpose, name of fund, and amount. Chronologically arranged and consecutively by order numbers. No index. Handwritten.
Condition poor. Average 390 pages. 16 x 11 x 2.5. Attic storeroom.

284. REGISTER OF ORDERS ISSUED
1869-1890. 4 volumes.

Auditor's record of orders issued on county treasurer by county auditor showing order number, to whom issued, purpose, name of fund, and amount. Chronologically arranged and consecutively by order numbers. No index. Handwritten. Average 480 pages. 18 x 11 x 3.5. Attic storeroom.

285. AUDITOR'S ACCOUNTS
1884-1904. 4 volumes.

Record of orders drawn on county treasurer and record of receipts certified into county treasury showing name of fund, credit, and debit. Chronologically arranged. No index. Handwritten. Average 470 pages. 22 x 15 x 4. Basement storeroom.

286. AUDITOR'S JOURNAL (Warrants)
1877—. 15 volumes. 1914-1917, missing.

Auditor's record of orders on which warrants have been issued showing name, purpose, warrant number, amount, and name of fund. Chronologically arranged. No index. 1877-1921, handwritten; 1922—, typed. Average 275 pages. 18 x 14 x 2. 5 volumes, 1877-1904, Attic storeroom; 3 volumes, 1904-1913, Basement storeroom; 7 volumes, 1918—, Auditor's office.

Vouchers and Warrants

287. (Sinking Fund) VOUCHERS
1925-1927. 1 volume.

Sinking fund voucher stubs going to whom issued and for what amount. Chronologically arranged. No index. Handwritten are printed forms. 292 pages. 9 x 15 x 2. Basement storeroom.

288. RECORD OF INFIRMARY BILLS FILED
1900-1913. 1 volume. Prior records missing.

Record of bills filed by the infirmary directors for expenses incurred in the operation of the institution showing date, to whom payable, for what purpose and number of voucher issued to meet bill. Numerically arranged by voucher numbers. No index. Handwritten on printed forms. 200 pages. 18 x 12 x 1.5. Auditor's office.

For subsequent records, see entry 282.

289. VOUCHERS
1823—. 65 file boxes (labeled by subjects). 1890-1900 and 1910-1914, missing.

Vouchers issued by various county officials to county auditor for payment of services rendered and material supplied. Chronologically arranged. No index. 1823-1837, handwritten; 1837—, handwritten on printed forms. 1823-1889, 45 cardboard file boxes, 11 x 5 x 4; 1901-1909, 1915-1930, 12 cardboard file boxes, 18 x 12 x 6; 1931—, 8 metal file boxes, 14 x 10 x 5. 45 file boxes, 1823-1889, Attic storeroom; 12 file boxes, 1901-1909, 1915-1930, Basement storeroom; 8 file boxes, 1931—, Auditor's office.

290. WARRANTS REDEEMED
1818—. 73 file boxes (labeled by subjects). 1889-1909, 1915-1921, missing.

Auditor's warrants redeemed by county treasurer. Chronologically arranged. No index. 1818—, handwritten and handwritten on printed forms. 49 cardboard file boxes, 11 x 5 x 4; 10 cardboard file boxes, 18 x 12 x 6; 14 metal file boxes, 14 x 10 x 5. 49 file boxes, 1818-1888, Attic storeroom; 10 file boxes, 1910-1914, 1929-1930, Basement storeroom; 14 file boxes, 1931—, Auditor's office.

291. AUDITOR'S WARRANTS

1884—. 51 volumes. 1886-1889, missing.

Record stubs of warrants issued on county treasurer by county auditor showing to whom issued, purpose, name of fund, and amount. Chronologically arranged and consecutively by warrant numbers. No index. Handwritten on printed forms. Average 470 pages. 14 x 10 x 3.5. 19 volumes, 1884-1885, 1890-1910, Attic storeroom; 23 volumes, 1911-1930, Basement storeroom; 9 volumes, 1931—, Auditor's office.

292. COURT WARRANTS

1921—. 2 volumes.

Auditor's record of court warrants issued showing what court, to whom issued, warrant number, purpose, and amount. Chronologically arranged and consecutively by warrant numbers. Handwritten. Average 250 pages. 18 x 12 x 2. Auditor's office.

Licenses

293. DOG AND KENNEL LICENSE REGISTER

1918—. 4 volumes. 1919-1924, missing.

Record of license tags issued showing owners name and address, description of dog, tag number, and fee. Alphabetically arranged under tabs by names of owners and chronologically thereunder. No index. 1918-1932, handwritten; 1932—, typed. Average 260 pages. 20 x 15 x 2. 2 volumes, 1918, 1925-1926, Basement storeroom; 2 volumes, 1927—, Auditor's office.

294. COSMETIC LICENSES

1933-1934. 1 file box. Discontinued.

Record of cosmetic licenses issued showing name of dealer, date, and amount of fee. Chronologically arranged. No index. Handwritten on printed forms. 14 x 10 x 5.

295. BEVERAGE LICENSES

1932-1935. 1 file box. Discontinued.

Record of beverage licenses issued showing name of dealer, date, and amount of fee. Chronologically arranged. No index. Handwritten on printed forms. 14 x 10 x 5. Auditor's office.

Bonds

296. AUDITOR'S RECORD OF OFFICIAL BONDS

1893—. 1 volume.

Record of bonds given by persons elected county treasurer and county prosecuting attorney with county commissioners' approval and copy of oath taken. Chronologically arranged. Alphabetical index by names of officials. Handwritten on printed forms. 304 pages. 16 x 11 x 2. Auditor's office.

For other records, see entries 15, 76, and 238.

297. BOND RECORD

1914—. 1 volume.

Record of bonds issued to provide funds in operating county projects showing date of issue, to whom sold, amount, rate of interest, number of coupons, date redeemed, date of maturity, premium received, amount of accrued interest, and for what purpose issued. Chronologically arranged and numerically thereunder by bond numbers. No index. Handwritten. 300 pages. 17 x 15 x 2. Auditor's office.

298. FORFEITED RECOGNIZANCE RECORD

1890-1910. 1 volume.

Record of bail bonds forfeited as certified to county auditor by county prosecutor. Chronologically arranged. Alphabetical index by names of defendants. Handwritten. 218 pages. 16 x 10 x 1.5. Attic storeroom.

Reports

299. AUDITOR'S RECORD OF INSPECTOR'S REPORTS

1902-1906. 1 volume.

Auditor's record of state examiner's report on financial condition of each county office or department showing amount of credit to each fund and overdraft. Chronologically arranged. No index. Handwritten. 190 pages. 20 x 14 x 1.5. Basement storeroom.

300. DAILY AND MONTHLY REPORT, MOTOR VEHICLE FEES
1925-1932. 2 volumes.
Auditor's records of reports of motor vehicle license fees received. Chronologically arranged. No index. Handwritten. Average 150 pages. 16 x 20 x 1.5. Basement storeroom.

301. FUND STATEMENTS
1925—. 2 volumes.
Statements by the depositories of public funds to county auditor each thirty-day period showing amount of deposits and withdrawals on order of fiscal officer of tax district; also balance on deposit. Alphabetically arranged by names of taxing districts and chronologically thereunder. No index. Handwritten on printed forms. Average 250 pages (loose leaf) 20 x 14 x 2.5. 1 volume, 1925-1930, Basement storeroom; 1 volume, 1930—, Auditor's office.

Miscellaneous

302. UNCLAIMED MONEY ORDERS
1912—. 1 volume.
Auditor's record of unclaimed money showing to whom due, purpose, amount, date paid into county treasury, and date certificate issued for recovery. Chronologically arranged and alphabetical thereunder by names that claimants. No index. Handwritten. 250 pages. 14 x 9 x 2. Auditor's office.

303. ENUMERATION RECORDS
1829-1911. 4 file boxes. 1838-1848, 1865, and 1878-1888, missing.
Record copies of reports by enumerators of school-age youths. Chronologically arranged. No index. 1829-1964, handwritten; 1866-1911, handwritten on printed forms. 3 file boxes, 11 x 5 x 5; 1 file box, 18 x 12 x 6. 3 file boxes, 1829-1877, Attic storeroom; 1file box 1889-1911, Basement storeroom.

304. INDEX OF MOTOR VEHICLE LICENSES
1926-1931. 2 volumes. Discontinued; subsequent records have been kept by the state bureau of motor vehicles.
Auditor's record of motor vehicle licenses issued showing to whom issued, make

of vehicle, model, type, and license number. Chronologically arranged and alphabetical thereunder by names of licensees. No index. Handwritten. Average 300 pages. 14 x 18 x 2.5. Basement storeroom.

305. MISCELLANEOUS RECORDS
1902—. 1 volume.

Auditor's record of miscellaneous items such as bonds of deputy officials, additional contractors' bonds, agreements with county commissioners concerning carrying out by contractors of stipulations in contracts, and reports from county highway superintendents to county commissioners. Chronologically arranged. Alphabetical index by names of principles. Handwritten and typed. 432 pages. 15 x 11 x 2.5. Auditor's office.

A budget commission was established in Brown County in 1915 under the act of 1911 which made provision for the establishment of a budget commission in each county to be composed of the county auditor, the mayor of the largest municipality, and the prosecuting attorney (102 O. L. 266). It was not until after the World War, when county expenditures steadily increased, that the importance of improved methods of finance were forcibly brought to the attention of the legislature. This new need was met in 1927 by the establishment of a budget commission in each county. This commission, consisting of the county auditor, the county treasurer, and the prosecuting attorney, receives and examines the annual budget of the county, municipal, township, and school authorities, with an estimate of the amount to be raised for state purposes in each subdivision (112 O. L. 399). If the total amount exceeds the sum authorized to be raised, the commission adjusts the amount to be raised and may change and revise the estimates. The commission may reduce all items in the budget, but it is prohibited from increasing the total of any budget or any item.

The adjusted budget is certified to the taxing authority in each subdivision. If the work of the commission is satisfactory, each taxing authority by ordinance or resolution authorizes the necessary tax levies and certifies them to the county auditor. (G. C. sec. 5625-25). On the other hand, the taxing authority in any subdivision may appeal, through its fiscal officer, from the decision of the budget commission to the state tax commission of Ohio, which is empowered to adjust the estimates of revenues and balance this in fixing the tax rate (G. C. Sec. 5625-28).

The county auditor, as secretary to the commission, is required to keep a full and accurate record of the proceedings of the commission.

306. BUDGET COMMISSION RECORD

1915—. 1 volume.

Record of minutes of meetings of county budget commission showing budgets for different subdivisions and for county as a whole. Chronologically arranged. No index. Handwritten. 300 pages. 16 x 11 x 2. Auditor's office.

The county board of revision, the object of which was to correct some of the defects and inequities of assessments, was established by the legislature in 1825. The first board of revision, or equalization as it was sometimes called, was composed of the county commissioners, the county auditor, and the assessor. The board was authorized to meet at the seat of justice on the first Monday in June annually "to hear and determine the complaint of any owner of property listed and valued by the assessor . . . and shall correct any list or valuation made by the assessor, either by adding to or deducting from his valuation." (23 O. L. 64). The act of 1831, repealing the act of 1825, left the duties and personnel of the board unchanged (29 O. L. 278).

In 1859 the legislature made provision for two county boards of equalization. One board, composed of the county auditor and the county commissioners, was directed to meet annually for the purpose of equalizing real and personal property, and moneys and credits in the county. The other board, composed of the county auditor, the county surveyor, and the county commissioners, was authorized to meet sexennially for the same purpose. (56 O. L. 57, 60).

The act of 1863, amending the act of 1859, left the personnel and duties of the annual county board unchanged. The second county board, although continuing without alteration and composition or duties, was directed to meet decennially, rather than sexennially. (60 O. L. 57, 69).

The annual and special boards of equalization were abolished, when, in 1913, the state tax commission of Ohio was given the task of supervising the assessment of real and personal property in the state. Under this arrangement each county constituted a district. In each district containing less than 60,000 inhabitants by which stipulation Brown County was included, there was to be appointed by the governor one state tax commissioner. In all other districts there was appointed, in the same manner, two state deputy tax commissioners. In each district there was appointed a district board of complaints. This board, appointed by the state tax commission with the consent of the governor, took over the duties and powers formerly invested in the boards of equalization. The county auditor, made secretary to the board of complaints, was required to present at each meeting in person or by deputy, and keep an accurate record of their proceedings to be kept in a book for that purpose. (103 O. L. 791). Moreover, the board was directed to take full minutes of all evidence given before it and might have such evidence taken in shorthand and extended into typewritten form. The auditor was required to preserve in his office separate records of all minutes and documentary evidence offered in each complaint. (102 O. L. 791).

This arrangement, after being in operation for two years, was abrogated by the legislature in 1915. In that year the county auditor, under the supervision of the tax commission of Ohio, became the chief assessing officer in the county. The county treasurer, the county prosecutor, the probate judge, and the president of the county commissioners were to constitute a board with the purpose of appointing three members to constitute a board of revision. Again the county auditor was made secretary to the board and was directed to keep a record of their proceedings and to preserve in his office a separate record of all minutes and documentary evidence offered in each complaint. (105 O. L. 257-258).

Under the present system, inaugurated in 1917, the county treasurer, county auditor, and president of the county commissioners constituted a board of revision. This board organizes annually, on the second Monday in June, by electing a chairman for the ensuing year. The county auditor serves as secretary to the board (G. C. secs. 3357, 5592). The county board of revisions may, with the consent and approval of the tax commission of Ohio, employ experts, clerks, and other employees (G. C. sec. 5587).

The duties of the board, not differing in detail from those prescribed in 1825, include the hearing of all complaints relating to valuation or assessments of real property as it appears upon the tax duplicate of the "then current year." The board is authorized to investigate all complaints and may increase or decrease any valuation or correct any assessment complained of, or may order a reassessment by the original assessing official. (G. C. sec. 5597). However, no valuation is increased without giving notice to the person in whose name the property affected is listed (G. C. sec. 5599). The board of revision, in all respects, is governed by the laws respecting the valuation of real property and makes no change of any valuation "except in accordance with such laws" (G. C. sec. 5596).

On the second Monday in June, annually, the county auditor lays before the board of revision the returns of assessments of any real property for the current year, and the board proceeds to review the assessment. The board of revision certifies its action to the county auditor, who corrects the tax list and duplicate according to the additions and deductions ordered by the board. The auditor is prohibited by statute of making up his tax list and duplicate, until the board has completed its work and has returned to him all the returns laid before it with revisions. (G. C. Sec. 5605). But in the event the tax duplicate has been delivered to the county treasurer, the auditor is required to certify such corrections to him and enter such corrections in his tax duplicate (G. C. sec. 5602).

In its investigations the board may examine, under oath, persons as to their or others' real property. In the event witnesses fail to appear or refuse to testify, the board by its chairman is authorized to make a complaint in writing to the probate judge, who, by statute, is directed to institute proceedings against them. (G. C. sec. 5596). The decision of the board are subject to appeal, within thirty days after a decision is served, to the tax commission of Ohio (G. C. sec. 5610).

The secretary of the board is required to keep "an accurate record of the proceedings of the board in a book to be kept for that purpose" (G. C. sec. 5592). The county auditor, as in 1913, is required to preserve in his office separate records of all minutes and documentary evidence offered in each complaint (G. C. sec. 5603). The records of the board are open to the inspection of the public (G. C. sec. 5591).

307. BOARD OF REVISION RECORDS

1880—. 4 volumes. Prior records and 1911-1913, missing. Title varies: 1880-1910, 1 volume, Board of Equalization Record; 1914-1933, 2 volumes, Board of Complaint Records.

Records of meeting of county board of revision showing assessments and valuations adjusted. Chronologically arranged. No index. 1880-1910, handwritten; 1914—, typed. Average 300 pages. 18 x 12 x 2. 1 volume, 1880-1910, Basement storeroom; 3 volumes, 1914—, Auditor's office.

The board of sinking fund trustees, composed of the prosecuting attorney, auditor, and treasurer, was organized in 1919 in each county owing a bonded debt. The records of Brown County were initiated in 1921. The county prosecuting attorney serves as president of the board and the auditor as secretary. It is the duty of the trustees to provide for the payment of all bonds issued by the county and the interest maturing thereon.

All bonds issued by the county must be recorded in the office of the trustees of the sinking fund, bear a stamp containing the words "Recorded in the office of the sinking fund trustees," and signed by the secretary before they become valid in the hands of any purchaser. Since 1922, in the event the secretary is unable to act, by reason of absence or disability, such recording and authenticating are performed by the county treasurer. (G. C. sec. 2976-25).

On or before the first Monday in May of each year, the trustees certify to the county commissioners the rate of tax necessary to provide a sinking fund for both the payment and maturity of bonds heretofore issued by the county and for the payment of interest on the bonded indebtedness. The amount certified by the trustees is set forth without diminution in the annual budget of the commissioners. (G. C. sec. 2976-26). Then, after each semiannual settlement of taxes and assessments, the county auditor reports to the trustees the amount of money in the treasury of the county charged to the credit of the sinking fund. Money drawn from county treasury for investment or disbursements is by the issuance of a voucher signed by all the members of the board and directed to the county auditor. The trustees are directed, by statute, to invest all moneys subject to their control in United States bonds, Ohio bonds, or bonds of a municipal corporation, school district, township, or county in the state.

The board members are required to keep "a full and complete record of their transactions, a complete record of the funded debt of the county specifying the dates, purpose, amounts, numbers, maternities, and rates and maturities of interest and installments thereof, and where payable, and an account exhibiting the amount held in the sinking fund for the payment thereof." (G. C. sec. 2976-24).

The meetings of the trustees are open to the public. All questions relating to the purchase or sale of securities for the payment of bonds or interests are decided by a yea and nay vote, which is recorded in their journal.

308. SINKING FUND JOURNAL
1921-1927. 1 volume. Discontinued.
Record of minutes of meetings of board of trustees of sinking fund. Chronologically arranged. No index. Typed. 104 pages. 15 x 9 x 1. Basement storeroom.

309. SINGING FUND LEDGER
1921—. 1 volume.
Auditor's record of county sinking funds showing receipts, expenditures, and balances. Chronologically arranged. No index. Handwritten. 300 pages. 18 x 10 x 2.5. Basement storeroom.

The county board of education, a modern administrative and supervisory agency developed during the last two decades, supplanted the smaller educational units, which, established during the early period of Ohio history, became inefficient and unable to meet the modern requirements as demanded by rural communities.

During the earlier period of Ohio history, educational administration, because of the newness of the state, the spareness of the population, and the undeveloped means of transportation was, by necessity, local in character. For fourteen years after the accession of Ohio to statehood, through the constitution stated that means of education could be encouraged by the general assembly no legislation was enacted for public schools (*Ohio Const. 1820,* Art. VIII, secs. 3, 25, 27). It was not until 1817 that the legislature authorized six or more people in the townships to form associations to build school houses and to be incorporated for educational purposes (15 O. L. 407). This was a beginning, but as yet the values of an educational system were not readily perceived by those engaged in subduing a stubborn wilderness.

The first permanent law for the organization of schools in Ohio was passed in 1821. Under the provisions of this act, the electors of the township were authorized to vote on the proposition of dividing the townships into school districts. If the proposal carried, there were to be elected three school commissioners, who, in turn, were authorized to select a clerk and a collector who should act as a treasurer. They were instructed also, to levy taxes for the support of schools and to hire teachers. (19 O. L. 54).

As education began to advance in the early years of the nineteenth century, some kind of state control was needed. Accordingly, in 1837, the office of state superintendent of schools was established. A year later an act was passed making the county auditor also the county superintendent of schools; and in each township the clerk became superintendent of the smaller unit. The county superintendent was made responsible to the state superintendent in all educational affairs. In the same year each incorporated city, town, or borough not regulated by a charter was made a separate school district. The voters in each division were authorized to elect three directors. (31 O. L. 21). The effectiveness of this organization, however, was destroyed in 1840, when the legislature abolished the office of state superintendent and the secretary of state took over his functions of tabulating and transmitting school statistics (38 O. L. 130). Seven years later, twenty-five counties exclusive of Brown were allowed to have county superintendents (45 O. L. 32), and in 1848 the provisions of the previous act were extended to all other counties in the state (46 O. L. 86).

Although marked changes were made in the curriculum of the schools, the history of education in Ohio from 1850 to the early part of the twentieth century was largely one of the gradual transference of powers from districts to townships, and from townships to county in the interest of a better system of education. It was not, however, until within the last three decades that the county became the unit for educational administration (70 O. L. 195, 204; 97 O. L. 354).

Although the county superintendent was known as early as 1838, the first permanent law for the establishment of a county board of education was enacted in 1914. Under this act the school districts were classified, and provision was made for a county school district, exclusive of the territory embraced in any city or village desiring exemption. The county district was to be under the supervision of five board members elected by the presidents of the village and rural school boards. Members were to hold office for one, two, three, four, and five years respectfully, and each year one member was to be selected.

The county board of education was authorized to change school district lines; afford transportation for children living more than two miles from a school house; appoint a county superintendent; and certify annually to the county auditor the number of teachers and superintendents employed, their salaries, and the amount apportioned for each school district. The county superintendent, acting as secretary of the board, was required to keep in a book provided for that purpose a full record of the proceedings of the board properly indexed. Each motion, together with the name of the person making it and the votes thereon, was to be entered on the record. (104 O. L. 133; 108 O. L. pt. i, 704).

The county was divided into administrative divisions containing one or more villages or rural school districts. Each district was to be under the supervision of a district superintendent, who was required to visit the schools in his charge, direct and assist teachers in the performance of their duties, and classify and control promotion of pupils. Moreover, he was required to report annually to the county superintendent on matters under his charge, and assemble teachers for the purpose of conferring on curricular matters, discipline, and school management. (104 O. L. 133-145).

Significant changes were made by the act of 1921, under which the board members became elective by popular vote. They were authorized to appoint one or more assistant county superintendents for a term of three years. Brown County, however, has no assistant. The board was authorized to publish, with the advice and consent of the county superintendent, a minimum course of study to serve as a guide to local board members. The same act abolished the office of district superintendent. (G. C. secs. 4728-1, 4729; 109 O. L. 242).

The county organization has placed the rural schools on a plane of equality with the city schools. The consolidation of the smaller units has eliminated the small, ill-equipped schools, and provides under one roof facilities and instructions suited to the needs of the rural children under the supervision of educational specialist.

All records are located in the office of the county superintendent of schools.

Journal and Reports

310 MINUTES OF BOARD OF EDUCATION

1914—. 1 volume.

Record of minutes of all meetings of county board of education showing each motion and the name of person making it. Chronologically arranged. No index. Typed. 560 pages. 14 x 9 x 4.

311. MONTHLY REPORTS

1934—. 3 file boxes.

Teachers' reports on enrollment and attendance records. Alphabetically arranged by names of schools. No index. Handwritten on printed forms. 12 x 11 x 7.

312. ATTENDANCE OFFICERS' REPORTS

1935 —. 1 file box.

Attendance officers' reports on investigation of teachers' reports of pupils' absences. Chronologically arranged. No index. Handwritten on printed forms. 15 x 9 x 3.

313. ANNUAL REPORTS

1931—. 5 file boxes.

Annual statistical reports by county superintendent listing average attendance for year and miscellaneous annual reports. Chronologically arranged. No index. Handwritten on printed forms. 15 x 9 x 3.

314. FINANCIAL REPORTS

1933—. 5 file boxes.

Annual financial reports by county superintendent to board of education. Chronologically arranged. No index. Handwritten on printed forms. 15 x 9 x 3.

Miscellaneous

315. APPROPRIATION LEDGER

1931—. 1 volume.

Financial records of county board of education giving source of funds, date, payee, purpose, warrant number, and unencumbered balance. Chronologically arranged. No index. Handwritten. 140 pages. 10 x 12 x 1.

316. RECORD OF OFFICIAL BONDS AND OATHS

1928—. 1 volume.

Record copy of bonds executed by clerk-treasurer of school districts and oaths of office. Chronologically arranged. No index. Handwritten. 140 pages. 11 x 8 x 1.

317. APPLICATIONS

1933—. 3 file boxes.

Applications for teaching positions with credentials and recommendations. Alphabetically arranged by names of applicants. No index. Handwritten. 15 x 9 x 3.

The general health district, or county health department, is one of the recent developments in county health administration. An act at the legislature in 1919 provided that townships and municipalities in each county, exclusive of any city with 25,000 or more population, should constitute a general health district; cities with 25,000 or more population a municipal health district; and municipalities of not less then 10,000 or more than 25,000 population, and maintaining a board of health meeting the qualifications of the legislative act, were authorized after examination by the state health department to continue operation as separate health districts (108 O. L. pt. i, 238).

An amendment in December 1919 made each city a health district; the townships and villages in each county were combined into a general health district; and a city and general health district might combine for administrative purposes (108 O. L. pt. ii, 1086). The mayor of each municipality not constituting a city health district, and the chairman of the trustees of each township, are authorized to meet at the seat of justice and by selecting a chairman and a secretary organize a district health advisory council which selects and appoints a district board of health composed of five members, one of whom must be a physician, who serve without compensation (108 O. L. pt. ii, 1085).

Within thirty days after their appointment the members of the district board of health–the county board of health–organized by appointing one of their members president and another president *pro tempore.* The board is authorized to a point as district health commissioner a licensed physician who is designated deputy state registrar of vital statistics and is required to report monthly to the state registrar of vital statistics, and who serves as secretary to the board. (G. C. sec. 1261-32; 108 O. L. pt. i, 242).

On recommendation of the district health commissioner the board appoints a whole-time public health nurse, a clerk, and such additional public health nurses, physicians and others as may be necessary for the proper conduct of its work. The board studies the prevalence of disease, especially communicable diseases, provides treatment of venereal diseases, and is authorized to make any and all regulations it deems necessary for the prevention or restriction of disease, and the prevention, abolition or suppression of nuisances. It provides for inspection of public charitable, benevolent, correctional and penal institutions; and may provide inspection of dairies, stores, restaurants, hotels, and other places where food is manufactured, handles, stored, sold or offered for sale. The board is authorized to carry on necessary laboratory tests by establishing a laboratory or contracting with existing laboratories, and all state institutions supported in whole or in part by public funds must furnish such laboratory service to a county board of health under the terms agreed upon (108 O. L. pt. ii, 1088-89).

The health department is financed by public taxation. The district board of health annually estimates in itemized form the amount needed for the fiscal year, and these estimates are certified by the county auditor and submitted to the county budget commissioners who may reduce any item but cannot increase any item or the aggregate of all items. The total amount fixed by the budget commissioners is apportioned by the county health department on the basis of taxable valuations in the townships and municipalities composing the district. (108 O. L. pt. ii, 1091).

All records of the county board of health are located in the office of the board.

Journal

318. MINUTES OF COUNTY BOARD OF HEALTH

1927—. 1 volume. Prior records missing.

Minutes of meeting and record of proceedings of county board of health. Chronologically arranged. No index. Handwritten. 152 pages. 9.75 x 7.75 x 1.

Vital Statistics
(See also entries 162-165)

319. BIRTH RECORDS

1926—. 1 file box and 24 volumes. 1922-1925 in Births and Deaths, entry 320.

Record of births showing names of infant and parents, place and date of birth, sex, registration district, and file number. File box, 1926-1929, alphabetically arranged by names of registration districts and alphabetical thereunder by names of infants; volumes, 1930—, alphabetically arranged by names of infants. No index. Handwritten on printed forms. File box, 16 x 4.75 x 4; volumes average 100 pages. 8.25 x 7 x .5.

320. BIRTHS AND DEATHS

1922-1932. 6 file boxes. Prior records missing. Discontinued.

Card record of births and deaths. Birth record shows maiden name of mother, full name of father, name of doctor, whether legitimate or illegitimate, and date received for record. Death record shows name and address of decedent, cause and date of death, name of attending physician, and date received for record. Contains: Birth Records, 1922-1925, entry 319; Deaths, entry 321. Alphabetically arranged by names of registration districts and alphabetical thereunder by names of infants or decedents. No index. Handwritten. 16 x 5.75 x 4.

321. DEATHS

1932—. 10 volumes. 1922-1932 in Births and Deaths, entry 320.

Record of place of death, registration district number, primary registration district number, file number, registration number where death occurred, name and address, and date. Alphabetically by names of decedents. No index. Handwritten. Average 100 pages. 8.25 x 7 x .5.

Miscellaneous

322. DIPHTHERIA IMMUNIZATION

1936. 1 volume.

Records names of persons immunized for diphtheria showing date of immunization. Chronologically arranged. Alphabetical index by names of patients. Handwritten. 280 pages. 13 x 8 x 1.

The Brown County poorhouse, now called the county home, was established in 1829 under the provisions of the legislative act of 1816 which authorized the county commissioners to purchase land and construct poorhouses in which to care for the county's indigent. By the same act the commissioners were authorized to appoint annually a board of seven directors which was authorized to make rules and regulations for the management of the institution and to appoint a superintendent. (14 O. L. 248-249). Accordingly, on January 15, 1828 the commissioners authorized the auditor to advertise for the purchase of land and to receive proposals for building a poorhouse. On January 16, 1829, the commissioner's purchased of Michael Weaver a farm for the use of the county, for which they paid $522. Soon a building was constructed in which to house those of the county who were financially unable to support themselves.

By the legislative act of 1831, the membership of the board was reduced to three. This board, like its predecessor, was authorized to appoint a superintendent. It was his duty, upon the order of the board, to discharge from the poorhouse any person who had been admitted because of illness when he had sufficiently recovered. Moreover, the directors were authorized to remove paupers to their legal place of residence. (29 O. L. 319). Besides this, any "pauper" rejected by the board of directors could be turned over to the township overseers to be cared for by contracting with the lowest bidder (29 O. L. 321-322).

In 1850 the name county poorhouse was changed to that of county infirmary. Fifteen years later, and 1865, the board of infirmary directors, consisting of three resident electors, were to be elected by the voters of the county for a three-year term. The board was still authorized to appoint a superintendent, and was still required to make inspection visits, and report their findings to the county commissioners. (62 O. L. 24-25).

Although reports have been required in previous years, it was not until the decade of the seventies that the legislature enacted measures looking forward to some business like management of this ancient institution. Accordingly, in 1872, an act was passed which required each infirmary director, as well as the superintendent, to give bond conditioned for the faithful performance of the duties of his office (69 O. L. 120-121). Under this act the directors were required to report semiannually to the county commissioners the condition of the infirmary, the number of inmates, and such other information as the county commissioners believe proper. Furthermore, the board of directors was required to file a full account "of all moneys received and paid out, together with the vouchers . . . from whence received, to whom and for what paid out" with the county commissioners, who, after examining it, entered the report in the minutes of their proceedings. This report, as well as the vouchers, was filed in the auditor's office, it was to be "safely preserved" by that officer. (69 O. L. 121-122).

The county infirmary served also as a place for the confinement of children, the mentally ill, and persons afflicted with epilepsy. Although the state assumed responsibility for the mentally ill in the early years of the nineteenth century, it was not until 1898 that it was made unlawful to confine the insane and epileptics in the county home (93 O. L. 274). In the meantime, in 1884, the legislature prohibited the housing of children in the county infirmary who were ineligible to a county children's home or to some other charitable institution. However, exceptions were made in the case of insane, idiotic and epileptic children. (103 O. L. 890). The latter provision is still effective in Ohio.

By an act of May 31, 1911, effective January 1, 1913, the board of infirmary directors was abolished and the powers formerly exercised by this body was transferred to the county commissioners and the infirmary superintendent (102 O. L. 433). The superintendent is still required to keep a record of the inmates, as prescribed by statute, and to report annually to the county commissioners. This report, the acceptance of which is evidenced by an entry in the minutes of the commissioners' journal, is filed with the county auditor and by him preserved (G. C. sec. 2535). In 1919 the name county infirmary was changed to that of county home (108 O. L. pt. i, 68).

The county commissioners still make provision for the establishment and maintenance of the county home, appoint a superintendent, and make regular inspection visits. Since December 1, 1932, the superintendent has been appointed from a list of names of persons eligible under civil service regulations. Moreover, since 1882, they have been authorized to appoint an infirmary physician, who, like the superintendent, is required by statute to report to the county commissioners. This report, made quarterly, includes such information as the nature and extent of medical services rendered, to whom, and the character of the disease treated. (G. C. sec. 2546; 73 O. L. 233; 79 O. L. 90; 102 O. L. 436; 108 O. L. pt. i, 269).

Since 1929 the commissioners have been authorized, whenever the buildings of the county home become unsuitable for habitation or whenever the population is too small for economical operation, to abandon the county home and provide for the care of inmates and others afterwards accepted as a county charge by boarding them with another county home. (G. C. sec. 2557).

Although corrective measures have been passed, the county home has remained one of the most unprogressive institutions of the county. There is no uniform system of administration of indigent relief. The state department of public welfare is authorized to inspect the county home, but is powerless to enforce its recommendations.

All records of this office are located at the institution in the office of the superintendent unless otherwise indicated.

Registers

323. INFIRMARY REGISTER
1862—. 2 volumes.

Register of persons admitted to county home showing date admitted, name, sex, age, physical condition, birthplace, from what township, date of birth, date of death, date of discharge, and remarks. Chronologically arranged. No index. Handwritten. Average 400 pages. 18 x 12 x 3.

324. DAILY RECORD
1932—. 6 volumes.

Daily record of movement of population at county home giving number registered, received, and discharged; number of deaths. Chronologically arranged. No index. Handwritten. Average 50 pages. 9 x 14 x .5.

325. VISITORS' REGISTER
1884—. 1 volume.

Record of visitors to see residents of home or to view institution showing date, name, address, and remarks. Chronologically arranged. No index. Handwritten. 250 pages. 16 x 12 x 4.

326. JOURNAL (Business transactions)
1888- December 31, 1913. 2 volumes.

Complete record of business transactions of county infirmary directors. Chronologically arranged. No index. Handwritten. Average 625 pages. 18 x 12 x 5. County courthouse, basement storeroom.

For other records, see entries 327 and 328.

327. JOURNAL (Expenses)

1905—. 2 volumes.

County home superintendent's record of expenses of county home. Chronologically arranged. No index. Handwritten. Average 575 pages. 15 x 9 x 4.5.

For other records, see entries 326 and 328.

328. (Bill) DOCKET

1904. 1 volume.

Infirmary directors' docket of bills showing date, name of claimant, purpose, amount, date allowed, amount allowed, and date paid. Chronologically arranged. No index. Handwritten. 350 pages. 16 x 7 x 2.5. County courthouse, basement storeroom.

For prior and subsequent records of expenditures, see entries 326 and 327.

Miscellaneous

329. INFIRMARY RECORD

1905-1906. 1 volume.

Copy of report of township trustees to infirmary directors concerning destitute persons. Chronologically arranged. No index. Handwritten on printed forms. 311 pages. 18 x 12 x 2. County courthouse, basement storeroom.

330. INFIRMARY ORDERS

1904-1905. 1 volume.

Stubs of orders issued by infirmary directors to county auditors showing name, amount, purpose, and date. Chronologically arranged. No index. Handwritten on printed forms. 125 pages. 15 x 10 x 1. County courthouse, basement storeroom.

Although the legislature made provision for the institutional care of the county's indigent as early as 1816, it was not until after the middle of the nineteenth century, when hundreds of Ohio children were left homeless by the scourge of civil war, that the legislature enacted measures for the care of dependent children. Previous to this time the Ohio statutes relative to the care of children had been taken from the territorial code which authorized the overseers of the poor, and later the trustees of the "poor house," to apprentice the children of the indigent, boys until eighteen and girls until twenty-one years of age (Pease, *op. cit.,* 219; 3 O. L. 276; 8 O. L. 223-224; 29 O. L. 318). The fact that this system was not only inhuman, but entirely unsatisfactory, is evidenced by the innumerable advertisements for runaway apprentices appearing in the press.

In 1865 the legislature authorized the county commissioners to receive bequests for orphans' asylums, and, when funds accumulated in sufficient quantities, to construct such a home, and appoint a board of directors consisting of six persons who were given the task of managing the institution, subject to the rules and regulations of the county commissioners. This board, electing a president and a treasurer from its own number, was required annually to make a report of the receipts and disbursements of the asylum, together with a number of orphans received into and discharge from the institution. This report was to be published by the commissioners in the newspaper having a general circulation. (62 O. L. 97).

A year later, in 1866, the commissioners were authorized, when in their judgment the best interest of the wards of the county would be served, to establish children's homes, and to provide by means of taxation, funds to be used for the purchase of a site, construct buildings, and maintain such charitable institutions (63 O. L. 46). Then, in 1876, an act, repealing all previous legislation was passed, which established the present duties of the county commissioners, trustees, superintendent, and matron in respect to children's homes. The act authorized the county commissioners to appoint a board of trustees and a superintendent of each children's home. (73 O. L. 64). The Brown County children's home was established in 1885 under the provisions of this act.

The board of trustees consists of five members appointed for a five-year term. The trustees, besides appointing a superintendent, hold annual meetings at which time they examine all accounts presented for payment, examine into the condition of the property and the matter of care offered to the wards. Annually or oftener, they are required to file with the state board of charities a detailed account giving the whereabouts of each child and the physical condition of each ward under their care. (G. C. sec. 3082-1).

The superintendent, operating under the rules and regulations of the trustees, has entire charge and control of the home and its inmates. He may appoint a matron, assistant matron, and other necessary employees, subject to the approval of the board of trustees. It is the duty of such employees to care for the inmates in the home, direct their employment and give suitable physical, mental, and moral training. Under the direction of the superintendent, the matron has general management and supervision of the household duties of the home. The matron, like other employees, receives such salaries as the trustees may direct and may be removed by the superintendent or at the pleasure of a majority of the trustees. (G. C. sec. 3085).

The county children's home serves as an asylum for the children under eighteen years of age who have resided in the county one year and who are, in the opinion of the trustees, eligible to admission by reason of orphanage, abandonment, or neglect by parents, or the inability of the parents to provide for them (G. C. sec. 3089). Children are admitted to the home on order of the juvenile court or upon the order of a majority of the board of trustees. Since 1876 each child committed to the children's home must be accompanied by a statement of the facts setting forth name, age, birthplace, and condition. These facts, recorded by the superintendent in a book kept for that purpose, are confidential and open to inspection only at the discretion of the board of trustees. (G. C. sec. 3098; 73 O. L. 64; 83 O. L. 196; 99 O. L. 187; 103 O. L. 864). All wards of the children's home who have been committed to the institution because of abandonment, neglect, or dependency by the juvenile court or who have been voluntarily surrendered by the parents are under the exclusive jurisdiction, guardianship, and control of the trustees until they have become of lawful age (G. C. sec. 3?93).

The county commissioners may, subject to the approval of the board of state charities, after an opportunity has been given to the electorate to demand a referendum on the proposition, abandoned the children's home. If the home is discontinued, they may sell the site and buildings and use the funds as they deem expedient, providing that the wards in the children's home who are placed in foster homes and those who are under the guardianship of the trustees are legally committed to the guardianship of the board and state charities. (109 O. L. 533). Under the provisions of this act the Brown County children's home was closed in 1925, and dependent and neglected children were, and continue to be, placed in private homes or institutions by the county commissioners.

Another method of carrying for juvenile wards is in use in Brown County. With the approval of the board of state charities, the county commissioners appointed in 1922 a child welfare board. This board has the same powers and duties relative to dependent and neglected children as are given by statute to the trustees of the children's homes. The board is authorized to appoint a visitor whose duty it is to find homes for children, and supervise their conduct and look after their welfare after they are satisfactorily placed. (G. C. sec. 3092).

All records are located in the probate court office.

331. JOURNAL

1885-1925. 1 volume.

Minutes of meetings held by board of trustees of the home, 1885-1921; minutes of meetings held by county child welfare board, 1922-1925; and the proceedings and financial records of both organizations. Chronologically arranged. No index. Handwritten.. 640 pages. 16 x 11 x 4.5.

332. RECORD OF INMATES

1885-1924. 1 volume.

Record of orphan or dependent children cared for by county given name, age, sex, birthplace, date admitted, date discharge, and reason for discharge. Alphabetically arranged by names of inmates. No index. Handwritten. 450 pages. 20 x 12 x 3.5.

The board of county visitors, an agency for the examination and inspection of county institutions supported wholly or in part by county or municipal taxation, was created by an act of the general assembly in 1882. Under this act, the judge of the court of common pleas was authorized to appoint five persons, three of whom were to be women, who were to visit periodically the county institutions as the county infirmary, county jail, municipal prisons, the children's home, and file annually a report of their proceedings and recommendations for changes with the clerk of courts, and to forward a copy to the state board of charities. The members, appointed for an indefinite period, were to serve without compensation. (79 O. L. 107).

By the act of 1892 the personnel of the board was increased to six persons, three of whom were to be women, and not more than three to have the same political affiliations. Furthermore the act made it the duty of the probate judge, whenever proceedings were instituted in his court to commit a child under sixteen years of age to boys' industrial home or to girls' industrial home, to have notice given to the board of such proceedings; and it was made the duty of the board of visitors to attend the meetings of the court, as a body or as a committee, to protect the interest of the child. (89 O. L. 161).

While the provisions of the act of 1892 were redefined by the acts of 1898 and 1900, these acts did not, in the main, affect the duties of the board (93 O. L. 57; 94 O. L. 70). The latter act, however, made the board a continuous body with two members serving for one year, two members serving for two years, and two members serving for three years. In addition to this, the board was allowed a minimum expense schedule for their services. (94 O. L. 70). Six years later the board was authorized to recommend to the county commissioners measures for more economical administration of county institutions. Their report, together with the recommendations, was to be filed each year with a judge of the probate court and with the county prosecuting attorney. (98 O. L. 28).

In 1913 the power of appointment of board members was transferred to the probate judge. Under this act the juvenile judge, like the probate judge under the act of 1892 was authorized to notify the visitors when any proceedings were instituted in his court for the commitment of any child to a state institution of correction. The act continued the practice of annually filing the reports of the board with the probate judge, prosecuting attorney, and state board of charities. (103 O. L. 173-174, 888).

Although the statue requires reports from the board of county visitors, no records have been found in Brown County.

County relief for the indigent, one of the most pressing problems of the twentieth century, was met in frontier Ohio. As early as 1805 there was passed an act, modeled from the territorial law, which was similar in all respects to the poor laws of the seventeenth century England (3 O. L. 272). Under the early enactments the township trustees were authorized to appoint overseers of the poor. In 1816 the county commissioners were authorized to construct "poorhouses" for the care of the county's indigent. As the system developed in succeeding decades the county was made responsible for those who have become permanently disabled, and for paupers who could not be satisfactory cared for except at the county infirmary, now called the county home. The township trustees and officials of municipal corporations were made responsible for providing temporary relief to needy residents of the state, or the county, township, or city. In the event any person became chargeable to a township in which he had not gained the legal residence, it was the duty of the overseers, later the township trustees, to remove him to the township where he was legally settled. With slight alterations, the principles of the system continued until the twentieth century. (For an excellent study, but biting criticism of the administration of relief in Ohio prior to 1934 see Eileen Elizabeth Kennedy, *The Ohio Poor Law and Its Administration,* Sophonisba P. Breckinridge, ed., *Social Service Monographs*, no. 22, University of Chicago Press, Chicago, 1934).

The unprecedented depression in the third decade of the twentieth century proved the antiquated, and uncentralized system was entirely inadequate. As a result of the abnormal employment and the crop failures following the drought of 1930, many local subdivisions of the county charged by law to administer support and medical relief to the indigent were unable to discharge their obligations. Accordingly, in 1931, the legislature passed an emergency act authorized the county, township, and municipal taxing authorities to borrow money and issue bonds for poor relief, providing the state tax commission found that no other funds were available (114 O. L. 11-12).

During the early months of 1932 the governor, aware of the widespread suffering in the state, called the legislature into special session (see message of the governor of the Eighty-ninth General Assembly in (114 O. L. pt. ii, 6-8). At this session the legislature authorized him to appoint a state relief commission composed of five members to study the relief situation. This commission was permitted to cooperate with the national, state, or local relief commission, which, in many counties, have been established and already functioning. Since the county and township treasuries were depleted, because of the excessive drain caused by the mounting relief load and it steady decline of tax collections, the legislature authorized an excise tax on utilities, for the years 1932-1937, to be used for relief purposes. This state tax was to be allocated to the counties on the basis of population, the tax duplicate, and the value of utilities property in the county as of 1930. (114 O. L. pt. ii, 19-20). The funds allocated to each county under this act were to be credited to the "county poor relief excise fund."

The county commissioners were authorized to borrow money for emergency relief and evidence such indebtedness by the issuance of negotiable bonds and notes. Upon submission of such resolution to the state tax commission, the commission was directed to estimate the amount which would probably be allocated to the county from the public utility excise taxes, and was directed to calculate the total amount of bonds, the principal and interest on which might be paid out of such estimated allocations. The date of maximum maturity of such bonds was to be on or before March 15, 1938. If, in the year 1932, additional funds were needed for poor relief, the county commissioners were authorized, after the state tax commission found that no other funds were available, to issue additional bonds in the amount not exceeding one tenth of one percent of the general tax list and duplicate of the county. The maturity date of such additional bonds was to be on or before September 15, 1940. (114 O. L. pt. ii, 20).

The proceeds of the sale of such bonds were to be placed in a special fund, denominated the "emergency relief fund." No expenditures were to be made from this fund except in accordance with the method and under the uniform regulations prescribed by the state relief commission, and in no case after December 31, 1933. The county commissioners were authorized to distribute, prior to the first of March 1933, portions of the fund to the political subdivisions of the county, according to their needs for poor relief determined by the county and set forth in such an approved budget. The money distributed to the subdivisions was to be expended in them for poor relief, including the renting of lands and the purchase of seeds for gardening by the unemployed. (114 O. L. pt. ii, 22). County poor relief included mothers' pensions, soldiers' relief, temporary assistance to nonresidents, maintenance of a county and children's home, and work and direct relief. In the townships and municipalities relief was interpreted to be the support of the poor and burial of the indigent dead. Each subdivision administering funds under the act was expected to require labor in exchange for relief given to any family where there resided an able-bodied wage-earner. (114 O. L. pt. ii, 17).

In February 1933, the tenure of the state relief commission was extended to March 1, 1935 (115 O. L. 22). In the same year, the legislature levied and additional stamp tax on the sale of bottled and bulk beer, malt, cosmetics, and toilet preparations to furnish additional funds for emergency relief (115 O. L. 642-646, 649; 115 O. L. pt. ii, 5, 33, 177, 200, 247, 256). The state treasurer was authorized to appoint the county treasurer as a deputy for the purpose of selling tax stamps to be affixed to such articles (115 O. L. 642-645).

When, in 1935, the state relief commission ceased to exist by reason of the term of the act creating it, the legislature passed a measure designed to coordinate and correlate all emergency poor relief work, activities, and administration with the federal emergency relief administration which was authorized to administer and direct the distribution and expenditure of federal funds for relief in the state. Accordingly, all powers previously vested in the state relief commission were transfered to the county commissioners. Whenever in their discretion such action was necessary in order to continue the coordination and correlation of state, local, and federal funds they were authorized to appoint, with the approval of the director of finance of the state of Ohio, a representative or representatives of such emergency poor relief. If such an officer was appointed, the representative succeeded to all powers and functions, which, under the act, were delegated to the county commissioners. This representative, however, was subject to such terms and conditions in respect to auditing, examinations, and reports as were directed by the county commissioners and such federal agency. The county commissioners were directed to conduct relief activities outside limits of municipal corporations through the township trustees, insofar as practicable, and were to be guided by the recommendations of the township trustees with respect to relief need in such political subdivisions. Again, as in 1932, the commissioners were authorized, if the state tax commission found that no other means existed to provide funds, to borrow money, and issue bonds in the year 1935-1936. The maximum maturity date of such bonds were to be on or before March 1, 1944. (116 O. L. 571). Other bonds, in addition to those secured by the county's share of the excise tax, might be issued not to exceed one fifth of one percent of the general tax list of the county (116 O. L. 575). If the county was unable to issue bonds by reason of the limitations imposed by the constitution (Art. XII, sec. 2), the taxing authority of each subdivision was authorized to submit the question of issuing bonds to the electorate either at a general or special election (116 O. L. 578).

The year 1936 saw the recreation of the state relief commission. Consisting of four members appointed by the governor, this body was authorized to serve until January 31, 1937. Again, as in 1932, the commission was directed to study problems of relief, receive advice from federal, state, and local governmental departments, cooperate with agencies of the national and local governments and private agencies engaged in the administration for financial support of direct or indirect relief, administer moneys appropriated to the commission for poor relief, examine the conduct of local governmental agencies in administering relief, and order the distribution and payment of moneys from the state treasury.

The county commissioners were authorized to administer all advances by the state to the relief commission and were directed to operate through duly authorized agencies of townships, municipalities, and school districts. Within the appropriations made by the commissioners and subject to the rules and regulations of the state relief commission, the commissioners were instructed to appoint assistants and such other employees as were necessary.

The county commissioners, like the state relief commission, were directed to cooperate with all agencies of the federal, state, county governments, and with private agencies which were engaged in administering relief for financial support to the needy. It was made the duty of all county, township, and municipal governments administering relief or assistance to dependents to report to the county commissioners, at their request, the names and addresses of all persons to whom they were providing aid ane the amount and character of aid given. (116 O. L. pt, ii, 133-148).

In the early months of 1937 the legislature authorized the staff relief commission to serve until April 1937. Under this act the county commissioners are authorized to give temporary support and medical relief to nonresidents and to all needy persons possessing a legal residence in the county. Funds may be expended for both direct and work relief. However, all persons on relief able and competent to perform labor who refuse to accept private employment under prevailing conditions and prevailing wages, may be dropped from the roles. This ruling does not apply, however, to areas where strikes are prevalent. On the other hand, any person receiving relief in the county is permitted to engage in any business without losing his relief status. During the period of such employment, he is required to forfeit the pro rate amount of relief received by him, and is eligible to his former relief status upon the conclusion of such employment.

The county commissioners are required to file with the state relief commission a budget and a detailed statement and plan showing how the funds to be received are to be expended, the purpose for which they are to be used, nature and kind of work to be carried on, and number of persons to be aided by such relief. Besides this, the county commissioners must file a complete analysis of their proposed expenditures, together with the estimate of all available resources, including the unencumbered proceeds of any bonds heretofore issued and the amount of bonds which the county commissioners have a right to issue without a vote of the people on the approval of the state tax commission of Ohio as authorized in 1935.

Of the funds allocated to the county by the state relief commission for direct relief, the commissioners may, when they believe that the cost of administration may be reduced, reallocate the funds on a percentage basis, of relief requirements of the various subdivisions (*Page's Ohio Cumulative Code Service*, Cincinnati, 1937, no. 20, 65-67).

The emergency relief measures passed during the period 1932-1937 gave the counties for the first time a centralized relief administration.

All records are located in the relief administration office.

333. CASE RECORDS

October 1933—. 7 file boxes (3 boxes labeled Active Cases; 3 boxes labeled Closed Cases; 1 box labeled Inactive Cases).

Complete record of each relief case giving family history, financial sheet, supplemental financial sheet, and commodities distribution record. All records of each case are contained in a folder. Alphabetically arranged by names of clients. No index. Handwritten and typed. 30 x 12 x 12.

334. CERTIFICATION RECORDS

1935—. 3 file boxes.

Record of certification of relief clients eligible for Works Progress Administration assignments. Alphabetically arranged by names of clients. No index. Typed. 22 x 6 x 5.

The soldiers' relief commission was established by an act of the legislature passed May 19, 1886, entitled "An act to provide for the relief of indigent Union soldiers, sailors and marines, and the indigent wives, widows and minor children of indigent or deceased Union soldiers, sailors and marines." Under the provisions of this act the commissioners of each county were authorized to levy a specified tax for the purpose of creating a fund for the relief of such beneficiaries; and the judge of the court of common pleas was authorized to appoint three county residents, at least two of whom were honorably discharged Union soldiers, to serve for a term of three years as members of the commission, which was organized by the selection of a chairman and a secretary and was known as the soldiers' relief commission. (83 O. L. 232).

An amendment passed on March 4, 1887, provided that councilmen of city wards, as well as the board of trustees of the townships, certified to the soldiers' relief commission the names of those requiring and entitled to aid under the act (84 O. L. 100).

By an act of the legislature, passed April 28, 1890, the soldiers' relief commission was required to appoint annually a committee of three in each township and a committee of three in each ward in any city in the county, whose duty it was to receive all applications for aid and to certify them to the soldiers' relief commission (87 O. L. 352).

Sections 2930 and 2933-4 of the General Code was amended, March 6, 1917, to provide for the appointment to each county commission of one member who is the wife or widow of an honorably discharged soldier, sailor or marine of the Civil War or of the Spanish-American War, the other two members to be honorably discharged soldiers, sailors, or marines of the United States; and for the appointment to each township and ward committee of a wife or widow of a soldier, sailor, or marine of the United States (107 O. L. 27). Two years later, in 1919, the provisions of the act were extended to include indigent veterans of the world War or to indigent parents, wives, widows, or minor children of such veterans (108 O. L. pt. i, 633).

Section 2930 and 2934 of the General Code were amended on April 6, 1929 to provide for the appointment by the court of common pleas in each county of a soldier' relief commission, to consist of three members, one to be the wife, widow, son or daughter of the honorary discharge soldier, sailor, or marine of the Civil War, of the Spanish-American War, or of the World War, the other two members to be honestly discharged soldiers, sailors, or marines of the United States, one of whom should, if possible, be a member of the Spanish-American War Veterans, the other a member of the American Legion (113 O. L. 466).

The soldiers' relief commission keeps no permanent records. For records of other officers, see entries 1 and 278.

SOLDIERS' BURIAL COMMISSION

In 1884 the legislature made provision for a soldiers' burial commission in each county, to consist of three persons in each township appointed by the county commissioners, which was directed to defray the expense incurred in the interment of any honorably discharged Union soldier, sailor, or marine, who died in poverty. The commission, serving at the pleasure of the appointing power, was required to report to the county commissioners the name, rank, and command of the decedent which report was transcribed to the county commissioners in a book kept for that purpose. (81 O. L. 146-147). The original act, amended in 1891, extended the provisions of the act to include the interment of the wives or widows of Union soldiers (88 O. L. 330-331). In 1893 the act was again amended to provide for the interment of mothers of Union soldiers, sailors, and marines, and army nurses (90 O. L. 177). In 1908 the personnel of the commission was reduced to two.

Under the present law which became effective in 1921 the county commissioners are authorized to appoint two suitable persons in each township and ward in the county, who are directed with the approval of the family or friends of the deceased, to contract with an undertaker and direct the burial in a respectable manner of the body of any honorably discharged soldier, sailor, or marine having at any time served in the United States army or navy, or the mother, wife or widow of any soldiers, sailor, or marine or that of any war nurse who served at any time in the army of the United States who died in poverty (G. C. sec. 2950; 108 O. L. pt. i, 31; 109 O. L. 211).

The burial commission is instructed to enforce all laws relative to the burial of indigent veterans, investigate the financial status of the decedent's family, and report its findings to the county commissioners, together with the name, rank, and command to which the deceased belong, date of death, place of burial, occupation while living, and itemized statement of the cost of burial (99 O. L. 100).

Upon receiving this report the burial commission, the county commissioners transcribe the information in a book kept for that purpose, and certify the expense to the county auditor who draws his warrant for payment to the person or persons specified by the county commissioners (99 O. L. 101).

The amount contributed by the county for burial of an indigent veteran set by the legislature at $35 in 1884 was increased to $75 in 1908 and to $100 in 1921(81 O. L. 146-147; 99 O. L. 99; 109 O. L. 212; G. C. sec. 2951). Since 1908 each member of the burial commission has been allowed one dollar for each service performed. (99 O. L. 99; G. C. sec. 2951).

335. SOLDIERS' BURIAL RECORDS

1884-1917. 4 volumes. 1918— in Commissioners' Journal, entry 1. Record of burial of indigent soldiers with itemized expense bills. Chronologically arranged. No index. Handwritten on printed forms. Average 281 pages. 15 x 9 x 1.5. 1 volume, 1884-1900, Attic storeroom; 3 volumes, 1901-1917, Basement storeroom.

Provisions for the relief of the indigent was made in 1805, but it was not until 1898 that the legislature provided separate relief for the indigent blind. The act authorized the township trustees to certify to the county commissioners an amount not to exceed $100 per person per annum for such relief, the certification to be made a record listing the name of the beneficiary and the amount required; and directed the county commissioners to levy on the townships to the amount certified, this amount to be paid into the county treasury and then to the township treasurer to be used for blind relief (93 O. L. 270).

Six years later, in 1904, certification authority was transferred from the township trustees to the probate judge, who was required to register the name and address of beneficiaries and to issue to each a certificate giving his name, address, and amount to be drawn. Persons eligible for relief were blind males over twenty-one and blind females over eighteen years of age, without property or other means of support. Not less than two county citizens, one a physician selected by the court, were required to testify that the applicant had been a resident of the state for five years and a resident of the county for one year immediately preceding the filing of an application for relief. (97 O. L. 392-394).

The act of 1904 was declared unconstitutional for the reason that it required spending for a private purpose public funds raised by taxation (*Auditor of Lucas County* v. *The State,* 75 O. S. 114-137). Hence, in 1908, an act was passed authorizing the county commissioners to levy a stipulated tax to create a fund for relief of the needy blind, the maximum benefits not to exceed $150 per person per annum to be paid quarterly; and authorizing the probate judge to appoint a blind relief commission consisting of three members for a three-year term, directed to meet annually in the office of county commissioners to examine applications recorded in order of their receipt in a book furnished by the county commissioners (99 O. L. 56-58).

The blind relief commission was abolished by the legislature in 1913 and its powers and duties were transferred to the county commissioners who were authorized, on evidence furnished by a registered physician or surgeon that the applicant for blind relief might have such disability benefited or removed by medical or surgical treatment, and with the written consent of the patient, to expand all or part of the year's relief allowance for this purpose (103 O. L. 60).

Six years later, in 1919, this allowance for blind relief was raised to $200 per person per annum, and the county commissioners were authorized to appoint such clerks as they might deem necessary to investigate applications and to serve at the pleasure of the county commissioners (108 O. L. pt. i, 421-422).

In 1927 the maximum benefit for blind relief was increased to $400 per person per annum, but in the event of a husband and wife both being blind and both applying for relief, the total maximum benefit for the two was fixed at $600 per annum (112 O. L. 109).

In April 1936 the state accepted the provisions of the social security act approved August 14, 1935, providing federal grants for state aid to the blind, and legislature designated the Ohio commission for the blind the administration agency in the state, and the county commissioners were made the administration agency in the county. The county commissioners were directed to appropriate from the general fund of the county a sum sufficient when supplemented by federal and state grants to provide for the blind a substance "comparable with decency and health," and if they fail to make such appropriations the attorney general was directed to bring *mandamus* proceedings against them.

The act of 1936 provides that those entitled to blind relief are persons not less than eighteen or more than sixty-five years of age, who has lost their sight while residents of the state, and who have resided in the state for a period of five years in the nine years immediately preceding application, the last year of which period shall have been continuous. Applications for blind relief are filed with the county commissioners who are required by statute to list such claims in their order of application in books kept for that purpose. At least ten days prior to action on a claim the applicant files a duly certified statement, including a certificate from a registered physician "skilled in disease of the eye' stating to what extent the applicant's vision is impaired, and written evidence from two reputable citizens that they know the applicant to be blind and that "he has the qualifications to entitle him to the relief asked." The county commissioners may allow the examining physician a fee not to exceed three dollars, and may employ an additional physician to examine the applicant. If after such inquiry the county commissioners are satisfied that the applicant is entitled to relief, they are directed by statute to issue an order for such sum as the board finds necessary, not to exceed the maximum fixed in 1927, such sum to be paid monthly from the fund created for that purpose. The ruling of 1913 concerning medical and surgical treatment for applicants remains in effect. Persons whose applications are denied by the county commissioners may appeal to the state commission for the blind which on its own motion may revise any decision of the county commissioners. Both the Ohio commission for the blind and the county commissioners have power to issue subpoenas, compel presentation of papers and examines witnesses.

At least once a year, oftener if directed by the Ohio commission for the blind, the county commissioners must examine the qualifications, disabilities, and needs of all persons on the list of the blind, and may increase or decrease the amount of relief according to the budgetary requirements within the limits fixed by law. If the county commissioners remove a name from the list of the blind they are required to notify the county auditor and the Ohio commission for the blind as to their action. (116 O. L. pt. ii, 195-200).

336. RECORDS OF BLIND RELIEF COMMISSION
1908-1915. 1 volume.
Minutes of meetings held by blind relief commission showing record of applicants received, granted, and rejected. Chronologically arranged. No index. Handwritten. 238 pages. 16 x 9 x 1.75. Basement storeroom.

For other records of applications and grants, see entry 337 and 339.

227. RECORD OF BLIND PENSIONS
1905-1936. 2 volumes.
Blind relief records showing application for pension, investigation date, physician's report on examination, amount granted, and record of payments. Alphabetically arranged by names of pensioners. No index. Handwritten. Average 160 pages. 16 x 11 x 1.25. Auditor's office.

For other records, see entries 336, 338, and 339.

338. REGISTER
July 1, 1936. 1 volume.
Register of blind persons receiving aid under the provisions of the Social Security Act showing name of client, date of application, address, age, color, date application approved, amount of award, and case number. Chronologically arranged by dates of applications. No index. Typed on forms. 100 pages. 18 x 12 x .75.

For other records, see entry 336, 337, and 339.

339. CASE RECORDS
July 1, 1936—. 1 file box.
Applications of blind aid, reports on investigation of application, and medical certificates, showing date, name of applicant, address, age, sex, date approved or rejected, and amount of award. Chronologically arranged by dates of applications. No index. Typed on printed forms. 12 x 12 x 22. Probate court's office.

For other records, see entries 336-338.

Old age pensions, although well known in Europe at the end of the nineteenth and beginning of the twentieth century and in a few American states during the same period, were not provided for in Ohio until recently (Arthur Lyon Cross, *A Shorter History of England and Great Britain,* New York, 1925, 746-747; J. Salwyn Schapiro, *Modern and Contemporary European History 1815-1925*, New York, 1923, 295). During the depression years the sight of thousands of aged persons who had lost their homes and savings, and as a result of such losses faced starvation, touch the sensibilities of Ohioans. Accordingly, in 1933, an "Old Age Pension" law, proposed by initiative petition, was voted upon at the general election of that year, providing for the granting of aid to the aged in Ohio under certain conditions. The law was adopted by a majority of electors voting thereon (115 O. L. pt. ii, 431-439). The act, as amended in 1936, provides, among other things, that any person sixty-five years of age or upward (unless confined in any penal or corrective institution or the state hospital) who is a citizen of the United States, who has resided in Ohio not less than five years during the nine prior to making application for aid, and who has resided for one year in the county wherein application for aid is made is eligible to receive a pension, providing his income from all and every source does not exceed $360 per year (116 O. L. pt. ii, 1st s. sess. H. 605; 116 O. L. pt. ii, 1st. S, sess. H. 558). Moreover the applicant must be unable to support himself, and have no husband, wife, child, or other person who is legally responsible for his support. In addition to this, the net value of all real and personal property of the unmarried applicant, less all encumbrances and liens, must not exceed $3,000; if the applicant is married the net value of the property of husband and wife shall not exceed $4,000. It may be required that such property, as a condition precedent to payment of aid, be transferred to the division of aid for the aged in trust. This provision does not, however, prohibit the applicant or his wife from occupying such property during their lifetime. (115 O. L. pt. ii, 431-439). An amendment to the act in 1937 eliminated the transfer of property as a possible condition precedent to granting aid, leaving the transfer optional. The amendment act further states that any property, either real or personal, which has heretofore been conveyed to the division in trust could be reconveyed to the grantor by the division (Amended G. C. sec. 1359-6).

For the purpose of administering the old age pension law there was created in 1933 in the state department of public welfare a division of aid for the aged. The chief of the division of the aid for the aged, appointed by the director of public welfare with the approval of the governor is authorized to appoint all necessary assistants, clerks, stenographers, and other employees and fix their salaries, subject to the approval of the director of public welfare. (115 O. L. pt. ii, 431-439).

In each county the commissioners constitute a board for administering the act. However, if the commissioners by a majority vote declined to serve in such capacity, the chief of the division of aid for the aged is authorized, with the consent of the director of public welfare, to appoint a board consisting of three to five members, who, like the county commissioners, serve without compensation. The local boards are required to keep such reports as the division may prescribe, and are also authorized to employ, subject to the approval of the division, such investigators, clerks, and other employees as are necessary for performance of their duties. (115 O. L. pt. ii, 431-439).

In 1937 the chief of the division was directed to appoint an advisory board in each county consisting of five citizens of such county. The members of the board, appointed for two years, are required to take an oath of office before entering upon their duties (G. C. sec. 1359-12).

Applications for relief were made annually to the local board but an act of the legislature in 1937, reorganizing the division of age for the aged, omitted the provision for annual reapplication. Each applicant is thoroughly investigated. In its investigations the local board is not bound by common law or statutory rules of evidence, but is authorized to make inquiries in such a manner as seems "best calculated to conform to substantial justice." For the purpose of its investigations, each county board has the power to compel the attendance and testimony of witnesses. Decisions of the local boards may be appealed to the division. (115 O. L. pt. ii, 431-439).

After the applicants have been investigated by the local board, "certificates of aid" are granted to persons entitled to relief in conformity with the provisions of the law. Each certificate, bearing the applicant's name and the pension allowed, as well as the records pertaining to the investigation, is forwarded to the division, which may approve, modify, or reject the certificate and findings of the board. (115 O. L. pt. ii, 435).

Under the provisions of this act the state became the general guardian of public and private welfare. The pension system relieves the increasing burden place upon county homes, which, even under the most favorable conditions, are a poor substitute for homes. Although $2,625,000 was appropriated by the legislature for old age pensions in the early part of 1935, the cost to the public, in the long run, should not be much greater than that of the antiquated system of support in charitable institutions (116 O. L. 510).

All the records are located at age for the aged office.

340. MINUTE BOOK

1934—. 3 volumes.

Record of minutes of meetings of executive board of aid for the aged. Chronologically arranged. No index. Handwritten. Average 80 pages. 11 x 8 x .5.

341. CASE RECORDS

1934—. 3 file boxes.

Original applications for aid showing case history, statement of relatives, property record, certificate for aid, and correspondence relative to each case. Each case is in a separate folder. Chronologically arranged and numerically thereunder by case numbers. Typed on printed forms. 30 x 12 x 12.

342. CARD INDEX

1934—. 1 file box.

Index to Case Records showing name of client, application and certificate numbers, address, date of birth, place of birth, date of award, and amount of award. Alphabetically arranged by names of clients. Typed. 30 x 12 x 6.

343. RECORD OF PROGRESS

1934—. 1 volume.

Complete record of progress on each case from date of application. Chronologically arranged. No index. Handwritten. 250 pages (loose-leaf). 10 x 14 x 2.25.

344. INVESTIGATORS' WORK SHEETS

1935—. 1 file box.

Records names and addresses of persons interviewed at office listing names and addresses of persons contacted outside of office, mileage, and application numbers. Chronologically arranged. No index. Handwritten on printed forms. 30 x 12 x 12.

345. DAILY REPORT OF TRAVEL EXPENSE

1935—. 9 volumes.

Duplicate copy of report showing mileage of investigator in contacting applicants or clients, meal cost, investigator's name, and total amount due. Chronologically arranged. No index. Handwritten on printed forms. Average 50 pages. 7 x 3.5 x 5.

346. LEDGER

1936—. 1 volume.

Records of reimbursements by relatives of deceased pensioners showing dates, names, and amounts. Chronologically arranged. No index. Handwritten. 100 pages. 12 x 8 x .5.

347. STATISTICAL REPORTS

1934—. 1 folder.

Copy of monthly report to state office showing number of active cases, number of cases added past month, number of cases closed, number of cases denied, and time reports. Chronologically arranged. No index. Typed on printed forms. 14 x 10.

Aid to dependent children, although provided for by the Ohio legislature in 1913 in the form of mothers' pensions, assumed a new significance, when, in April 1936, the Ohio Legislature accepted the provisions of the Social Security Act. With the acceptance of the act, the sections of the General Code (1683-2 - 1683-10) relative to mothers' pensions were repealed.

The administration of the act in the state is delegated to the department of public welfare through the division of charities. In the administration of the act, the department was authorized to prescribe forms, certificates, reports, records, and accounts to be kept by the local departments.

The administration of the act in the counties is delegated to the juvenile judge or to the judge of the court of domestic relations, excepting in counties in which by charter or by law the powers were vested in or imposed upon "a county department, board or commission, or officer other than the juvenile judge." In Brown County the juvenile judge (see p. 69) performs this function. When he serves in the capacity of county administrator, the juvenile judge is directed to utilize the services of the employees of the court exercising juvenile jurisdiction. In the performance of his duties the judge is authorized to compel the attendance of witnesses and the production of books, and may institute contempt proceedings against persons refusing to testify. Except for this, powers conferred upon a judge are administrative powers only.

Those entitled to aid under the act include, among others, a child residing in the state less than sixteen years of age who has been deprived of parental support or care by reason of death, continued absence of a parent, or mental or physical incapacity of a parent. However, a child more than sixteen but less than eighteen years of age may receive aid at the discretion of the county administration.

Application for aid is made to the juvenile court by the parent or a relative, with whom the child must be living. Before aid is granted, a careful examination of the home is made by the employees of the juvenile court. If the child is found to be eligible, the court may grant such amount as it is deemed proper. The amount of aid payable to any child is determined on the basis of actual needs "and shall be sufficient to provide support and care requisite for health and decency." In the event aid is granted, the home of such a child must be visited four times during each year. Each month the county auditor issue warrants upon the county treasurer for the payment of the warrants certified by court. The decisions of the juvenile judge are subject to abrogation or modification by the department of public welfare. Any person attempting to receive aid on behalf of any child unentitled to such aid is deemed guilty of a misdemeanor and upon conviction may be punished by fine or imprisonment or both.

The provisions of the acts are financed by federal, state, and local funds. The county commissioners are required to include in the annual tax budget an amount not less than that computed to yield a levy of fifteen one-hundreds of one mill on each dollar of the general tax list of the county. If the commissioners failed to comply with the provisions of the act relative to appropriations, the state department of public health is directed to request the attorney general to institute *mandamus* proceedings against them. (G. C. sec. 1359-31 - 1359-45; 116 O. L. pt. ii, 188-195).

All records of this office are located in the probate court office.

348. MOTHERS' PENSION DOCKET

1915-1936. 1 volume. Prior records missing.

Records names of mothers of dependent children granted pensions showing case history and amount of grant. Chronologically arranged. Alphabetical index by names of mothers. Handwritten. 300 pages. 16 x 11 x 2.5.

For other records, see entries 349-351.

349. MOTHERS' PENSION RECORD

1915-1936. 1 volume. Prior records missing.

Record of mothers' pension accounts showing amount allowed, name and address of mother, and case and warrant numbers. Chronologically arranged. Alphabetical index by names of mothers. Handwritten. 300 pages. 18 x 12 x 2.5.

For other records, see entries 348, 350, and 351.

350. REGISTER

July 1, 1936—. 1 volume.

Register of names of mothers receiving aid under the provision of the Social Security Act show name of applicant, address, date of application, case number, names and ages of children, amount of award, and date application approved. Alphabetically arranged by names of applicants and chronological thereunder by dates of applications. No index. Typed. 160 pages. 18 x 12 x 1.

For other records, see entries 348, 349, and 351.

351. CASE RECORDS

July 1, 1936—. 2 file boxes.

Original applications of mothers for aid; also investigators' reports on applications showing name of applicant, address, date of application, date approved, and amount of award. All papers and records of each case are together in a folder. Alphabetically arranged by names of clients. No index. Typed on printed forms. 12 x 12 x 2.

For other records, see entry 348-250.

(State Deputy Supervisors of Elections)

The responsibility for supervising and conducting elections in the county is delegated to state deputy supervisors of elections, the county board of elections. This board, created by the legislature in 1891 and consisting of four qualified voters in the county, is appointed for a four-year term by the secretary of state, who, by virtue of his office, is the chief election official of the state. (88 O. L. 449). On the first Monday in March in the even numbered years, the secretary of state appoints two board members, one of whom is from the political party which cast the highest number of votes in the state for the office of governor at the last preceding state election, and the other from the political party which cast the next highest vote at such election (G. C. sec. 4785-8). (For the method of appointment when the term of each of the four members of the board expires on the same date see G. C. sec. 4758-8a). The board members may be removed by the secretary of state for the neglect of duty, malfeasance, misfeasance in office, for willful violation of the election laws; or for other good and sufficient causes (G. C. sec. 4785-11). The compensation of the members is determined on the basis of population of the county and is paid by the county (G. C. sec. 4785-18). Similarly the expenses of the county board are paid from the county treasury, "in pursuance of appropriation by the county commissioners," in the same manner as other expenses are paid (G. C. sec. 4785-20).

The persons so appointed by the secretary, meeting five days after their appointment, select one of their members as chairman and a resident elector of the county as clerk who is not a member of the board (G. C. sec. 4785-10). The board is vested with authority to establish, define, and provide election precincts; fix places of registration; provide for the purchase, preservation, and maintenance of voting booths, ballot boxes, books, maps, flags, blanks, cards of instruction, and other equipment used in registration and to issue rules, regulations, and instructions consistent with the law or contrary to the rules and regulations as established by the chief election official (G. C. sec. 4785-13).

Besides providing places of voting and equipment, the board is authorized to appoint clerks and other officers of elections. On or before the first day of September before each November election the board by a majority vote is authorized, after careful examination and investigation as to their qualifications, to appoint for each precinct six "competent persons, four as judges and two as clerks, who shall constitute the election officers of such precincts." Not more than two of the judges and one of the clerks, states the law, "shall be members of the same political party." Precinct election officers, appointed for a one-year term, may be removed by the board for neglect of duty, malfeasance or misconduct in office. (G. C. sec. 4785-25).

The county board of elections is authorized to receive and examine and certify the sufficiency and validity of nominating petitions. They receive the election returns, canvas the returns, then make abstracts therefrom and transmit them to the proper authorities. They issue certificates of elections on forms prescribed by the secretary of state and report annually to the same officials, on the forms prescribed by him, the number of voters registered, elections held, votes cast, and such other information as the secretary of state may require. Moreover, the board prepares and submits to the proper authorities a budget estimating the cost of elections for the ensuing year. (G. C. sec. 4788-13).

Finally the board is empowered to investigate irregularities, nonperformance of duty, or violation of election laws by election officials. For the purpose of conducting investigations they may administer oaths, issue subpoenas, summon witnesses, and compel the presentation of books, papers, and records in connection with any investigation and report the facts to the prosecuting attorney. (G. C. sec. 4785-13).

The secretary of state, in 1930, ruled that the members of the various board of elections were to be considered as state officers. This had reference to appointments made under sec. 4785-8a of the General Code. (See George C. Trautwein, ed., *Supplement to Page's Annotated General Code 1926 to 1935,* ed., Cincinnati, 1935, note on p. 688).

All records are located in board of elections office unless otherwise specified.

352. MINUTE BOOK

1891—. 4 volumes. 1919 and 1923-1933 missing.

Minutes of meetings of county board of elections. Chronologically arranged. No index. Typed. Average 200 pages. 15 x 10 x 1.5. 3 volumes, 1891-1918, 1920-1922, Basement storeroom; 1 volume, 1934—, Board of elections' office.

353. POLL BOOKS

1934—. 160 volumes.

Record names of electors, number of ballots voted, different issues voted on, and summary of votes cast. Alphabetically arranged by names of electors. No index. Handwritten. Average 55 pages. 17 x 10 x 1.

354. REGISTER OF ABSENT VOTERS
1920—. 3 volumes. 1923-1929, missing.
Record showing application number, name of disabled or absent voter, ballots delivered, sex, voting place, return envelope received, address, and date of election. Chronologically arranged. No index. Handwritten. Average 150 pages. 14.5 x 8 x 1. 1 volume, 1920-1922, Basement storeroom; 2 volumes, 1930—, Board of elections' office.

355. ABSTRACT OF VOTES CAST
1934—. 10 file boxes.
Abstract of votes cast for different candidates. Alphabetically arranged by names of candidates. No index. Handwritten. 17 x 14 x 10.

356. CERTIFICATE OF APPOINTMENTS
1936—. 1 volume.
Record copy of certificate of appointment to precinct boards. Chronologically arranged. No index. Typed. 192 certificates and volume. 15 x 15 x 2.

357. RECORD OF APPOINTMENTS AND PAYROLL
1931—. 1 volume.
Records name, office, residence, party, date term begins, services at election, calling for returning ballots, mileage, rate per mile, total due, date order issued, and remarks. Chronologically arranged. No index. Handwritten. 110 pages. 16 x 11 x 1.25.

358. CASH BOOK
1931—. 1 volume. Prior records missing.
Records date received, from whom received, for what purpose, annual salary upon which filing fee is computed, amount paid, date paid into county treasury. Chronologically arranged. No index. Handwritten. 200 pages. 14.25 x 11.25 x 1.

359. ORDERS FOR WARRANTS

1930—. 1 volume.

Record of vouchers issued to county auditor authorizing him to pay bills. Chronologically arranged. No index. Handwritten. 200 pages. 16.25 x 13 x 1.5.

360. RECEIPTS

1916-1922. 1 volume.

Duplicate of receipts for fees received from candidates. Chronologically arranged. No index. Handwritten on printed forms. 200 pages. 15 x 12 x 1.5. Basement storeroom.

The office of county surveyor, another English institution transplanted to America during the colonial period, became an important office in frontier Ohio where land titles and boundary lines were often in dispute. The office is purely a creature of statute, there being no constitutional provision for its establishment.

The first act of the general assembly pertaining to the surveyor was passed during the first legislative session of 1803. Under this act the court of common pleas was authorized to appoint a person well qualified to act as county surveyor. He received his commission from the governor, was required to give bond conditioned for the faithful performance of the duties of his office, and was directed to survey all lands which were sold or were to be sold for taxes, and was authorized to appoint chainmen or markers whose function it was to establish corners. The surveys made by the surveyor or his deputies were the only ones to be accepted as legal evidence in any court of law or equity. For remuneration, the surveyor was permitted to retain all fees collected by him in the operation of his office. (1 O. L. 90-93).

Although it made no fundamental change in the duties of the surveyor, the act of 1816 fixed his term of office at five years; authorized him to appoint deputies, and made him responsible for their official acts; and made him liable to removal by the court for negligence or incompetency, and liable to suits by persons believing themselves damaged by his negligence or that of his deputies (14 O. L. 42-425). A year later, in 1817, provision was made for the appointment of a successor in the event the office became vacant because of death, resignation, or removal (15 O. L. 65).

The act of 1831 consolidated the previous acts, redefined the duties of the surveyor, increased the amount of his bond, and authorized him, when directed by the county commissioners, to procure from the surveyor general's office a "certified plat, together with the field notes of corners, and bearing trees to each section, quarter section, lot, or original survey in his county, and cause the same to be preserved in a book by him provided for that purpose; which shall be deposited in the county auditor's office, for the use of the landholders in the county." It provided further, that the surveyor shall keep "a fair and accurate record of all official surveys made by himself or by his deputies," in a suitable book to be kept by him for that purpose, and that he should number his surveys progressively. (29 O. L. 402). More significantly, however, was the fact that the office was made elective for a three-year term by the act of 1831. The term remained at three years until 1906 when it was reduced to a two-year period, and in 1928 the term was increased to four years. (29 O. L. 399; 98 O. L. 245-247; 112 O. L. 179).

During the years of the development of the office other duties have been delegated to the surveyor. In 1842 he was given the duty of ascertaining and reporting trespassing of public lands (40 O. L. 57). Ten years later, he was given the same powers as the justice of the peace to take and certify deeds, mortgages, powers of attorney, and other instruments affecting real estate, to administer oaths, and to take and certify affidavits (52 O. L. 70). In 1867 he was given authority, when directed by the county commissioners, to transcribe any and all dilapidated maps, records of plats, and field notes of surveys in other counties (64 O. L. 216-217; 78 O. L. 258). Similarly, in 1881, he was authorized to procure from any office in the state a certified plat together with the field notes of corners, quarter sections, lots, or original surveys and place them in a book provided for that purpose. Certified copies from his books were to be taken as *prima facie* evidence. (29 O. L. 399; 78 O. L. 285).

With the increase in modern means of transportation, there developed a growing need for more efficient methods of road construction and maintenance. Accordingly, in 1906, the surveyor was directed to act, whenever the services of an engineer were required, in the capacity of an engineer with respect to roads, turnpikes, bridges, or ditches, except in cities of the first grade (98 O. L. 245-247). He was directed by statute to perform all duties in his county which would be done by a civil engineer or surveyor, to prepare all plans, specifications, and estimates of cost, and to submit forms or contracts for the construction and repair of all bridges, culverts, roads, draws, ditches, and other public improvements (except buildings) over which the county commissioners had authority. At the same time, he was made responsible for the inspection of all public improvements, and was directed to keep a complete list of all estimates and bids received for such work, as well as of contracts awarded for improvements. (98. O. L. 245-247).

Similarly, another measure enacted in 1919 increased the duties of the surveyor regarding road construction and road maintenance. Under this act the surveyor was authorized to designate one of his deputies as maintenance engineer. This engineer, under the direction of the surveyor, was to have charge of all "road maintenance and repair work" in his county. Furthermore, when authorized by the county commissioners, the surveyor was to appoint a maintenance supervisor or supervisors to have charge of the maintenance of improved highways within a district or districts established by the commissioners or the surveyor, and containing not less than ten miles of improved roads. ((108 O. L. pt. ii, 497). In 1923 the surveyor was delegated to assist the county planning commission whenever such commission was established (110 O. L. 312).

Thus the general responsibility of planning and directing county road construction is vested, by statute, in the county surveyor. Because of this increased responsibility placed on this office there has been an attempt to raise the general qualifications of those seeking election to it. Accordingly, in 1935, an act was passed changing the title of the office to that of "county engineer," and eligibility to the office was restricted to "professional and registered surveyors listed to practice in the state of Ohio" (116 O. L. 283). This act was amended in 1936 to permit the incumbent to continue in office upon re-election, regardless of a lack of these qualifications (116 O. L. pt. ii, 152).

All records are located in engineer's office unless otherwise specified.

Surveys

361. RECORD OF SURVEYS

1818—. 8 volumes.

Record of land surveys giving description of each tract with boundary lines, and amount of surveyor's fee. Chronologically arranged. For index, 1818-1914, see entry 362; 1915—, alphabetical index by names of landowners. 1818-1934, handwritten; 1935—, typed. Average 350 pages. 15 x 12 x 2.5.

362. GENERAL INDEX OF SURVEYS

1818-1914. 1 volume.

Index to Record of Surveys, entry 361, showing landowners name, volume and page numbers of record, acreage, number of survey, names of original owner and surveyor, and date of survey. Alphabetically arranged by names of landowners. Handwritten. 464 pages. 16 x 11 x 3.5.

363. RECORD OF TOWNSHIP LINES

1879—. 1 volume. Last entry 1901.

Record of township lines as established by surveyor with maps showing boundaries and markers. Chronologically arranged. Alphabetical index by names of townships. Handwritten. 348 pages. 18 x 12 x 4. Basement storeroom.

Bridge and Road Records
(See also entries 3-7)

364. FREE TURNPIKE RECORDS
1866-1910. 6 volumes. Discontinued.

Record of specifications, construction, and repair of turnpike and bridges, including both force account and contract work until 1906. Chronologically arranged. Alphabetical index by names of improvements. Handwritten. Average 470 pages. 18 x 12 x 3.5.

365. RECORD OF COUNTY ROADS
1818—. 6 volumes.

Record of establishing county roads showing petitions, notices, hearings, and surveys. Chronologically arranged. 1818-1902, handwritten; 1903-1913, handwritten and typed; 1913—, typed. Average 500 pages. 16 x 10 x 4.

366. INDEX TO ROAD RECORD
1818—. 1 volume.

Index to Record of County roads showing names of townships, name and number of road and remarks by engineer. Alphabetically arranged by names of roads. Handwritten. 320 pages. 16 x 11 x 2.75.

367. ENGINEER'S RECORD OF COUNTY PIKES, ROADS, AND BRIDGES
1895—. 1 volume.

Record of proceedings, specifications, and construction in the matter of county pikes, roads, and bridges. Chronologically arranged. Alphabetical index by names of roads and bridges. Handwritten. 590 pages. 18 x 12 x 4.5.

368. ENGINEER'S ESTIMATE RECORD
1895-1932. 1 volume. Discontinued.

Record of estimates and specifications, contracts, and contractor's bonds. Chronologically arranged. Alphabetical index by names of roads, bridges, or contractors. Handwritten. 600 pages. 15 x 10 x 5.

369. CONTRACT AND SPECIFICATION RECORD
1906—. 3 volumes.
Record of engineer's estimates as advertised, listing bids received, contracts awarded, and names of contractors. Chronologically arranged. Alphabetical index by names of contractors. Handwritten. Average 400 pages. 16 x 11 x 3.

370. CONTRACT RECORD
1933—. 1 volume.
Record of estimates, specifications, contracts, contractors' bonds, and cost of project. Chronologically arranged and alphabetical thereunder by names of roads, bridges, and contractors. No index. Typed. 560 pages. 11 x 14 x 4.5.

Business Administration of Office

371. ENGINEER'S RECORD
1931-1933. 1 file drawer.
Records of county force account work and township gas tax payroll records. Chronologically arranged by months. No index. Handwritten. 16 x 13 x 6.
For other records, see entries 374 and 375.

372. SURVEYOR'S CASH BOOK
1922—. 1 volume.
Record of cash items received by county engineer listing from whom, for what purpose, and account. Chronological arranged. No index. Handwritten. 200 pages. 15 x 12 x 1.25.

373. SURVEYOR'S RECORD OF ACCRUED FEES
1922—. 1 volume.
Record of service showing date of service, to whom charged, per diem and fees of surveyor, mileage, recording total, and date paid. Chronologically arranged. No index. Handwritten. Average pages. 15 x 12 x 1.5.

374. ENGINEER'S RECORD AND JOURNAL

1925—. 4 volumes. Record initiated 1925.

Record of all payrolls and bills for labor and material in construction and maintenance of county roads and bridges by force account. 1925-1934, alphabetically arranged by names of townships; 1935—, chronologically arranged. 1925-1934, no index; 1935—, alphabetical index by names of townships. Handwritten. Average 517 pages. 15 x 13 x 4.

For other records of gas tax rolls, see entries 371 and 375.

375. JOURNAL (Gas and Tax Funds)

1929-1930. 1 volume.

Record of township gasoline tax and pay rolls charged against gasoline tax funds. Alphabetically arranged by names of township. No index. Handwritten. 498 pages. 16 x 10 x 3.5.

For subsequent records, see entry 374.

The Brown County agricultural society, an aggregate corporation whose object is the promotion of agriculture in the county, was established in January 1850, under provisions of sections 9880 - 9921-1c of the General Code, authorizing such county societies and defining their powers and duties. The first fair was held in October 1850. (Beers, Brown County, p. 309).

County agricultural societies in Ohio were provided for by statute as early as 1846. On February 28 of that year the legislature passed an act authorizing the forming of such societies and making provisions for their aid by the counties. (44 O. L. 70). On February 15, 1853, the legislature declared such society's to be bodies corporate and politic, capable of suing and being sued, and capable of holding in fee simple such real estate as they might purchase for sites whereon to hold fairs, the same to be paid for by the county commissioners (51 O. L. 333).

By act of the legislature passed February 20, 1861, county agricultural societies were required to report annually to the state board of agriculture, and to meet with the state board at Columbus once each year (58 O. L. 22). In 1883 the legislature provided for the organization of district or county agricultural societies. The act making this provisions stipulated that when thirty or more persons, residents of any county or district embracing two counties, organized themselves into an agricultural society, under the rules and regulations of the state board of agriculture, the county might aid such societies with a grant not to exceed $400 per year (80 O. L. 142). By Act of April 21, 1896, provision was made for representation in a county society of thirty or more residents of any county or district embracing two or more counties (92 O. L. 205). In 1900 the legislature extended the amount of county aid to $800 per year (94 O. L. 395). Later, May 6, 1902, the legislature passed an act authorizing thirty or more residents of the county or of a district embracing one or more counties, to organize themselves into an agricultural society (95 O. L. 403).

On April 17, 1919, the legislature provided for the organization of county and independent agricultural societies, the payment of class premiums; defined the duties of persons competing for premiums; prescribed the publication of treasures' accounts and the list of awards by societies; authorized the society to elect a board of directors consisting of eight members, and prescribed their term of office and the manner of their election. The act first stipulated how such societies might obtain state aid, and authorize the county commissioners to insure all buildings belonging to agricultural societies (108 O. L. pt. i, 381-385).

The legislature in 1921 passed an act stipulating that the total amount of county aid to county agricultural societies should not exceed one hundred percent of the amount paid by the society in regular class premiums (109 O. L. 240). By act of March 27, 1925, the county commissioners were authorized to purchase or to lease, for a term of not less than twenty years, real estate whereon to hold fairs under the management of county agricultural societies, and to erect thereon suitable buildings (111 O. L. 238). On March 10, 1927, the legislature authorized the county commissioners to appropriate annually on the request of the agricultural society a sum not less than $1,500 or more than $2,000 from the general fund for the purpose of "encouraging agricultural fairs" (112 O. L. 84).

The most recent legislation affecting agricultural societies were that of March 19, 1935. This act provides that where no duly organized county agricultural society existed, and when no fair was held by a duly organized county agricultural society which had held an annual exposition for three years previous to January 1, 1933, the county commissioner should, on the request of the independent society, appropriate annually from the general fund a sum not more than $2,000 or less than $500 for the encouragement of independent agricultural fairs (116 O. L. 47).

376. JOURNAL

1869—. 4 volumes. Prior records and 1892-1906, missing.

Record of minutes of meeting of county agricultural society (county fair board) showing order of business, copy of rules and regulations governing the annual county fairs, as classes of exhibits and schedule of prizes offered for best exhibits of agricultural, floral, and art products. Chronologically arranged by dates of meetings. No index. 1869-1934, handwritten; 1925—, typed. 1869-1891, 2 volumes, condition fair. Average 300 pages. 16 x 11 x 2. 2 volumes, 1869-1891, County courthouse attic storeroom; 2 volumes, 1909—, at residence of secretary of the association, Mr. Edgar Quinlan, one mile north of Georgetown on State Route 68.

377. LEDGER
1907—. 2 volumes.

County agricultural association's record of receipts and expenditures showing names of donors and amount of cash or merchandise subscribed and amount of gate receipt admissions to annual fair; itemized account of expenditures showing date, to whom, for what, amount; also list of exhibitors winning prices and prizes awarded to each. Chronologically arranged by dates of entries. No index. Handwritten on printed forms. Average 360 pages. 14 x 10 x 2. Records are at the residence of the secretary of the association, Mr. Edgar Quinlan, one mile north of Georgetown on State Route 68.

378. RECORD BOOK, BROWN COUNTY AGRICULTURAL SOCIETY
1857-1894. 1 volume.

Record of the minutes of the meetings of the board of directors giving detailed account of the agricultural fairs. Chronological arranged. No index. Handwritten. Condition fair. 500 pages. 22 x 14 x 5. Basement storeroom.

In 1914 the federal government passed an act providing for cooperative agricultural extension service between the state agricultural colleges and the United States department of agriculture. The purpose of the extension service was to give instructions and practical demonstrations in agriculture and home economics to persons not attending college, and to give such information through field demonstrations, publications, and other means. The funds for such work were to be supplied in part by the federal government and part by the state. (*U. S. Statutes at Large*, XXXVIII, pt. i, 372-374).

A year following the federal legislation, the Ohio legislature accepted the provisions of the act by providing that when twenty or more residents of a county organized themselves into a "farmers institute society for the purpose of teaching better methods of farming, stock raising, fruit culture and business connected with agriculture," accepted a constitution and bylaws conforming to the rules and regulations prescribed by the trustees of the Ohio State University, and elected proper officers, the institute shall be a corporate body. The Ohio State University was required to furnish speakers for their annual meeting. At the close of the session the trustees were authorized to publish the lectures in pamphlet or book form.

Besides maintaining an institute, the society was authorized to maintain a county experiment farm. Furthermore the county commissioners were authorized to select a county agent subject to the approval of the dean of college of agriculture of the Ohio State University. The first agent in Brown County was appointed on July 1, 1919. It is the duty of the agent to inspect and study the agricultural conditions in his county, distribute agricultural literature, cooperate with United States Department of Agriculture and the College of Agriculture of the Ohio State University. In the event the commissioners failed to make such an appointment, the electorate could require them to do so on a referendum vote. (106 O. L. 356-359).

In 1929 the original legislation was amended so as to authorize the trustees of the Ohio State University to employ home demonstration agents and boys' and girls' club agents. The county extension agent was given the additional duty of carrying the teachings of the college of agriculture of the Ohio State University in agriculture and home economics to the residents of his county through personal visits, bulletins, and practical demonstrations. Furthermore it was his duty to render educational service not only in relation to agricultural production, but also in relation to economic problems including marketing, distribution, and the utilization of farm products. (113 O. L. 82-83).

The initial legislation contained a clause which required the county commissioners to appropriate annually one thousand dollars if they wished to obtain the services of an agricultural agent. This amount was to be matched by the state. Under the present system the commissioners are empowered to levy a tax and to appropriate from the premium thereof or from the general fund to be paid to the state treasury to the credit of the agricultural extension fund an amount not in excess of three thousand for each agent. Amounts in excess must have the unanimous consent of the commissioners. (113 O. L. 82-83).

All the records are located in the office of the agricultural extension agent.

379. 4-H CLUB RECORDS

1934—. 60 folders in 2 file boxes.

Record of registration and membership in 4-H clubs showing accomplishments of each boy or girl. Folders marked as to type of activities. No index. Typed. Folders, 12 x 9 x .5; file boxes, 30 x 14 x 14.

380. TOBACCO RECORD

1934—. 1600 folders in 12 file boxes.

Record of tobacco growers complying with Agricultural Adjustment Administration. Each case in separate folder. Alphabetically arranged by names of growers. No index. Folders, 12 x 9 x 1; file boxes, 30 x 14 x 14.

381. CORN-HOG PROGRAM RECORDS

1934-1935. 450 folders in 4 file boxes.

Record of farmers complying with Agricultural Adjustment Administration requirements under the corn-hog program. Each case in separate folder. Alphabetically arranged by names of farmers. No index. Typed. Folders, 12 x 9 x 1; file boxes, 30 x 14 x 14.

382. WHEAT PROGRAM RECORDS

1933-1936. 127 folders in 3 file boxes.

Record of farmers complying with Agricultural Adjustment Administration requirements under wheat program. Each case in separate folder. Alphabetically arranged by names of growers. No index. Typed. Folders, 12 x 9 x 1; file boxes, 30 x 14 x 14.

383. RECORD OF EXTENSION WORK

1934—. Approximately 1,500 folders in 10 file boxes.

Record of all extension work activities supervised by county agent. Folders marked as to type of work or program. No index. Typed. Folders, 12 x 9 x 1; file boxes, 30 x 14 x 14.

Reports

384. 4-H CLUB REPORTS

1934—. 1 file box.

Copies of county agent's monthly and annual reports to Ohio State University extension department on 4-H club activities. Chronologically arranged. No index. Typed. 30 x 14 x 14.

385. NARRATIVE REPORTS

1934—. 1 file box.

Copies of county agent's narrative reports to Ohio State University extension department on extension work activities. Chronologically arranged. No index. Typed. 30 x 14 x 14.

386. COUNTY AGENT'S REPORTS

1934—. 1 file box.

Copies of county agent's detailed summation of daily work of county agent's office and monthly and annual reports to Ohio State University extension department and United States department of agriculture. Chronologically arranged. No index. Typed. 30 x 14 x 14.

The county dog warden, appointed by the county commissioners, has as his duty the enforcement of the provisions of the General Code relative to licensing dogs, the impounding and destruction of unlicensed dogs, and the payment of compensation for damages to livestock inflicted by dogs. This officer, like other county officials, is required to give bond conditions for the faithful performance of the duties of his office. This bond, in the sum of not less than $500 nor more than $2,000, is filed with the county auditor. His compensation and tenure, like that of his deputies, is determined by the county commissioners.

In Brown County the duties of the dog warden were under the jurisdiction of the sheriff from 1917 to 1927 as provided by Statute (107 O. L. 535). In 1927 an act authorized the commissioners to appoint a county dog warden responsible to the commissioners (112 O. L. 348), but for reasons of economy, no dog warden has been appointed. The commissioners administer affairs of the office, commissioning a sheriff's deputy to respond to all complaints and investigate all claims for injury or loss by stray dogs and dispose of such animals as provided by law. Since 1927 the commissioners have entered all records of such activities in the Commissioners' Journal, entry 1.

The warden is required to make a record of all dogs owned kept, or harbored in his county; to patrol the county; to seize and impound dogs more than three months of age found not wearing a valid registration tag. The latter provisions do not apply, however, to dogs kept in a regular licensed kennel. Moreover, he is required to make weekly written reports to the commissioners of all dogs seized, impounded, redeemed, and destroyed. Then, too, he is required to report all claims for damages to livestock inflicted by dogs.

The dog warden and his deputies have, in the performance of their legal duties, the same police powers as are conferred by statute upon sheriffs and police. They may summon the assistance of bystanders in performing their duties, serve writs and other legal processes in any court in the county with reference to enforcing the provisions of the laws relating to dogs. (G. C. sec. 5652-7).

Documentary Sources

Acts of the General Assembly, 1803-1938 (117 volumes, published annually under authority of the state of Ohio).

Baldwin, William Edward, ed., *Throckmorton's Ohio Code* (certified edn., Cleveland, 1936).

Chase, Salmon P., comp., *Statutes of Ohio and the Northwest Territory, 1788-1883* (3 volumes, Cincinnati, 1833-1935).

Commissioners' Journal [Brown County], 1843—. 19 volumes. This journal, as well as other records listed under the various offices included in the inventory, constitutes the most important source material on the history of Brown County.

Hammond, Charles, and others, eds., *Reports of Cases Argued and Determined in the Supreme Court of Ohio in Bank* . . . (20 volumes, Cincinnati, 1824-1952).

Howe, Henry, *Historical Collections of Ohio* (2 volumes, Norwalk, 1896). Contains much valuable material.

McCook, G. W., and others, eds., *Reports of Cases Argued and Determined in the Supreme Court of Ohio* . . . (132 volumes, Cincinnati 1852—).

Ohio Auditor of State, *Annual Report,* 1836-1936 (72 volumes, published under state authority).

Ohio Department of Agriculture, *Annual Report,* 1846-1903 (68 volumes, published under state authority).

Ohio Department of Banks and Banking, *Annual Report* 1908-1937 (published under state authority).

Ohio Secretary of State, *Annual Report,* 1857-1937 (90 volumes, published under state authority.

__________, Commission Register, 1858—. 3 volumes.

Ohio Study of Local School Units, *A Study of the Public Schools of Brown County* (mimeographed, Columbus, 1937).

Pease, Theodore Calvin, comp., *Laws of the Northwest Territory, 1786-1800 (Illinois State Bar Association Law Services,* no. I, Springfield, 1925).

Report of the Geographical Survey of Ohio (10 volumes, Columbus, 1873-1894).

Report of the Joint Legislative Committee on Economy and Taxation of the Eighty-Sixth General Assembly (Columbus, 1926). In chapter xiii the Committee condemns the organization of county government in Ohio.

Shepherd, Vinton R., ed., *The Ohio NISI PRIUS REPORTS* (32 volumes, n. s. Columbus and Cincinnati, 1894-1934). Cases decided by common pleas, probate, and municipal courts of the state of Ohio.

Trautwein, George C., ed., *Page's Ohio Cumulative Code Service* (22 volumes, Cincinnati, 1927-1938).

__________, Supplement to Page's *Annotated General Code 1926 to 1935* (Cincinnati 1935).

United States Statutes at Large, 1776-1936 (49 volumes, United States Government Printing Office).

Biography, Journals, and Letters

Monica, Sister Mary, *The Cross in the Wilderness, A Biography of Pioneer Ohio* (New York, 1930). It is to be regretted that the author failed to document her excellent narrative.

Rankin, John, *Letters on Slavery* (Ripley, Ohio, 1926).

Strickland, W. P., Ed., *Autobiography of Reverend James B. Finley; or Pioneer Life in the West* (Cincinnati, 1853). Contains significant observations of a circuit rider.

Secondary Sources

Adams, George Burton, *Constitutional History of England* (New York, 1921). A standard work.

Ayer, N. W., and Son's, *Directory of Newspapers and Periodicals* (Philadelphia, 1937). A guide to publications printed in the United States and its possessions, the Philippines, dominions, etc.

Beers, W. H. and Company, comp., *The History of Brown County, Ohio* (Chicago, 1883).

Bond, Beverly W., Jr., *The Civilization of the Old Northwest: A study of Political, Social, and Economic Development, 1788-1812* (New York, 1934). An excellent study in which the author develops the thesis that the Northwest was a laboratory in which the America colonial system was developed.

Cross, Arthur Lyon, *A Shorter History of England and Greater Britain* (New York, 1925). A standard textbook, but too sharp in outline.

Downes, Randolph Chandler, *Frontier Ohio, 1788-1803* (Ohio Historical *Collections,* no. 3, Columbus, 1935). One of the most satisfactory treatments of the Ohio Frontier– well-documented.

Fess, Simeon, D., ed., *Ohio Reference Library* (4 volumes, New York, 1937),

Heiges, R. E., *The Office of Sheriff in the Rural Counties of Ohio* (Findlay, Ohio, 1933). This volume has the usual limitations of a doctoral dissertation.

Hockett, Homer C., *Western Influence on Political Parties to 1825: An Essay in Historical Interpretation* (Ohio State University Bulletin XXII, no. 3, Columbus, 1917). An excellent study.

Kennedy, Aileen Elizabeth, *The Ohio Poor Law and its Administration* (Sophonisba P. Breckinridge, ed., *Social Service Monographs* no. 22, University of Chicago Press, Chicago, 1934). A bit biting criticism of the administration of poor relief in Ohio prior to 1932.

Kerraker, Cyrus Harreld, *The Seventeenth Century Sheriff: A Comparative Study of the Sheriff in England and the Chesapeake Colonies, 1607-1699* (Chapel Hill, 1930). Although interesting, this volume does not supersede the earlier studies made of that office.

Leggett, J. C., *The Flood in Ohio, February, 1884, Report of the Citizen's Relief Committee of Ripley, Ohio* [Ripley[, 1884, pamphlet).

Mills, William C., *Archaeological Atlas of Ohio* (Columbus, 1914),

Peattie, Roderick, *Geography of Ohio, Geological Survey of Ohio,* Bulletin XXVII (Columbus, 1923).

Peters, W. E., *Ohio Lands and Their Subdivision,* 2d edition (Athens, 1918).

Pollock, Sir Frederick, and Maitland, Frederic, *The History of English Law Before the Time of Edward I* (2 volumes, Cambridge, 1895). A standard work.

Randall, Emilius O., and Ryan Daniel J., *History of Ohio: The Rise and Progress of an American State* (5 volumes, New York, 1912). Inaccurate in detail.

Robinson, Louis N., *Penology in the United States* (Philadelphia, 1922). Although an old work, this volume contains many significant conclusions.

Roseboom, Eugene Holloway, and Weisenburger, Francis Phelps, *A History of Ohio* (New York, 1934). The most satisfactory history of Ohio–scholarly and impartial.

Schapiro, J. Salwyn, *Modern and Contemporary European History 1815-1825* (New York, 1923). A standard textbook. Especially good on the intellectual and social history of the period.

Sutherland, Edwin H., *Principles of Criminology* (Chicago, 1934). An excellent study.

Van Waters, Miriam, *Youth in Conflict* (New York, 1926). An excellent study of the causes of delinquencies written by the reference in juvenile court, Los Angeles.

Williams, Byron, *History of Clermont and Brown Counties Ohio* (2 volumes, Millford, Ohio, 1913).

Magazine Articles

Boyd, W. W., "Secondary Education in Ohio Previous to the Year 1840," *Ohio Archaeological and Historical Quarterly,* XXV (1916), 118-134.

Downes, Randolph Chandler, "Evolution of Ohio County Boundaries," *Ohio Archaeological and Historical Quarterly,* XXXVI (1927), 340-447.

Evans, Nelson W., "Colonel John O'Bannon," *Ohio Archaeological and Historical Quarterly,* XIV, (1905), 319-327).

Fowke, Gerard, "Stone Graves in Brown County, Ohio," *Ohio Archaeological and Historical Quarterly,* IX (1901), 193-204.

Galbreath, C. B., "Centennial Anniversary of the Birth of Ulysses S. Grant," *Ohio Archaeological and Historical Quarterly,* XXXI, (1922), 221-288.

Grim, Paul R., "The Reverend John Rankin, Early Abolitionist," *Ohio Archaeological and Historical Quarterly,* XLVI, (1937), 215-256.

Hart, Albert Bushnell, "The Westernization of New England," *Ohio Archaeological and Historical Quarterly,* XVII, (1908), 259-274.

King, Rev. I. E., "Introduction of Methodism in Ohio," *Ohio Archaeological and Historical Quarterly,* X (1902), 165-219.

MacLean, J. P., "The Kentucky Revival and its Influence on the Miami Valley," *Ohio Archaeological and Historical Quarterly,* XII (1903), 242-286.

Miller, Edwin A., "The History of Educational Legislation in Ohio from 1803-1850," *Ohio Archaeological and Historical Quarterly,* XXVII (1918), 1-271.

Morris, William A., "The Office of Sheriff in the Anglo-Saxon Period," *Ohio Archaeological and Historical Quarterly,* XXXI (1916), 20-40.

Sherone, H. C., "The Indian in Ohio," *Ohio Archaeological and Historical Quarterly,* XXVII (1919), 274-510.

Siebert, Wilbur H., "The Underground Railroad in Ohio," *Ohio Archaeological and Historical Quarterly,* IV (1895), 44-63.

James Wells	1818-1820
John Lindsey	part of 1818
William White	part of 1818
Walter Wall	1818-1824
John Evans	1818-1826
William W. Clark	1820-1822
Robert Breckenridge	1822-1824
William Humphreys	1824-1830
John Lindsey	1824-1825
William Legitt	1825-1830
Robert Allen	1826-1829
Henry Chapman	1829-1835
Joseph Stableton	1830-1833
James McCall	1830-1833
John Lindscy	1833-1837
William Parker	1833-1834
J. D. McCarty	1834-1835
Jephtha Beasley	1835-1836
Noah Ellis	1835-1841
Samuel Ross	1836-1839
Samuel Kerr	1837-1843
Richard W. Ditto	1839-1845
Michael Pindell	1841-1844
Joseph Dugan	1843-1846
William Norris	1844-1846
William P. Allen	1845-1848
Robert W. McClain	1846-1853
James F. Thompson resigned	1846-Feb 29, 1848
Peter L. Wilson	unexpired term
Charles W. Reed	1848-1852
John Wright	1850-1856
Shary Mooore	1852-1855
Joseph Briant	1853-1855
Thomas Hunter resigned	1855-Apr 1857,
Samuel M. Blair	Apr 1857, unexpired term and to 1861
William F. Pickrell resigned	1855-Feb 1856
Shary Moore	unexpired term
David Keithler	1856-1857
John Brady	1856-1863
William B. Logan	1857-1864
James Campbell	1861-1864
James F. Davis	1863-1865
Husotn Bare	1864-1868
Samuel McNown	1866-1869
C. A. Linn	1867-1870
James Camptell	1868-1871
William Fulton	1869-1875
William Vance	1870-1873
Peter L. Wilson	1871-1874
John Wright	1874-1879
James L. Burger	1874-1877
W. B. West	1875-1881
Daniel McCann	1877-1880
Jefferson Fite	1879-1882
Farmer Thornton	six months of 1878
Jefferson Fite	1879-1882
John A. Jennings	1880-1886
Ross Wise	1881-1887
S. W. Pickerill	1882-1888
R. C. Drake	Jan 1888-Jan 1894
Frederick Bauer	Jan 1888-Jan 1894
Homer F. Pindell	Jan 1889-Jan 1895
Thomas A. Glaze	Sep 1896-Sep 1890
Lee J. Evans	Sep 1897-Sep 1900
James B. Holman	Sep 1898-Sep 1901
W. A. Rist	Sep 1899-Sep 1902
J. M. Devore	Sep 1900-Sep 1903
John McCann	Sep 1901-Sep 1907

*Compiled from: W. H. Beers and Co., *The History of Brown County, Ohio* (Chicago, 1883), 361-366; Ohio Secretary of State, *Annual Report*, 1880-1938.

Commissioners, continued

W. A. Rist	1902-Sep 1905
J. M. Devore	1903-Sep 1906
W. E. Hare	1905-Sep 1909*
W. E. Hare	Aug 1909-Sep 1911
S. A. Davis	Sep 1909-Sep 1911
William Wahl	1909-Sep 1911
R. R. Stratton	1911-Sep 1913
John H. Neu	1911-Sep 1913
John Evans	1911-Sep 1913
John Evans	1913-Sep 1915
John H. Neu	1913-Sep 1915
R. R. Stratton	1913-Sep 1915
Perry Cahall, Jr.	1915-Sep 1917
John Griffith	1915-Sep 1917
P. W. Pence	1917-Sep 1919
Perry Cahall, Jr.	1917-Sep 1919
Lucien Borden	1919-Sep 1921
Joseph H. Richey	1919-Sep 1921
G. V. Hughes	1919-Sep 1921
Joseph H. Richey	1921-Jan 1923
W. L. Borden	1921-Jan 1925
G. V. Hughes	1921-Jan 1925
W. H. Dawley	1923-Jan 1927
George Frank	1925-Jan 1929
W. A. Pindell	1925-Jan 1929
H. E. Tweed	1927-Jan 1931
W. A. Pindell	1929-Jan 1933
V. K. Thompson	1929-Jan 1933
M. B. Glassco	1929-Jan 1933
A. J. Kennedy	1931-Jan 1935
Arch Pitzer	1933-Jan 1937
J. E. Weisbrodt	1933-Jan 1937
J. E. Griffith	1935—
Mrs. Fannie Kennedy appointed Aug 1937, vice A. J. Kennedy, deceased	
Arch Pitzer	1937—

*Term of incumbent extended to allow for change from three-year to two-year term, by 1905 amendment to Ohio Constitution, Art. XVII, Sec. 2.

Recorders**

Amos Ellis	1819-1822***
David Ammen	1831-1834
Charles White	1834-1837
David Crawford	1837-1843
Thomas M. Barker resigned	1843-Jul 1847
David Ferrier deceased	Jul 1847-May 28, 1850
James T. Morgan	May 28, 1850-1853
John P. Biehn	1853-1856
John H. Dugan deceased	1856-Aug 1857
Robert H. Higgins	Aug 1857-Oct 1857
James T. Morgan	1857-1863
Amos T. Ellis	1863-1866
John F. Black	1866-1869

**Under the law of 1803 the associate judges of the court of common pleas appointed the recorder for seven years. The office became elective for a term of three years in 1829, two years im 1905, and four years in 1937.

***Data for the years 1823-1830 could not be located.

Recorders, continued

John W. Evans	1869-1875	M. J. Clark	Sep 1913-Sep 1917
Grandison Pinckard	1875-1881	Wilbur W. Hendrixson	Sep 1917-Sep 1921
George L. Ellis	1881-1883	Charles E. Kelly	Sep 1921-Sep 1925
G. C. Reisinger	Jan 1883-Jan 1890	May Thompson	Sep 1925-Jan 1931
C. C. Chaney	1890-Jan 1896	J. Robert Owens	Jan 1931-Jan 1935
L. P. Schweickart	Sep 1896-Sep 1902	Luther F. Waits	1935—
W. R. Johnson	Sep 1902-Sep 1908		
William McMichael	Sep 1908-Sep 1913		

Clerks of the Court of Common Pleas*

Abraham Shepherd	1818-1824	C. C. Blair	1882-1888
William Shepherd	1824-1830	Young Stephenson	Feb 1888-Feb 1894
James Finley	1830-1833	Thomas W. Weaver	Aug 1894-Aug 1900
George W. King	1833-1841	Hiram Tyler	Aug 1900-Aug 1906
A. C. Stewart	1841	A. J. Kirkskaddon	Aug 1906-Aug 1911
John H. Blair	1841-1849	Frank P. Kendle	Aug 1911-Aug 1915
Gideon Dunham	1849-1855	W. F. Kinnett	Aug 191-Aug 1919
Harvey McKibben	1855-1858	L. P. McBeth	Aug 1919-Aug 1923
R. H. Higgins	1858-1864	Fred Innis	Aug 1923-Aug 1925
R. C. Mitchell	1864-1867	Charles O. Yochum	Aug 1925-Aug 1929
R. H. Higgins	1867-1876	Kelsie S. Harover	Aug 1929-Jan 1935
John Lafabre	1876-1882	Herbert L. Sanders	1935—

Judges of the Court of Common Pleas

President judges under the constitution of 1802, in District VII which includes Brown County

Francis Dunlevy**		John T. Thompson	1820-1824
Joseph H. Crane**		Joshua Collett	1824-1826
John T. Thompson**		George P. Torrence	1826-1833
Joshua Collett	1818-1820	John M. Goodenow	1833-1834

*Under the state constitution of 1802 the court appointed its own clerk for a seven-year term; under that of 1851 the office became elective for a three-year term. The term was changed to two years in 1905, and to four in 1935.

**Prior to 1818, when Brown County was organized.

Judges of the Court of Common Pleas, continued

John W. Price	1834-1841	Shepherd F. Norris	1851-1852
Owen T. Fishback	1841-1848	unexpired term	
George Collins	1848-1851		

Associate judges under the constitution of 1802 in District VII

Joseph N. Campbell	1818-1823	Hugh B. Payne	1832-1838
James Moore	1818-1825	Benjamin Evans	1836-1840
William Anderson	1818-1832	Henry Martin	1838-1852
William White	1823-1824	Micah Wood	1840-1847
James Finley	1824-1831	John Kay	1845-1851
Robert Breckenridge	1825-1836	Isaac Carey	1847-1852
David Johnson	1831-1845	Benjamin Sells	1851-1852

Judges under the constitution of 1851 in District VII which included Brown County

Shepherd F. Norris	1852-1861	John M. Markley	Feb 1897-Feb 1913
Thomas M. Lewis	Feb - Oct 1861	John S. Parrott	Oct 1898-Oct 1908
Thomas A. Ashburn	1861-1876	Frank Davis, Sr.	1908-Dec 1914
David Tarbell	1872-1882	Galleib Banbach	1907-Feb 1913
Allen T. Cowen	1878-1888	James Tarbell	1913-1931; deceased
D.W.C. Loudon	1881-1887	Harry E. Parker	unexpired
Frank Davis	1887-Oct 1892	term to Feb 1931	
DeWitt Loudon	Feb 1887-Feb 1892	Joseph Walter Bagby	1931—

Judges of Probate Court

John J. Higgins	1852-1855	S. H. Stevenson	1870-1876
John W. King	1855-1857, resigned	John P. Biehn	1876-1882
James H. King	1857-1858	George P. Tyler	1882-1888
D.W.C. Loudon	1858, resigned	Eli B. Parker	Feb 1888-Feb 1894
J. H. Marshall	1858-1859	Lewis F. Walther	Feb 1894-Feb 1900
James H. Fyffee	1859-1861, resigned	R. E. Campbell	Feb 1900-Feb 1906
Charles F. Campbell	1861-1862	W. W. Pennell	Jan 1906-Feb 1913
William P. Allen	1862-1864	Harry E. Parker	Feb 1913-Feb 1921
Charles F. Campbell	1864, deceased	Howard D. Waters	Feb 1921-Feb 1929
George W. King	1864	John G. Quinlan	Feb 1929—
David Tarbell	1864-1870		

Prosecuting Attorneys

Thomas Morris	Mar 1818-Jul 1818
George W. King	1818-1826
Alexander Gilliand	1826-1835
A. Leggitt	1835-18396
Thomas H. Linch	1836-1838
David G. Devore	1838-1840
Andrew Ellison	1840-1843
C. F. Campbell	1843-1845
William Boyle	1845-1849
C. W. Blair	1849-1852
C. A. White	1852-1855
John G. Marshall	1855-1856
William H. Sly	1856-1858
William F. Wylie	1858-1860
Thomas T. Taylor	1860-1867
E. C. Devore	1863-1867
J. W. Bailey	1867-1870
W. J. Thompson	1870-1875
C. A. Linn	1875-1877
W. W. McKnight	1877-1879
John R. Moore	1879-1883
W. R. Evans	1883-1888
D. V. Pearson	Jan 1888-Jan 1831
David Tarbell	Jan 1891-Jan 1897
James W. Tarbell	Jan 1897-Jan 1903
John Q. Waters	Jan 1903–Jan 1906
George C. Barnes	Jan 1906-Jan 1911
F. X. Frebis	Jan 1911-Jan 1915
John M. Markley	Jan 1915-Jan 1919
J. W. Bagby	Jan 1919-Jan 1923
E. B. Stivers	Jan 1923-Jan 1927
John H. Houston	Jan 1927-Jan 1935
Thomas G. Johnson	Jan 1935-Jan 1937
David P. Tarbell	Jan 1937—

Coroners

Henry Lacher	Dec 1858-1860
Henry Lacher	Oct 1860-1861
Sylvester Shaw	1861-1864
A. B. Sidwell	1864-1868
Jacob Herzog, Jr. removed	Nov 1868-Mar 1870,
Adam Hensel	Oct 1870-1872
Sylvester Shaw	1872-1876
William S. Norris	1876-1880
Sylvester Shaw	Nov 1870-Nov 1882
D. B. Young	Nov 1882-Nov 1886
John W. Adkins	Nov 1886-Jan 1889
Alfred Sidwell	Jan 1889-Jan 1893
John L. Fritz	Jan 1893-Jan 1897
James B. Albright	Jan 1897-Jan 1901
Mike Gray	Jan 1901-Jan 1905
A. S. Holland	Jan 1905-1909
F. P. Shaw	1909-Jan 1913
Charles Miller	Jan 1913-Jan 1917
William H. Dowdney	Jan 1917-Jan 1921
Mike Breen	Jan 1921-Jan 1923
Dr. r. L. Chambers	Jan 1923-Jan 1927
Dr. George P. Tyler, Jr.	Jan 1927—

Sheriffs

William Butt	1818-1823	George R. Shields	1867-1871
Robert Allen	1823-1827	John T. Brady	1875-1877
James Loudon	1827-1831	John Carringan, Sr.	1877-1881
Jeremiah Purdum	1831-1835	Lee Richey	Jan 1889-Jan 1893
John H. Blair	1835-1839	John Wood	Jan 1893-Jan 1897
John J. Higgins	1839-1843	R. H. Campbell	Jan 1897-Jan 1901
William Shields	1843-1847	Ed. H. Kennedy	Jan 1901-Jan 1905
Thomas Middleton	1847-1849	Perry Cahall	Jan 1905-Jan 1909
William P. Allen	1849-1853	Charles McBeth	1909-Jan 1911
Henry Young	1853-1855	C. C. McBeth	Jan 1911-Jan 1913
John S. Foster	1855-1857	J. N. Bower	Jan 1913-Jan 1717
Charles Oursler	1857-1861	Stephen D. Miller	Jan 1917-Jan 1921
Alfred Jacobs	1861-1865	Edgar H. New	Jan 1921-Jan 1925
William C. Howard	1865, part of a year	George P. Kellum	Jan 1925-Jan 1927
		John H. McCollum	Jan 1927-Jan 1929
George R. Shields	Oct 1865-1866	John E. New	Jan 1929-Jan 1933
William C. Howard	1866-1867	Steven D. Miller	Jan 1933—

Treasurers

William Humphreys	part of 1818	J. P. Richey	Sep 1884-Sep 1890
George King	1818-1820	E. A. Tissandier	Sep 1890-Sep 1894
William Humphreys	1820-1822	James H. Markley	Sep 1894-Sep 1898
Amos Ellis	1822-1829	Louis Mischler	Sep 1898-Sep 1902
William Middleton	1829-1836	W. R. Waters	Sep 1902-Sep 1906
Thomas Middleton	1836-1846	Samuel Kantz	Sep 1906-Sep 1911
John D. White	1846-1854	W. B. Albright	Sep 1911-Sep 1915
Reason J. Bennett	1854-1856	CorneliusWilson	Sep 1915-Sep 1919
Benjamin W. Whiteman	1856-1858	W. W. Cooper	Sep 1919-Sep 1923
John McColgins	1858-1862	William T. Wilson	Sep 1923-Sep 1927
John P. Louiso	1862-1866	W. E. Mullen	Sep 1927, deceased
William Norris	1866-1870	Mrs. Flora Mullen	unexpired term until successor elected
Alfred J. Parker	1870-Mar 1874		
Peter L. Wilson	Mar 1874-Sep 1874	Edna Sroufe	vice W. E. Mullen, deceased, term expired Sep 1931
George W. Drake	1874-1878		
Enos B. Fee	1878-1880	Mrs. Flora Mullen	Sep 1931-Sep 1933
B. F. Dyer	1880-1884	Virgil L. Prickett	Sep 1933—

Auditors*

William Middleton	1821-1827	James A. Stephenson	1865-1867
William Butts	1827-1829	Alonzo G. Quinlan	1867-1871
Benjamin Evans	1829-1831	William P. Elsberry	1871-1875
Samuel Glaze	1831-1838	Enoch E. Roney	1875-1880
Hezekiah Lindsey	1838-1841, resigned	William J. Jacobs	1880-1885
Peter L. Wilson	6 months of 1841 unexpired term	John W. Helbling	Sep 1885-Sep 1893
		H. L. Jennings	Oct 1893-Oct 1899
James L. Smith	1841-1845	Robert McCall	Oct 1899-Oct 1905
Stephen T. Brunson	1845-1849	Charles E. Biehn	Oct 1905-Oct 1911
John McColgin	1849-1853	Wayne Cahall	Oct 1911-Oct 1915
Lewis J. Egbert	1853-1855	John E. Penny	Oct 1915-Oct 1919
P. Ellis	1855-1857	John P. Stephan	Oct 1919-Oct 1927
John W. Purdom	1857-1861	John E. Penny	Oct 1927-Mar 1931
J. W. Heterick	1861-1863	Charles E. Biehn	Mar 1931-Mar 1935
William P. Ellsberry	1863-1865	Mrs. Mabel Yochum	Mar 1935—

Infirmary Directors**

John G. Brose	Dec 1858-Dec 1859	B. J. Woods	Nov 1877-1878, to fill vacancy by death of John Brose
Charles Richards	Nov 1859-1862		
Robert Hunt	Oct 1860-1863	Jacob Hanselman	Nov 1877-1880
John G. Brose	Oct 1861-1864	William Jacobs	Oct 1878-1881
John E. Ellis	Dec 1861-1864	Phillip J. Miller	Oct 1879-1882
Matthias Arn	Feb 1864-1867	Jacob Hanselman	Nov 1880-1883
Saul P. King	Dec 1864-1867	William Jacobs	Oct 1881-1884
John E. Ellis	Dec 1865-1868	Philip J. Miller	Nov 1883-1886
John G. Brose	Nov 1866-1869	Charles Andrews	Oct 1883-1886
John Allen	Oct 1867-1870	A. D. Ellis	Oct 1884-1887
William Jacobs	Nov 1868-1871	George K. Weaver	Oct 1885-1889
John G. Brose	Nov 1869-1872	Randolph Waters	Dec 1887-Dec 1888
John Allen	Oct 1870-1873	Charles Andrews	Jan 1887-Jan 1890
William Jacobs	Nov 1871-1874	A. D. Ellis	Jan 1888-Jan 1891
John G. Brose	Oct 1872-1875	Randolph Waters	Jan 1889-Jan 1892
Jacob Hanselman	Oct 1875-1876	Thomas Weaver	Jan 1890-Jan 1893
Philip J. Miller	Oct 1876-1879	J. A. McElroy	Jan 18921-Jan 1894

*The duties of this office were discharged by the commissioners' clerk until 1821.

**The board of infirmary directors was abolished in 1913 and its duties transferred to the county commissioners.

Infirmary Directors, continued

Jesse Cahall	Jan 1898-Jan 1901	John R. Burris	1908-Jan 1911
S. D. Teeters	Jan 188-Jan 1902	Bob Heterich	1908-Jan 1911
George W. Murray	1900-Jan 1903	Philip Miller	1908-Jan 1911
Jesse Cahall	1909-Jan 1911	Fred Noll	1911-Jan 1913
S. D. Teeters	1908-Jan 1911	W. T. Wilson	1911-Jan 1913
George W. Murray	1900-Jan 1903	Philip Miller	1911-Jan 1913
W. T. Wilson	1909-Jan 1911		

Surveyors*

James Pilson	1818-1824	Charles H. Gore	Jan 1889-Jan 1895
William Wall	1824-1828	Charles M. Gordon	Sep 1895-Sep 1901
Jephtha Beasley	1828-1836	Lewis H. Wolfe	Sep 1901-Sep 1907
John D. White	1836-1844	George R. Hoss	1907-Sep 1911
Abraham Sallee	1844-1847	D. G. Devore	Sep 1911-Sep 1913
William Tatman	1848-1854	Carl H. Thomas	Sep 1913-Sep 1915
Abraham Sallee	1854	John R. Moore, Jr.	Sep 1915-Sep 1917
William Hays	1854-1857	Carl H. Thomas	Sep 1917-Sep 1919
O. P. Ralston	1857-1864	John R. Wright	Sep 1919-Sep 1921
J.R.C. Brown	1864-1867	Herbert Klinker	Sep 1921-Se[1924
James M. Stivers	1867-1872	A. P. Cooper	Dec 1924-Sep 1925
Jacob M. Bower	1872-1878	Charles M. Gordon	Nov 1924-Jan 1929
H.L.P. Vance	1878-1881	N. R. Scott	Jan 1929-Jan 1937
G. L. McKibben	1881-1885	John Kay	Jan 1937—
J. R. Wright			

*From 1803 to 1831 the surveyor was appointed by the court of common pleas and commissioned by the governor. From 1831 to 1906 he was elected for a three-year term, from 1906 to 1928 for a two-year term, and since 1928 for a four-year term.

Governmental

All addresses refer to Georgetown, Ohio, unless otherwise noted.

Auditor
https://browncountyohio.gov/index.php/auditor47
800 Mt. Orab Pike Suite 181

Board of Elections
https://www.browncountyohio.gov/index.php/board-of-elections
800 Mt. Orab Pike Suite 111

Brown County Educational Service
https://www.brownesc.us/
9231 Hamer Road

Clerk of Courts
https://browncountyohio.gov/index.php/clerk-of-courts46
210 E Grant Ave

Commissioners
https://browncountyohio.gov/index.php/commissioners42
800 Mt. Orab Pike Suite 101

Common Pleas
https://browncountyohio.gov/index.php/common-pleas-judge33
101 South Main St.

Coroner
https://browncountyohio.gov/index.php/coroner
800 Mt. Orab Pike Suite 161

Dog Warden, Brown County Humane Society/Dog Shelter
https://bchsohio.org/animal-control/
100 Veterans Blvd.

Engineer
https://browncountyohio.gov/index.php/engineer41
25 Veterans Blvd.

Health Department
https://www.browncountyohio.gov/index.php/health-department
826 Mt. Orab Pike

Municipal Court
https://browncountyohio.gov/index.php/municipal-judge38
770 Mt. Orab Pike

Probate/Juvenile
https://browncountyohio.gov/index.php/probatejuvenile-judge36
510 East State St., Suite 1

Prosecutor
https://browncountyohio.gov/index.php/prosecutor45
740 Mt. Orab Pike, Suite 1

Recorder
https://browncountyohio.gov/index.php/recorder44
800 Mt. Orab Pike
Suite 151

Sheriff
https://browncountyohio.gov/index.php/sheriff39
750 Mt. Orab Pike

Treasurer
https://browncountyohio.gov/index.php/treasurer43
Administration Building
800 Mt. Orab Pike Suite 171

Non-governmental

FamilySearch
https://www.familysearch.org/search/catalog

FamilySearch is a free website with digitized records. Court records located for Brown County include: Auditor (Duplicate tax records), Brown County Children's Home (Indentures), Common Pleas (Court records, Law records, Naturalization records, Partition records), Probate Court (Court records, Declaration of Intention, Final record, Marriage records, Probate records, Vital statistics, Wills), Recorder (Deed books, Soldier's discharge records), Supreme Court (Chancery).

Brown County - Rootsweb.
https://homepages.rootsweb.com/~teri/OH/brown-co.htm

This site gives abstracts of the county, records from high schools and public schools, vital records, cemeteries and obituaries, genealogical help. This is an easy site to access and is the website for the Brown County Chapter, Ohio Genealogical Society.

Ohio Genealogical Society
611 State Route 97 West
Bellville, OH 44813
https://ogs.org

The Ohio Genealogical Society is known as "The Premier Gateway for Discovering Ohio Family History Roots." The Samuel D. Islay Library offers over 70,000 volumes alphabetically arranged by state, county, and subject; over 250,000 ancestor cards are filed by surname, over 4,000 Bible records (indexed), over 23,000 high school and college yearbooks, plus over 5,000 lineage society applications for First Families of Ohio, Settlers & Builders of Ohio, Century Families of Ohio, The Society of Civil War Families of Ohio, and the new Society of Families of the Old Northwest Territory.

The library catalog is available online. Check also the Library Special Collections.

The library is free for OGS members, while non-members pay only $5.00 per day to use the facilities.

Heritage Books by Jana Sloan Broglin:

Additions and Corrections to the W.P.A. Inventory of Adams County, Ohio: West Union

Additions and Corrections to the W.P.A. Inventory of Allen County, Ohio: Lima

Additions and Corrections to the W.P.A. Inventory of Ashland County, Ohio: Ashland

Additions and Corrections to the W.P.A. Inventory of Athens County, Ohio: Athens

Additions and Corrections to the W.P.A. Inventory of Belmont County, Ohio: St. Clairsville

Additions and Corrections to the W.P.A. Inventory of Brown County, Ohio: Georgetown

Additions and Corrections to the W.P.A. Inventory of Cuyahoga County, Ohio: Cleveland

Additions and Corrections to the W.P.A. Inventory of Fulton County, Ohio: Wauseon

Additions and Corrections to the W.P.A. Inventory of Geauga County, Ohio: Chardon

Additions and Corrections to the W.P.A. Inventory of Hamilton County, Ohio: Cincinnati

Additions and Corrections to the W.P.A. Inventory of Hancock County, Ohio: Findlay

Additions and Corrections to the W.P.A. Inventory of Lake County, Ohio: Painesville

Additions and Corrections to the W.P.A. Inventory of Lorain County, Ohio: Elyria

Additions and Corrections to the W.P.A. Inventory of Lucas County, Ohio: Toledo

Additions and Corrections to the W.P.A. Inventory of Medina County, Ohio: Medina

Additions and Corrections to the W.P.A. Inventory of Montgomery County, Ohio: Dayton

Additions and Corrections to the W.P.A. Inventory of Muskingum County, Ohio: Zanesville

Additions and Corrections to the W.P.A. Inventory of Ross County, Ohio: Chillicothe

Additions and Corrections to the W.P.A. Inventory of Seneca County, Ohio: Tiffin

Additions and Corrections to the W.P.A. Inventory of Trumbull County, Ohio: Warren

Additions and Corrections to the W.P.A. Inventory of Washington County, Ohio: Marietta

Additions and Corrections to the W.P.A. Inventory of Wayne County, Ohio: Wooster

Hookers, Crooks and Kooks, Part I: Hookers
Hookers, Crooks and Kooks, Part II: Crooks and Kooks
Lucas County, Ohio, Index to Deaths, 1867–1908
Mason County, Kentucky Wills and Estates, 1791–1832, Second Edition